Number 366 i

reprint of 1000 c

Worldwide

THE AUTHOR.

Titanic

and other ships

Commander Lightoller

Historia Press

This reprinted edition of *Titanic and Other Ships* first published by:

Historia Press
P.O.Box 937
Hull
Humberside
HU6 8WW
United Kingdom

This edition © Historia Press 2007
All rights reserved.

Date of original publication: 1935

Historia Press specializes in books on neglected figures and events from the past, and in the reprinting of lost classics. Every effort is made to ensure compliance with copyright law.

Any correspondence should be addressed to the publisher.

Email: historiapressuk@yahoo.com

Website: www.historiapress.com

ISBN 978-1-906187-02-6

DEDICATED TO
MY PERSISTENT WIFE
WHO MADE ME DO IT

CONTENTS

CHAPTER		PAGE
One	OFF TO SEA	1
Two	65° SOUTH	8
Three	'FRISCO IN THE 'EIGHTIES	15
Four	FLYING FISH WEATHER	20
Five	THE "HOLT HILL"	25
Six	RIO AND REVOLUTIONS	29
Seven	SMALLPOX	35
Eight	WRECKED ON ST. PAUL'S	39
Nine	A DESERT ISLAND	46
Ten	A FIGHT WITH ALBATROSSES	55
Eleven	A TIMELY RESCUE	64
Twelve	HOME IN A TEA CLIPPER	69
Thirteen	SEA FIGHTS AND CYCLONES	74
Fourteen	"SHARKS"	82
Fifteen	I GET MY "TICKET"	87
Sixteen	FIRE AT SEA	93
Seventeen	THE NITRATE COAST	106
Eighteen	DERELICTS	113
Nineteen	"BULLY" WATERS	120
Twenty	A SURFBOAT TRAGEDY	125
Twenty-One	TRAIL OF '98	133
Twenty-Two	CROSSING THE ATHABASKA	141
Twenty-Three	NO GAME . . . NO GOLD	154

CHAPTER		PAGE
Twenty-Four	THE RETURN TRAIL	162
Twenty-Five	BACK TO SEA	176
Twenty-Six	SHANGHAIED	182
Twenty-Seven	WHITE STAR LINE	190
Twenty-Eight	ALMOST A PENALTY	199
Twenty-Nine	GREYHOUNDS OF THE ATLANTIC	204
Thirty	LOSS OF THE "TITANIC"	214
Thirty-One	LEAVING SOUTHAMPTON	220
Thirty-Two	COLLISION WITH AN ICEBERG	227
Thirty-Three	WOMEN AND CHILDREN—ONLY	237
Thirty-Four	SHE FOUNDERS	244
Thirty-Five	THE RESCUE	251
Thirty-Six	THE WAR	262
Thirty-Seven	SEAPLANES AND GRASS LINES	276
Thirty-Eight	DOVER PATROL	281
Thirty-Nine	THOSE DAMNED "R" WORDS	294
Forty	BLUNDERING THROUGH A MINE-FIELD	303
Forty-One	SCROUNGING LEAVE	309
Forty-Two	LOSS OF H.M.S. "FALCON"	318
Forty-Three	NORTH SEA CONVOYS	325
Forty-Four	DESTROYER v. SUBMARINE	333
Forty-Five	I "BURY THE ANCHOR"	343

TITANIC AND OTHER SHIPS

CHAPTER
ONE *OFF TO SEA*

I DON'T think my relatives ever knew how amazed I was when I obtained their consent to go to sea. I chuckled at my good luck, as they no doubt chuckled at their good riddance.

I had long since made up my mind (or what, at the mature age of thirteen, I was pleased to call my mind) that I would go to sea. And to sea I went, knowing little and caring less about those prospective first few years of hellish servitude, during which experience must be gained—experience that, like a corn, had to grow, become hardened, and most damnably hurt.

My Dad didn't enter into it, as he was settled in New Zealand, having seen the best days in cotton. In fact we had been "in cotton" for generations, and I had fully expected that I should have to "follow in father's footsteps."

For my part the "going to sea" was just a bluff, but it worked. I hear some say, to my sorrow. Not a bit of it. The sea is a hard, unrelenting mistress, always ready to whip up the fools (as I was soon to discover). She tried to drown me several times, yet I beat her; she nearly broke my neck on more than one occasion, but we still remain the best of friends, and I never regret that my bluff was called.

I had a distant relative, a one hundred per cent sailor to the tips of his stub-ended fingers, so I suppose it was only natural that my near relatives should start me off in his footsteps. The fact remains that I found myself a brass bound apprentice on board the famous *Primrose Hill*, a four-masted barque, and three skysail-yarder.

It was not long before I learned exactly how to throw out my chest as I described my ship as a "three skysail-yarder." There weren't many of them about, as most owners considered skysails more ornamental than useful.

If you had been near the half-deck door when one of the Mates sang out, "Now one of you youngsters, up and stop the main skysail buntlines," then you would have known just what we boys thought of them! The sole reason for their existence, in our opinion, lay in the fact that they formed a ready to hand punishment for first voyagers. But skysails undoubtedly did give that finishing touch to a ship with her towering piles of canvas rising, tier on tier, a full two hundred feet above the deck. Courses—as the three big lower sails were called—lower and upper topsails, lower and upper t' gallant sails, royals, and finally, the boys' pet objection, those skysails. These were exactly forty-five feet from yard-arm to yard-arm, just half the length of the main yard; a comparative pocket handkerchief, but making for perfect symmetry, and taking away that chopped off look that either stump t' gallant masts, or even royals alone are apt to give. Our great objection to these sails was that there was no way of getting up the final fifteen feet to this yard except by shinning up the back stays, (the mast being greased). As far as the royal yard the going was not so bad; one had the rigging and a Jacob's Ladder. But swinging around on a wire back-stay, half way to heaven, may have some attraction but it also has its drawbacks, particularly when she was rolling heavily.

OFF TO SEA

Having arrived at the summit of one's present ambition and standing there on the footrope of the skysailyard, looking down two hundred odd feet, always carried a thrill. To a first voyager it seemed inconceivable that such an almighty spread of canvas, as then lay below one, should not put that slight strip of deck on its beam ends.

In addition to the square sails, the *Primrose Hill* carried fifteen fore and aft sails, in the way of jibs, staysails, spanker and gaff topsail, each with the definite set purpose of adding its drive to that long, narrow hull. She was a great ship, and even in the days when a forest of masts was a common sight in dockland, the tapering spars of the old *Primrose Hill* always stood out like one of the tea clippers of old.

I know the skipper was a mighty proud man, and we boys almost reverenced him, pacing his lonely beat up and down that poop, lord of all he surveyed. His slightest word was law absolute and immutable. We thought that even such as we, might with luck, some day, walk the poop with that deep sea roll. But that was too far in the dim distant future for boys of our age to consider seriously.

Fourteen years of age found me beating down the channel in the teeth of a Westerly gale. My first voyage horribly seasick—and sick of the sea. That seemingly objectless and eternal beat from side to side of the Channel, driving along with every stitch she would stand, trying to make to the westward. Once in the fog we almost succeeded in running down the Royal Sovereign Lightship, and then on the other side we got into a jam with the notorious Race of Alderney.

At long last, clear of the Chops of the Channel, we squared away to a fine Nor'-Nor'-West breeze, and tore down through the Roaring Forties towards good old "flying fish" weather. Shirts and pants the order of the day; the ship heeling over with a bone in her teeth, ropes fore and aft cracking like a machine gun as they surged round the green-heart belaying pins. Day after day, and week after week, snoring along without touching halyard or sheet; bending fine weather sails, holystoning decks, scrubbing bright work and painting ship. Never a lazy moment aboard any sailing ship in fine weather, and the man with the forenoon or afternoon Trick at the wheel, is the man to be envied. At night it is the other way about, as the watch on deck can always find the soft side of a deck plank, for an hour's " caulk."

This was a new world to me, and the first time in my life that I had seen real sunshine. Steadily the mercury rose as it grew hotter and hotter, until the pitch boiled up out of the seams in the deck, to stick to and blister our still tender feet. It brought other things also; not exactly out of the deck, but from below deck, in the shape of rats and cockroaches. Where they all came from goodness knows. We used to kill rats with belaying pins, and later even became expert in stamping on them with our bare feet! At night in our bunks, the little beasts would come and eat our toe-nails, and the hard flesh off the soles of our feet, and this without awakening us. We knew nothing about it until we got on deck and put our feet in some salt water. Then we knew!

Cockroaches near two inches long. These must have come aboard when she was loading somewhere out East. They had the same happy habit of browsing on our feet, although not quite to the same extent. For their benefit we kept a tin of very strong caustic soda and a small brush with a handle two feet long, and when they started to make themselves objectionable a dab with the brush settled their hash.

We were soon out of the Forties and into the Trades and it was here we were to see our first flying fish rising in shoals out of the water and flying anything up to a quarter of a mile. Some have a spread of 14-16 inches from tip to tip, and to watch them bank and skim the surface of the water makes it hard to believe they are fish at all. In fact, one can sympathise with the old lady whose son, returning from his first voyage, was telling her yarns, true and stretched, and eventually told her about flying fish. She replied "John, there may be mountains of sugar, and rivers of rum, but you can't tell me that fish fly!"

My life, in common with other first voyagers, was made a misery until I knew, not only every sail, but every rope used in furling, setting or trimming, and they average a round dozen per sail, in all well over five hundred. Even on pitch dark nights and in blinding rain, you must be able to put your hand on any individual rope, and the consequence of letting go the wrong one may be pretty disastrous to both the ship and the culprit.

The Third Mate is usually the boys' mentor, and hikes them away from their sky-larking in the second dog-watch, to learn the ropes—whence no doubt the saying originated. A second and third voyager, to say nothing of the salt-horse A.B. knows his ropes, and that almost by the feel. These are the men to rely upon when it comes to shortening down in bad weather.

With fine weather sails bent, and decks like snow we drew down the Line and into the region of Bonito, Dolphin, and Albacore. Always a keen fisherman, I was sure of a call if there were fish under the bows. Watch on deck mustn't think of anything so frivolous, but someone always managed to sneak into the half-deck and give me a shout in hopes of fish for tea; a mighty welcome addition to the Liverpool pantiles and salt junk, if there *should* be any left over from dinner. Beautiful ships, but badly found.

With us boys, sneaking grub was no crime, it was a religion, and heaven help the chap that let a chance go by. This led some of us into queer scrapes, for cooks, and particularly stewards were all out to catch the hungry hound, and haul him before the Captain. On one occasion we located some biscuits in a spare cabin, and I was told off for foraging. I got into the cabin and got the biscuits all right, but when I came to open the door, which I had closed so that it couldn't slam with the roll of the ship, I found I had landed into a trap. The handle turned, but not the catch; that was the *catch* so to speak! I got the port open in hopes of scrambling out on to the cro' jack braces (ropes that were used to trim that yard) but when I did eventually get my head and one arm out, I found that not only could I get no further out but I could not get back, and I had horrible visions of them having to cut away part of my anatomy, or part of the ship. Anyhow there was nothing for it but to ignominiously call for help. I did get my head back, finally with the loss of a bit of scalp,—and though I succeeded in convincing the Second Mate, who rescued me, that I had walked in my sleep, it wouldn't go down with the Skipper. Six solid weeks of the night watch on sentry go, capstan bar on shoulder, and a six foot elm bar at that!

Another time we discovered a loose plank in the bulkhead of the lazarette, and, after some nights of hard work, gained through. The chap told off for the work, Austin, nicknamed Beaky on account of his nose, was a bit deaf. What he had to do was to get the grub (in this case onions, to put in our Cracker Hash) and climb up over the cargo until he came to No. 4 Booby Hatch, the doors of which opened right facing the half-deck door, inside which we were waiting. He came up all right, but just as he started to shy the onions across the intervening four feet of space between hatch and half deck, the Mate must come along, and, be it known, they were Cabin onions. We sang out cave! when we heard the Mate coming, but Beaky heard neither us nor the Mate, and continued to shy the onions. The Mate was bound through the four foot passage, and, as he turned the corner of the hatch, he stopped one! Stepping back, he viewed the procedure, no doubt inwardly amused at our frantic efforts to put Beaky wise. Beaky smiled serenely, and continued to shy the onions, all of which had to be duly returned, and in their place we, once again, took what was coming to us.

However, that was all in the day's work, and we would, and frequently did, risk our necks crawling along cro' jack braces to pinch a bit of pie or what not from the steward's pantry. Few boys that go to sea are born to be drowned.

CHAPTER TWO
65° SOUTH

WE crossed the Line, with the usual formalities, into the S.E. Trades, and a long leg down to the Horn. Here a westerly gale drove us South and further South; colder and colder it grew until we fetched in amongst the Antarctic ice. I've seen plenty of it since, both down there and up on the Banks, but one's first sight is always the most impressive. That long ghostly outline of white, in places blue, and, of every conceivable shape and size.

By this time we had bogies going—when the sea did not put them out.

Despite all our efforts we were steadily driven down south until we eventually fetched the sixty-fifth parallel. The month was June, in other words, mid-winter. The conditions men had to endure almost beggar description. Ropes and blocks frozen up, and solid with ice. Sails iron hard with frozen rain and spray, often ice an inch thick, requiring belaying pins to break it. I have seen all hands on the topsail yard for hours on end of a bitter night, blowing a living gale, fighting with canvas like cast-iron, finger nails turned back, and knuckles raw, battling to get it gathered in and a gasket round. It is difficult to realise how any human being could survive the days and weeks with never a dry stitch. Don't think this applied merely to the clothes we wore; it included both blankets and bedding.

Long before one reaches the latitude of the Horn all maindeck doors are as near hermetically sealed as is possible. Usually with the close application of a sheath knife and quantities of rag and paper. One gains access to the different living quarters, the galley and so forth, by means of a skylight; watching one's chance, opening the skylight, dropping down and closing it again. A breath of the atmosphere in these close quarters becomes almost as good as a meal. Huge seas, scores of tons in weight, come thundering on board over the bulwarks, sweeping anything movable before them. It is often a case of days without a hot meal.

Added to all this, there is always the intense anxiety as to whether one is going to happen across an iceberg during the night. The only means of detecting them, when there is no moon, is from the white foam at the base of the berg. If there is a moon one can sometimes get a glint or glimpse of what is called "ice blink." Ice down in these latitudes becomes more in the nature of ice-fields, and may extend for miles, and become a veritable island. There is one well-known case of a sailing ship running into a huge bay with a fair wind, and, finding herself unable to beat out. Back and forth she thrashed, trying to work her way clear, till finally she missed stays and crashed on the ice, to be battered to pieces and all hands lost. Boats are of little or no use in these conditions, for men can hardly survive on board ship, let alone in an open boat.

After six weeks battling with Cape Horn greybeards, as those huge rollers are called, at last we got our slant. With the wind backing well to the south-west we crammed on every stitch she would carry in our endeavour to get up to the north-west and weather that dreaded old Cape Stiff. There was every indication that we should make it, and be able to stretch away for fine weather. Lower t'gallant sails and t'gallant staysails set. Steering full-and-by, with all sails drawing strong, her nose pointing well up to windward, everyone's spirits rose with each mile reeled off. Every man and boy counted the hours to when he would be able to hang out his dunnage and have some dry clothing, though it was still a bit too soon to be looking forward to real warmth, but that would come later. All we longed for from the bottom of our hearts was that the wind would hold and not head us off by hauling any more to the westward. The very first question asked each time the watch was called was "How's the wind?" and it was a cheery crowd that answered to the names called over at each relief. Now another forty-eight or sixty hours at the most would see us with old Stiff astern, and we would be safe.

That night we were still snoring along, dark as pitch but with every stitch on her that she could possibly bear. There *was* the risk of hitting an iceberg, yes, but one that we were all willing to take. Still, with the sea that was running, there was every chance of seeing it before hitting and in good time to either go about, or run her away. However, it was not to be. Our luck was out, and a long way out. Soon after the watch had been relieved at midnight, the wind to our great disappointment started to fall light. Nothing too bad in that, so long as it did not head us. Better much, than blowing up one of those seemingly eternal gales with which we were absolutely fed-up.

Lighter and lighter the wind fell, and to an extraordinary degree baffling, a thing most uncommon in those latitudes. You expect, and do get, baffling winds in the tropics but not down in the sixties. The cold became intense, in fact, piercing. Not a great deal of difference from what we had had, yet somehow it was a distinctive cold and it seemed to have a dry, penetrating drive with it. We certainly connected the cold with ice, but not seriously. It was the vagaries of the wind we couldn't understand, and no wonder.

At four bells as the wheel and look-out was being relieved, the two look-out men stood for a few minutes talking and discussing the rotten luck in losing the wind. The man relieving was a real old-timer, and presently he walked up to the weather rail of the foc's'tlehead, and sort of stuck his nose up into the wind. Suddenly he whipped round and bellowed out, "Ice right ahead, sir." Instinctively the Second Mate, aft on the poop, gave the order, "Put your helm down and shake her up," with the idea of taking the wind out of the sails, and the way off the ship, until he could get a clear grasp of the situation.

The vital question was, in what direction did the ice extend. Were we to windward, or to leeward of the main body? As she ran up into the wind, both lookout men saw the ice still coming into sight ahead, and on the weather bow. Old Heron, with his vast experience, and knowing that everything right ahead and to some distance on the bow, was completely blotted out by the sails from the Second Mate on the poop, now roared out, "Put your helm up, sir. The ice is to windward."

On a sailing ship you get to know your man to the very fibre of his being, and the Second Mate *knew* Heron and ordered the helm "Hard up." It was a big risk to take, for if once she filled again and got way on her, and the ice should chance to be leeward as well as windward then, we should undoubtedly strike and sink. There being little wind, however, she payed-off slowly.

The Captain was now on deck and quickly rapped out his orders "All hands on deck. Stand by the braces." Sure enough, old Heron was right, and by now we could all see the ghostly and threatening outline of a massive berg, extending as far as the eye could see. Furthermore, it was this monstrous berg that had been taking the wind out of our sails. This we realized, and with the realisation the knowledge that it must be the father of all bergs, if it was responsible for the extraordinary baffling of the wind, which we had now experienced for over four hours, and during which time we must, in the darkness, have been sailing parallel along this block of Antartic.

Quickly we rounded in the weather braces in the hopes of filling on her, and making an offing. We must take the chance as to whether we had run into an ice bay in the dark, for it must be remembered we could not see more than quarter of a mile, and the ice was less than *half* that distance from us. At one time, just before she commenced to gather way and draw off we were no more than a hundred yards from that towering cliff of ice which looked as if our yardarms were going to touch. Being right under the lee, the wind was utterly unreliable, and kept catching her aback and drifting her nearer and nearer those threatening white walls of ice.

An added anxiety, was the query in our minds as to whether there were any protruding ledges below the water which might hold us below the water line, and sink us. Goodness knows what the temperature was at this time. Fortunately our anxiety blotted out all sense of the cold, except when we tried to use our hands. Everything that carried or showed the slightest moisture, was all just solid ice, clothing included.

Steadily, inch by inch, we clawed off and, at last, gained sea room; then we hove-to till daylight broke and we should be able to see to where the ice extended and what was the best hope of saving the ship. With the first streak of dawn it was easy to see what a narrow shave it had been, and, with the increasing daylight, the cliffs of ice just extended and extended. As the light became better and better, till with the full day there was revealed an impenetrable wall of ice for close on fifteen miles astern, and more than double that distance ahead. As it turned out, we sailed the best part of two solid days before we could safely round the end of that island of ice. But, what was worse, we were all the time slowly but surely being forced off our course, and away to the eastward; for ever lessening our chances of rounding the Horn on this leg.

A magnificent sight, cruising slowly along these blue-black cliffs. Pinnacles, bays, chasms and cathedral like structures, huge ravines and bridges, bridges of ice, looking for all the world as if they had been built by some clever engineers, and would have done credit to them at that. Unfortunately we were in no mood at that moment to appreciate these beauties. Curses, deep, sincere and universal were hurled at this one insurmountable bar, which prevented us from stretching away with a fair wind to fine weather.

At long last when we did finally get round the ice, it was too late to weather the old Cape, so once again we heard that well-known order, "All hands wear ship," and commenced another long leg to the southward.

It might well be proverbial amongst sailing-ship men of those days that one was not entitled to the name of sailor until the Horn had been rounded three or four times. I know I felt all of a sailor after rounding it once. Six weeks to the day, from the time we first made the Horn bound south, till we again brought it abeam bound north.

A good clean run up through Trades and Tropics soon removed all traces of our trials down south, whilst with all the goodwill in the world we said good-bye to those harbingers of high latitudes, albatrosses, Cape pigeons, Molly hawks and Mother Carey's chickens.

Heavy weather-sails were sent down and fine weather canvas bent in place. Running gear re-rove, and heavy weather spare spar-lashings removed. All dunnage (Anglice, clothing and bedding) out on deck drying and airing. Everyone revelling in the sun and even welcoming the bubbling pitch, though it should stick to our toes.

The very ship herself seemed to spring into greater life as the flying kites were once again hoisted and set; each adding the urge and drive which a few weeks later carried us through the Golden Gates of San Francisco, on to the broad, smooth waters of the Sacramento.

CHAPTER THREE   'FRISCO IN THE 'EIGHTIES

WHAT a strange mixture we found in that city of mushroom growth. Beautiful broad streets and magnificent buildings, but almost entirely without law or order,—unless you could pay for it. One section of the city, known as Chinatown, was literally a young China. Rarely, if ever, did any white man attempt this locality at night time. We boys cared little about the reputation of the place; in fact, we did not realise the perfectly appalling reputation it bore, and we spent lots of our time hunting up curios from John Chinaman. The great fire of San Francisco has cleared away this well-known landmark, and the Chinese are scattered to the four winds of heaven. Certainly one does not find them now in 'Frisco. Whether 'Frisco is any better off without her young Chinatown than with, is an open question. For my part I much prefer John Chinaman to many other races. At least his word is his bond, and you can rely on it to the bitter end. Get him to give you his brief "Can do" and you need no attorneys, stamps nor seals.

'Frisco at this time, had the honour of bearing the worst reputation of any sea port in the world for lawlessness, not excepting New York. It was bad enough for the landsman to be on the streets at night, if it was even, suspected that he was carrying more than a very few dollars. Even in broad daylight it was no uncommon thing for a man to be sandbagged and robbed. Judge then, what it was for a sailor coming out of the shipping office, *known* to have his pay-day in his pocket. He was lucky if he could get as far as the nearest Post Office, always allowing he had the sense to go there, which was seldom.

The water front of 'Frisco was held and run by a lot of soulless crimps. These human vultures didn't wait for a man to get as far as the Shipping Office; in fact they were indifferent as to whether a man was even paying off or not. All *they* wanted was his body, and they would fight amongst themselves for possession. Red Jake for a long time held unquestioned sway. He derived his name from his lurid complexion and crimson nose; one might even include his language,—it suited his name.

A ship arriving within the Golden Gates (was there ever such a misnomer?) was at once overrun by a horde of these wretched crimps' runners. The Captain was powerless to stop them. The men might be on the capstan heaving in the tow rope, and the crimps would just join up and heave round also on the capstan bars, hauling out of their pockets flasks of whisky, and once a man has accepted a drink, he is theirs,—and it was more than another crimp's life was worth to alienate that man's affections.

Red Jake would have perhaps half a dozen of the toughest runners to each ship, and so held a monopoly. After the drink, the sailor chap is given money. No receipt or anything, is asked in return, but *now* they have bought him, and he must be slick indeed, to get out of their toils. He goes ashore that night under the wing of the crimp's runner to have a good time. He has everything he asks for, and eventually goes to the boarding house that every crimp keeps.

If there is a ship ready to sail and short of a crew, he will be one of them. Heavily doped, his body is delivered on board and a receipt taken, which, in turn, is cashed for a month's pay, deducted from the sailor boy's pay sheet; having already sacrificed all his earnings of the outward passage.

Who profits?

The crimp gets a month's pay. The shipowner gets the whole of the outward passage's pay, and the Captain gets his crew, and, let it be known, he will get them no other way.

Who should kick?

The skinflint shipowner, thousands of miles away, lining his pockets and increasing his dividends?

Not he.

Furthermore, the skipper with a conscience, who manages to keep his crew together, will get no bouquets when he arrives home and faces "ship's expenses" at the office.

The 'Frisco police also get their rake off, according to a printed and accepted schedule, agreed with the boarding house runners.

I am glad to say our Skipper was one with a conscience. I'll go further and say, such men were not difficult to find in British ships. He gave the crew to understand they would get money out of his own pocket the moment the ship was fast, and if they deserted that night, well, he would be the loser. He told them, "Go ashore, and have a good time. But for God's sake men don't let those crimps get hold of you." We did lose a couple of men before we left. Men we could afford to lose, as a matter of fact, but of the real good crowd we lost none.

Of course it was good to be ashore for a time. To stretch our legs, and feed the inner man, and see the sights. What sights some of them were!!! Old Dupont Street with its green shutters and painted hags.

The Underground rabbit warren that honeycombed Chinatown.

Beach Street on the river edge with its rows of Dives, where more men went in than ever came out.

Hard, bitter hard, though ship life often was, yet we were glad to see the Golden Gates, with all they stood for, fading away and finally disappearing below the horizon. At least the sea was clean.

The only good thing about 'Frisco as far as I, a first voyager with an eternal hunger, could see, was the biscuits. "'Frisco biscuits" are known the world over. Big, crisp, and eatable. A good six inches across, and even the ship's margarine could not altogether spoil their flavour. Why the food, supplied by the British shipowners, should have been so notoriously bad, barely sufficient to keep body and soul lashed together, seems inconceivable. Ships were paying, and paying well, yet they screw the old salt horse shellback down to the last ounce—and a poor one at that. In fact, the outstanding feature of my first voyage seems to have been the state of semi-starvation we boys lived in, until we got the 'Frisco biscuits.

One of the squarest meals I ever remember enjoying was on an occasion, in the port we had just left. Standing outside a restaurant, a very small and very hungry boy, just thinking what I could do with a dollar and some of the good things in front of me—if I had the chance. When a voice with the broad, drawling, Western accent, spoke from away up above me, "Say, Sonny, could you go a feed?" I looked up to see a man about six feet five inches, and big in proportion, wearing the rough rig of a miner or rancher, just up to town. Could I go a feed! when money was doled out to all and sundry at the munificent rate of a dollar a week! A.B.'s, apprentices, or petty officers, it was just the same, though why on earth we should not have been allowed to have some of the money that was already ours, heaven and the owners alone knew.

He took me in and gave me the meal of my young life. Lashings of ham and eggs (a sailor's staple diet when ashore), cups of thick chocolate and apple pie. He just grinned as it all disappeared, till, at last, despite his earnest persuasion, I could eat no more.

Next day he was down on board with pockets full of apples, asking for "that youngster with the gaff-topsail collar." Western generosity!

CHAPTER FOUR *FLYING FISH WEATHER*

WE left the Golden Gates behind us homeward bound, with a cargo of grain. About half way down to the Horn we discovered that she had sprung a leak somewhere. We could tell this by the frightful stink coming up from below. Rotting grain has worse contemporaries, but they are not so easy to find. Evidently there was water getting in somewhere on the starboard side, for that was obviously where the stench came from.

There was nothing for it but to open up the hatches, and break down. Fortunately we were still in fine weather so we could pile the decks with sacks of grain, and loose wet grain laid out drying. The leak was located and found due to a bit of flint getting into the red lead packing around one of the side ports!

Poor old Chips, he was for the carpet all right. A few thousand pounds worth of damage done, all on account of a little stone! All the same, it was lucky it happened where it did. Ships are known to have had their sides burst out by the swelling grain, when the leak could not be got at.

It was shortly after we had the grain stowed again that Olsen, the Swede, got moonstruck, through sleeping out on deck in the full rays of the tropic moon. He woke up, one middle watch, to muster with the rest, and at the sight of him, with his face all twisted on one side, everyone burst out laughing. Poor devil, he didn't know what was the matter. It was full moon, and as light as day; in fact, one could easily see to read a book by the light, yet old Olsen went stumbling about the decks, as if it were pitch dark. As it turned out, he thought it was dark, and that gave us the first inkling that something had gone wrong. We heard him say, half to himself, "*Gosh!* it's dark," and then someone asked him what he meant, and it came out that not only was his face all twisted up, but he could not see his hand in front of him. When daylight came he was all right, but as soon as it got a bit dusk, he was finished. He got over it to a certain extent before we arrived home, but he never fully recovered his sight at night time.

Most sailors have a hobby of some sort—making mats, carving models out of wood, with beautifully cut sails, thin as a wafer, and bellying out in the most natural way. Olsen's strong point was making planes for planing wood—Spoon planes, Jack planes, and all sorts of planes. It was just marvellous to sit and watch him fashioning them out of pieces of hard wood he brought away with him, fitting the irons and polishing them off. Most Swedes are good carpenters, and, though an A.B. he was a jolly good chippy man. After he got twisted up, he just moped, and would do nothing. It was pitiful to see him feeling his way round the decks when it was light enough for the rest of us to pick up a pin.

On a long sailing ship voyage each man knows the other better than he knows himself. Funny little characteristics develop. He tells a bit here, and a bit there, until, whether he likes it or not, you can piece his life story together, like fitting a jig-saw puzzle.

Knut, the Dane, had been a whaler in Nova Scotia, and had killed a man with a harpoon. He never told us in so many words, and of course, his secret was quite safe.

If it had happened in a Yankee whaler, he would not have had to bother—always supposing no one else laid him out. It would merely have resolved into a matter of paying so many dollars in to the right quarter, and nothing more would have been heard of it. But, as he came under British law, it was a different matter, and he was lucky to change over at sea, as he did, and eventually work his way back to Denmark. Knut wasn't his name; we all knew that. He hadn't meant to kill the man; in fact, the man went for Knut with the steering oar, just when Knut was going to make his strike, and, as he turned suddenly away from the whale to defend himself, the boat gave a lurch, and he drove the harpoon into the steerman's stomach. It *might* have washed in a Court of Law but for the bad blood that was known to exist between the two. Wisely, or unwisely, he took the chance when it was offered of getting right back home.

It wasn't until the passage home that we could get him to even take a shot with the harpoon. He certainly was an artist with it, and three out of four times he would hit a chip of wood thrown from the bowsprit end. In fact, I saw him put the harpoon through a three-inch rope grummet, three times in succession—and this with the ship laying over, and doing a good seven knots. He could pick up a porpoise every time, and that is not easy, for there is only one place where you can harpoon a porpoise and be certain that it is going to hold.

Lying becalmed one day, a whole shoal of these greybellies came thundering over the horizon; each one anything up to ten feet long, all leaping straight up out of the water, and flinging themselves sideways, landing flat on to the surface, with a report like a 4.7 gun. There were thousands and tens of thousands of them. Thunder was mild compared with the row. They covered, at a rough guess, a rectangle, about half a mile long, and five hundred yards wide. The sea was like glass, and when they were first sighted, we could see just a patch of foam, growing rapidly bigger and bigger: then bodies shooting up in the air, the roar growing louder and louder, until we couldn't hear each other speak.

The average weight must have been well over a ton and a half. The one Knut nailed was purposely a small one, otherwise the line would not have held him. Of course it would have been a different matter if Knut had been in a small boat and so could have let the porpoise tow him before the line ran out. As it was, the $2\frac{1}{2}$ inch rope was taxed pretty severely when hauling it up by sheer brute force, tail first, to the cat-head.

I was told the wind always came from the direction where a shoal of porpoises was heading. But first voyagers are fair game for all sorts of yarns; one remembers some, and if wise, believes about half of what one remembers. All the same, sailors do believe the wind will come from the direction indicated by porpoises. Personally I think they gather together from far and wide at certain times, simply to migrate; going thousands of miles to fresh hunting grounds.

They jump out of the water and drop smack on to it again partly for sheer sport, and partly in an endeavour to knock off suckers. Anyhow, they're good eating and a mighty welcome change from sailing-ship salt horse where the fat is often going, or gone, green—and that's no exaggeration.

The *Crofton Hall* had cholera break out through eating some such junk and lost half her crew before she could get back to Calcutta. Admittedly the stuff had been slowly going rotten lying in the harness cask for two months under a tropical sun. Still, they had the usual sailor's choice; eat it or leave it.

Fish hung up in the light of the moon will go the same way and must on no account be touched. If the moon does get at it you see the whole fish, or what may be left of it, become phosphorescent. That is the danger signal, and I've never seen anyone hardy enough, even amongst sailing-ship men, to tackle it after that.

Neither will sailors touch a fish that has come out of what is called "Blood Water." This is a case when the sea turns deep red, often crimson, in the sun. Really, it's nothing but countless millions of animalculae like cochineal. You will be slipping along through beautifully blue water (never seen within two hundred miles of our English coast) when suddenly you will run into this Blood Water (it does look just like blood) and may so continue for a couple of days.

As for the yarn about never eating fish out of it; well, I've never seen fish in it, and that's a pretty sound reason to my mind.

Sailing-ship life, even on one's first voyage, is cram full of incidents, but they are irrelevant, and would fill a good sized book in themselves.

At long last we arrived in Liverpool, just a few days short of a year from the time we left; and such was my first voyage in sail.

CHAPTER FIVE — *THE "HOLT HILL"*

FOR some reason I changed over to the *Holt Hill*, sister ship to the *Primrose Hill*, and of the same Line. My cousin was Third Mate; I was then second voyage apprentice, and beginning to feel my feet. We were bound for Rio, and proud to sail under Captain "Jock" Sutherland, one of the greatest crackers-on out of Liverpool; in fact, he made a boast that he never allowed a ship to pass him with any of his sails furled. He certainly was a sailor to his finger tips; and it was great to see him lying that ship over in half a gale of wind, with scupper holes and wash-ports well under water, the water even swirling through the sheave-holes half way up the bulwarks; this used to thrill us boys to the bone.

He knew exactly, to the last ounce, what she would carry, and woe betide anyone who voiced a thought that sail might be shortened. To first voyagers it was pretty terrifying I'll admit, for many a time and often it seemed as though nothing could save the ship from going over on her beam ends, or, alternatively, the masts being taken out of her.

On one occasion old Jock heard some of the crew cursing at the way he was carrying on. He just went down below, and arrived back on deck, with a camp chair and a revolver, and dared any man to even whisper about shortening sail, much less touch a halyard. He followed this up with a threat that, unless they went about their work and stopped their grousing, he would "put the helm up and sail the whole damn lot of you to hell." And, knowing the man, I wouldn't have put it past him. It was not exactly that he was altogether a daredevil in his cracking-on, it was just sheer knowledge of his ship, and confidence in what she could stand.

Beyond minor incidents that will happen to any good cracker-on, old Jock had, up to that time, run free of any serious smash up, but this voyage proved to be his undoing. The first bad break (and, as it turned out afterwards, there were to be three) was off the Western Isles, one filthy dirty night; carrying on as usual to the last ounce, under six t'gallant sails, when really she should have been under six topsails—backstays like harpstrings, and every rope straining to its limit. Suddenly a man got washed overboard from the lee braces. In response to old Jock's whip crack orders, we dropped the upper t'gallant yards with a run, and let fly the lower t'gallant sheets, as he flung the ship up in the wind, nearly taking the masts out of her; but the case was utterly hopeless.

We even got a boat away, by sheer good luck, but in the pitch darkness, and in that sea, it was a wonder we didn't lose both boat and boat's crew as well.

It was no fault of old Sutherland's that the man went overboard, except that the ship had far too much canvas on her—but who would blame him for that? All sailors know the danger in shipping a lee sea. Each man must look out for himself. On the other hand, to be dubbed a cracker-on should be the ambition of every skipper worth his salt. We lost our man, but he was the first and last to lose his life, from being washed overboard whilst under Sutherland's command.

The second misfortune came about just outside Rio, off Cape Frio, at eight o'clock one morning, driving hard as usual, every stitch of canvas set. A sudden squall sent the ship heeling over, ropes and chains cracking, yard parrels groaning, till she was ripping it up like the proverbial Flying Dutchman.

Whether what happened was due to a sudden shift of wind, or to the skipper giving the order to luff, and the man at the wheel giving her too much helm, was never known—(Sutherland would never explain, nor make any attempt to justify himself)—but the fact remains, without a moment's warning, we were caught back, and then a moment later, the sails suddenly filled again and twisted the fore and main t'gallant masts clean out of her.

That meant both fore and main t'gallant, royal and skysail masts with all their attendant yards and gear, came crashing down on or near the deck. No one was hurt, marvellous to relate, though the main skysail yard dropped and hung within a few feet of a bunch of us boys, who, despite the fact that it was our watch below, had turned out to see the fun, and, to be perfectly frank, in the hopes that something *would* happen.

It did, and no one had another meal, or spell for twenty-four hours. The gale, which had been brewing, and of which the squall was the forerunner, came down on us, and did its best to put us under altogether. Nothing but the superhuman efforts of Mates and crew saved the ship (as it turned out, only for a later fate). It was in emergencies like this, that one appreciated a British crowd. As a rule they are the greatest grumblers on earth, but you can always rely on them when the time comes, and you are in a tight corner; which you can't on Dutchmen—the broad term applied to all Continental foreigners.

On one ship of which I was Second Mate, the Mate was a Dutchman (actually a Swede) and had a watch of his own kidney. Down round the Horn one night, with the Skipper laid up, the Mate had to "wear ship" himself, an "all hands" job. I had to take his Watch at the Main Braces, and the Third Mate take mine at the Cro'jack Braces. Wearing Ship is a ticklish job at the best of times, particularly the bracing up when she comes to. At the crucial moment, the whole Watch got a dose of sheer funk and cowered at the braces, and when I got amongst them with hands and feet, cursing them to all eternity, they simply vanished, and hid in what they considered safety.

We saved her, but only because half the British Watch broke off and did the "Dutchmen's" job at the Main, whilst the other half of the Watch carried on at the Mizzen.

Having, at last, cleared the wreckage of masts, yards, and sails, cut away the last wire back stay, saved what we could, and let the remainder go by the board, we squared away the remaining yards, and limped into Rio.

CHAPTER SIX — *RIO AND REVOLUTIONS*

Rio is a marvellous harbour, second only to Sydney, and at that time full of sailing ships, though many of them were swinging to an anchor without a soul on board. Cholera and smallpox were at their worst, with little facilities, and less energy on the part of the natives, to hold the disease in check. Deaths were averaging about two hundred a day ashore, whilst "Dead boats" continually patrolled the harbour with their gruesome cargoes collected from the various ships. Still, there was plenty of enjoyment to be got out of life, and with the usual youthful indifference, one paid little heed to the horrors around.

I cannot say the British were ever favourites in Rio, and little blame can be attached to the natives, for the ill-concealed hate with which they regarded us. "Incidents," happened pretty frequently, important and unimportant; many of them were just skylarks. One night we had been ashore on duty, and returning without the Captain we were chased by a police boat; owing to the revolution the inhabitants were indulging in at the time no one was allowed on the water after sunset.

Ours was a six-oared mahogany gig, very light and very fast, and we led that police boat a dance round that harbour, they were not likely to forget. All they wanted was to know which ship we belonged to, so that they could drop on the Skipper, and that was the very thing we were determined they should not find out. They tried a few shots with their revolvers, but we knew they didn't mean to hit us. The result was, they pulled and we pulled, but their crew had not got their muscles and sinews developed in the hard school of a British sailing ship. After a couple of hours they had to give it up, absolutely exhausted, and next morning yet another complaint was carefully noted—and filed—by that tactful warden of British prestige: the good old British Consul.

On another occasion a British Man-o'-Warsman had a knife stuck into him, and, as a result, died on his ship. The British Fleet out there at that time, consisted of two comparatively small ships, but what it lacked in size, the Admiral certainly made up for in grit and determination. Having ineffectually demanded the surrender of the murderer, after forty-eight hours he stood over, opposite the town, cleared for action, and landed an armed party. We boys were in at the steps, in our own ship's boats at the time, and nothing would please us but we must abandon our boats, and follow the naval party up the town, to see the fun. No resistance at all was made to the Bluejackets, who marched right up to the jail, extracted the murderer, put him on board the cruiser, and sailed out of the harbour, to return a few hours later with his remains swinging at the yard arm! Later, the body was lowered, and landed at the steps, and left for the authorities to collect.

Pretty high handed, I'll admit, but the British were both feared and respected in those days.

Another time the Port Authorities refused, for some reason, to give the *Thetis*, a full rigged British ship, her papers, and, after delaying her for a week, the Captain threatened to take her out without papers. The authorities ashore told him that they would blow her out of the water, if he attempted to pass the forts.

He threatened to go and fetch the British Fleet (consisting of these two small cruisers) and turn them loose. Their reply was that they would blow the British Fleet out of the water also.

This appeared to be good enough to be getting on with, so, commandeering a steam launch, the Captain carried the glad tidings to Admiral—— who was cruising outside the harbour, not wishing to get mixed up in a revolution then in progress, and by which they hoped to unseat Don Pedro. The two British cruisers came in; made fast on either side of the British sailing ship, and told the Captain to heave up his anchor. Then steamed with him out of the harbour. We cheered ourselves pretty well hoarse at the success of this manœuvre. Needless to say, not a shot was fired from the forts.

A common form of amusement amongst us boys, in which the *Holt Hill* played a leading part, was swimming around "ship visiting." In most ships swimming over the side was absolutely prohibited; in others, only allowed for half an hour or so in the evening, with very strict precautions, such as boats in the water, and look-outs aloft for sharks. Old Jock Sutherland was a sport to his finger tips, and simply left us to use our own good common sense. So, when the work of the day was over, decks had been washed, —and ourselves—tea finished, then, in the cool of the evening, over the side we would go and swim away to the next ship. If nobody was watching, their boys would come over the side and join us, and so we would go on from ship to ship, until perhaps close on fifty of us, would be swimming and singing round the harbour, in water like warm milk. Sharks are cowards, anyway, always excepting tiger sharks, and as it turned out, we were perfectly safe and never lost a soul.

As a matter of fact, a fish that is far more dangerous

than a shark in Rio harbour is a Blanket Fish, often called a Sun Fish; sometimes misnamed a Devil Fish. It frequently lies asleep on the surface, covering an area of anything up to ten or fifteen square yards. One of these fish is apt to heave itself almost bodily out of the water, and land on top of its objective, which may be a man swimming. They have only one motion, and that is forward, so there is not much danger really,—providing you are fairly quick in the uptake, dodge sideways, and don't lose your head.

Coming off in the gig one night, we ran right up one of these chaps, much to the annoyance of the Skipper. It was shortly after midnight, and pitch dark. I think the Skipper had had a pretty good time; anyhow, he was feeling quite pleased with himself. We pulled six oars, and the custom is to judge your distance from the gangway, say a hundred feet, and on the order "give her weigh" get in about half a dozen good strokes, then smartly toss the oars, while the boat, with her own impetus, runs alongside. We had just given her the half dozen, when she ran her nose high and dry, on one of these great slabs of sleeping fish, lying on the surface. He awakened in a hurry, and, tossing his stern, dived down. Being a long narrow boat, *our* stern was already well down, and the result of the Sun Fish's kick up, was that the skipper found himself sitting up to his armpits in water. On our lives we dared not laugh, so we just hustled him up on board out of the way, and howled our heads off.

Another amusement, for the boys forming the boats' crews from the different ships in harbour, was to muster up at the landing steps ashore, and, leaving one in charge of all the boats, do a cruise round the market, buying what we couldn't steal. I dare say we were a bit of a trial, and the natives certainly did not overtax their patience with us; in fact, they often used to turn out *en masse* and kick us out of the market. I don't blame them altogether, but when, on occasions, they drew knives, then it got beyond a joke. One time they chased us half way across the square before we got reinforcements from the boats with stretchers, and we were able to return their good wishes—and quite a good account we gave. This time I not only collected two very nice little cuts, but actually left a small piece of flesh, off one hand, on the ground. Several of us had got cut about, when, to add insult to injury, the mounted police turned up, but charged us boys, if you please, instead of charging the mob!

Rio is also rather noted for its podgy little bum-boats, which cruise round the harbour visiting the ships, and are anxiously looked for by the hungry hordes of apprentices. In exchange for money, or a shirt if you hadn't cash,—as was usually the case, you got glorious bread, coffee, oranges, bananas, and "alligator" pears, as they are now known, though their proper name is Avocada. This sort of trading is stopped by the Mates if it can possibly be detected. But when the sun shines, and a fellow is hungry, seaboots and thick underclothing seem quite superfluous. Many's the chap that has left Rio, bound round the Horn, with barely enough clothes for tropical weather, let alone the rigours of Cape Stiff. To have been round the Horn a few times you are a "sailor," but to have been round without seaboots, you are a real "hard case."

We rigged up stump t'gallant masts in Rio, for the simple reason, I suppose, they had no spars long enough for t'gallant, royal and skysail masts. They were terrible misfits, but the best we could get from a town in the turmoil of eternal revolutions. The sails were of No. 1 canvas and had forty-two feet of a drop. Lowered down and clewed up. At least they were supposed to lower down, but when needed never would, so it was usually a case of "Lower away t'gallant halyards," and, as nothing ever happened, "Haul taut and clew up." Finally, we would have to take up a downhaul, and pull the infernal yard down by brute force, on to the lifts. That done, then it was "up aloft and furl them"—a sixty by forty sail, No. 1 canvas, and wet at that. It was more like trying to roll up a piece of rhino hide than anything else I can imagine. You manage to beat a crinkle in the belly, so that you can get all your fingers fastened on to it, then, all together, you haul in and tuck that particular bit of sail under your stomach and lie on it, hard. All this time the sail is banging and thrashing about, and you are balanced on the foot rope, so named because it is under your feet, and all else there is under you is the deep blue sea, or worse still, the deck, if you do come down. After two or three bights of the sail have been tucked under each man, someone may inadvertently ease up, or the sail will give an extra kick, and away goes the whole damn lot, and you start all over again—if you've been lucky enough to catch the jackstay in front of you as the sail went bellying up over your head. How heartily we cursed those sails!

Finally, with all our ballast on board, a round thousand tons of sharp edged granite, every ounce of which we had man-handled from lighters to the hold, we were ready for sea. With sails bent, tug alongside, we hove up and said "so long" to them and their oranges, their cholera and their revolutions.

With a fair wind and light ship we sailed out of Rio harbour bound for Calcutta—or so we thought.

CHAPTER SEVEN *SMALLPOX*

It was almost a dead beat in the teeth of the Trades, so we reached away to forty odd degrees south, where we hoped to pick up the prevailing westerly wind, and stretch away for the Cape. We had to send down the mizzen skysailyard and unbend the mizzen royal staysail, as it gave her far too much canvas aft with only stump t'gallant masts forward; in fact, with the mizzen royal, and the wind anywhere abaft the beam, it took two hands at the wheel to keep her from broaching-to at the best of times. Whereas ordinarily with a ship of her class you could steer with one hand and a few spokes of the wheel. And, take it from me, to have in your hands the eight foot wheel (diameter, not circumference) and a twenty-five hundred ton ship, and she with a bone in her teeth, is a thing never to be forgotten. You can "feel" her just as closely as you can a horse with the most delicate mouth, and to be a helmsman worthy of the name, you must know what she is going to do, before she does it. She lifts to this sea, straightens herself up and goes down to the next, with the unmistakable motion that tells you she is going to run up in the wind on the following sea. If you don't get the helm against her before she does it, up she comes with all the upper sails shaking in the wind and the Mate howling out to know, "Where the hell are you going to, you soldier?"

Although we had left Rio, we were not to forget it in a hurry.

We had been out about a fortnight when some of the crew commenced to go down with some sort of sickness. The first chap we said was loafing, until he died. That's nearly always the verdict on a sailing ship, anyway. A man is invariably "mouching" until he dies, and then we say, "Oh, he must have been bad after all." It was smallpox.

Old Sails was the first to go under, and, even then, I don't think we were by any means sure what we were up against. No medicine, and no doctor, of course; in fact, the last medicine on board, which consisted of half a cup of castor oil, was drunk by one of the patients in mistake for water. As there was nothing to check it, we just had to rely upon our cast iron constitutions and stick it out. I seemed to be immune both from smallpox and yellow fever. I once had a chap die in my arms of Yellow Jack, and I used to wear a fur coat belonging to one of our smallpox convalescents. He used to wear it during the day, and I borrowed it at night! I'll admit I wasn't popular with the watch whilst I did wear it.

Twice I read the burial service, or such parts as I could find, in a gale of wind when the Mate couldn't leave the poop. Sometimes we couldn't get the body over the rail,—then it was beastly.

We reached away down into high latitudes in the hopes of freezing it out. This was a mixed advantage, as on one hand we had to shorten down, and keep her shortened down, for the simple reason that if we did crowd the canvas on, we had not the hands to take it in, if it came on to blow. This left us battling around under six topsails instead of stretching out for the Cape under full sail.

After several memorable weeks of struggle, under appalling conditions, we at last got our anchor down

SMALLPOX

in Capetown Quarantine ground. Made up our losses and left again. I think everyone was glad to see the last of us, as the reason for our being there had somehow leaked out ashore, although, by that time we had lived down the scourge.

From time immemorial sailing ships have what is termed "Run their Easting Down." That is, after rounding or leaving the Cape, they ran on a parallel of latitude, and sometimes worked south, keeping down till they reach St. Paul's, or thereabouts. The prevailing winds are westerly and strong, and St. Paul's serves to check chronometers for longitude, and the run north to the East Indies. We had left Rio in ballast, and mighty little of that, and therefore were in no case for cracking-on, but that made no difference to old Jock Sutherland.

We were nearing St. Paul's, when, in the afternoon, a big fourmaster barque hove in sight on our port quarter, overtaking us, under six t'gallant sails, whilst we were flying along under six topsails, but the other ship was loaded and we were light, and in no shape, with our stump t'gallant masts, to try to get away from her. The wind was well aft, which made it worse for us, owing to our makeshift rig. But all that didn't matter a bean to Jock.

"He'd never had a ship pass him with any of his sails furled, and he was not going to start now."

"*Set everything.*"

We set everything, and before dark ran her right out of sight. And small wonder, for when we hove the log at eight bells (eight o'clock) that night, we were reeling off thirteen and a half knots. Two hands at the wheel, and then all they could do to hold her on her course and prevent her broaching to; the mizzen royal, and the mizzen royal staysail doing their utmost to force her up in the wind. One thing, being in ballast, she was dry, though why on earth she didn't turn right over, heaven and old Jock alone knew—and he said nothing. As a matter of fact, the Mate and he were walking up and down the poop, each waiting for the other to make the first suggestion for shortening down, and neither would. Both good chums; both crackers-on, and you've got the situation!

At last eight bells came, and the relief of the watches. We all heard the Mate, Mr. Williams, say, "Keep a good look-out for land ahead and on the lee bow. Relieve the wheel, and look out. That will do the watch," and my watch went below. The Second Mate, taking over, said to the Mate, "Just as soon as you get below I'm for having some of these sails in."

"Just as you like," the Mate replied, "and the sooner the better."

It was blowing a gale, and he knew quite well the risk we were running in that sea, which by this time was like a house side, and the ship nearly unmanageable.

As I turned in I heard the Second Mate go forward, along the fore and aft bridge, which links up the poop to the half deck, midship house and fo'c'sle, so that anyone could get fore and aft without touching the main deck. On the fo'c'sle head he found the lookout man coiling down the flying jib downhaul, a new rope, just rove off the day before, and which eventually saved our lives.

We should have seen the land before, only for a heavy squall of rain that passed ahead, just at eight bells. The Second Mate, looking up, with the squall clearing, suddenly saw the loom of the land right ahead, and the ship rushing for it at racehorse speed.

One of our chaps had just got up to blow out the light in the half deck, when we heard Mowatt come thumping along the bridge roaring out: "Hard down. All hands on deck. Let go royal and t'gallant halyards."

CHAPTER EIGHT *WRECKED ON ST. PAUL'S*

POOR old Mowatt! He'd got the shock of his life, and in his excitement had given the wrong order; though he wasn't to know that. His idea was to bring her up in the wind, and either reach clear of the land or go about and stand off on the other tack. He had not seen, up till then, that there was four miles of land to windward, (the way he was turning the ship,) but only two to leeward.

Old Jock, with his experience, when he got on deck a moment later, took all this in, and countermanded Mowatt's order with:

"Hard up. Square away the Cro'jack yard."

The wind had been two points on the port quarter, therefore Jock also saw she would, if brought up to the wind, and being in ballast, just sag to leeward, and take the rocks broadside. Then nobody would have had a ghost of a chance. (Not that anyone would have given a brass farthing for our chances, as it was.) Jock saw that by putting the helm up he could clear the two miles to leeward, if—and it was a big if—he could get her round in time.

Under ordinary circumstances, or given the time, he would have done it, but conditions were dead against him. She had started to come up, and had been carrying the helm nearly hard up all the time, in consequence of the terrific pressure of sail aft. So that by the time she checked coming up, and started to pay off a bit, it seemed too late. She had just gone off so far that she was back on her original course, heading straight for the land, and the decision then had to be made, was it or was it not too late, to continue the manœuvre? Jock decided it was too late, (and certainly his decision was right), but he had had to make the hardest possible choice the Captain of a ship is ever called on to make. Continue to try and save his ship and thus risk everyone's life, by the ship being driven on broadside? Or, to put his ship straight at it, and deliberately throw her away.

I firmly believe that it was in taking that last desperate chance to drive her straight at that mountain of rock, rising sheer out of the darkness ahead, that later on broke him up, though by doing it he saved the lives of pretty well everyone on board.

All this had taken place within a few minutes.

When I got on deck, the land was towering right up above us. It was just then that old Jock made his irrepealable decision, and I heard him give the heart-breaking order, "Steady the Helm. Put her straight at it. Steady as she goes. Belay everything."

I had only stayed in the half deck long enough to get into my shirt, pants and shoes. Even then, it was a sight to make me feel as though I had missed my breakfast. Gigantic seas were tossing her high in the air, to let her drop next moment like a stone into an almost bottomless trough, whilst the unrelenting rocks loomed nearer and nearer.

Scared, yes scared stiff, but I don't think I was rattled, in fact I don't think anyone was rattled, Jock least of all. You certainly would not have thought so to hear him say to the Mate in a casual sort of way, "Well, she is in the breakers now. She won't be long before she bumps."

Yet his heart must have been breaking. I know mine was sinking lower and lower, as she tore at those forbidding black cliffs.

Only sixteen and every prospect of my bright young life coming to the end of the chapter within the next few minutes. A queer, hardly describable sensation of semi-suspended animation. Everyone waiting without movement or word for the crash that must almost immediately be followed by the short sharp struggle. Then . . . what? I don't advise anyone to try it as an experiment. Take it from one who knows. It's unpleasant, mighty unpleasant.

Jock's one last word of advice was to, "Stand aft under the break of the poop clear of the falling gear."

We expected all four masts to come down like a row of ninepins. A moment later we heard, "Every man for himself!" freeing everyone to follow their own devices—only, there were none to follow. There was nothing anyone could do, but just wait, wait, wait, whilst the gale still roared and the ship laboured in the gigantic seas, racing on to her impending doom. One could almost describe it as a relief from the racking suspense when at last she struck. With a shuddering crash she hit an outlying rock. The shock of that terribly alien feeling, when a ship strikes the ground, went through everyone like a knife. This was instantly followed by another terrific bump, then the sickening, rending crash, as she tore up the rocks, ripping the bottom right out of herself.

Up to that moment we had thought she was going to sail right up to the cliff, hit it like a wall, close up like a telescope, and go down with all hands. However, she didn't, though, as we discovered later, had she been a couple of hundred yards to the northward, this is exactly what would have happened. On the other hand, had she been the same distance to the southward, she would have struck outlying rocks half a mile or more out to sea. In either case it would have meant a swift and sure exit for all of us.

As it was, she struck a gradual rise, right on the top of high water, up which she went till her bowsprit was almost over the dry land. Then, as though to make doubly sure, a gigantic sea came rolling up, lifted her bows up, and dropped them between two huge pinnacles of rock, staving them both in, but holding her in a vice-like grip, and preventing any possibility of slipping back into deep water.

So there she was, with every stitch of canvas set, a slight list to port, sidelights burning, ropes coiled down, and everything in shipshape order. The sea at the moment we struck, was right aft, so all the power it had, was to smash in the stern, which it promptly did.

I recollect a lot of gear coming through the saloon; also an infernal cackling from a crate of hens, that had been on the after hatch—then blank, until I picked myself up forward. I suppose I got a crack over the head with some piece of wreckage that came through the gutted saloon and State rooms. I had not earned the soubriquet of "Woodenhead" (through my ability to sleep soundly) for nothing. I felt no ill effects anyway, and so I clambered up on the foc's'le head where, by this time, the crew had got the flying jib downhaul hitched to the end of the bowsprit, and were sliding down on to the rocks. As almost everybody was on the starb'd side of the boom, I nipped along to the port side. Caught hold of the rope with one hand and let go. With the result, that, I came a terrific cropper on the rocks below. I can only assume it was the rubber in one's limbs at that age, and that alone, which prevented both legs being broken.

As I landed on the rocks, a huge sea came over my head. I knew quite well that it was in the backwash the danger lay, so I quickly took a turn round one wrist, and round one leg, jamming it with the other, and held on like grim death. When the backwash came, I could feel that rope dragging through my hands, inch by inch. If it were possible to squeeze the heart out of a rope,

I should think I did. So great was the drag of the water that it sucked my shoes off.

However, the backwash expended itself at last, and, half drowned, I swung over the rocks again, and let go sharp, for I could feel the rope vibrating, which indicated that somebody else was coming down to try their luck. He also landed with a pretty good bump, and together, we scrambled up the rocks, to get out of the way of the next breaker. It was black dark, blowing, raining, and bitterly cold, though it wasn't until later on that we noticed the cold.

Our scramble brought us up against the face of a wet, perpendicular, and particularly slimy, rock. The sides we could not see; the top we could only reach. Leonard, the chap with me, had his wits about him, and barked,

"Give me your foot. Up you go youngster."

No sooner said than done. I landed on the top, then turned to reach for him.

"I'm all right," he called, out of the darkness.

Evidently he had found a way round, and at this moment, as I got to my feet, along came a breaker, roaring up the rocks, and just deep enough, to lift me off my feet, and carry me bodily forward. A few moments, then again the backwash, and I was swimming for dear life, at odd times trying to dig my fingers into the slimy, slippery stone, knowing that I was going backwards and backwards, towards the edge of that big rock up which I had just climbed. Over that edge, and it would be all up for me. I put every ounce of swimming into it that I ever knew, and ended with my legs, from the knees downward, dangling over the edge. But I was safe, and the next sea did *not* catch me, for I was high and dry.

We only lost one man, and that was Mr. Williams, the Mate, a great favourite with us boys, partly because he was so good natured,—although a strict disciplinarian,—and partly because he was such a fine wrestler. At one time he had, I believe, wrestled for the championship of Cornwall.

The flying jib downhaul down which we slid to the rocks was a new rope, half manilla and half jute, and when that grade of rope gets wet, it oozes oil for the first week or so. All I can think is that the Mate came down by the run, as I did, and probably broke his legs at the bottom. Or else he was not as lucky as the rest of us in dodging the backwash. However, we never saw him again. It was a marvel that half of us ever saw daylight again.

What a night. Bitterly cold, blinding rain and heavy sprays breaking right over us. If we had not been made of cast-iron we certainly could not have stuck it.

My cousin and I—he was third mate—did a little exploring to see if we could find some sort of shelter from the wind and rain. In great delight I sang out that I had found a cave, and he replied: "Well, get into it, and see what it is like."

So we got in, and crawled, and crawled, but it did not seem to afford much shelter, and, eventually, we crawled out the other side. It was only a huge boulder thrown up against the cliff. Still, it helped.

The old ship made a most wonderful picture there, with a slight list to port, every stitch of sail set (even our precious t'gallant sails), and side lights still burning, looking for all the world, with the foam at her bows, as if she were still tearing along, running her Eastern down.

About two o'clock in the morning, the wind suddenly shifted to the north-west, and with it, the sea. Up to this time the waves, coming from right aft, had only power to smash her stern in, and nothing more. The first sea, after the sudden shift, caught her on the quarter, and broke her back; the second sea parted her amidship, and brought down the Mizzen and Jigger masts; in fact, the whole after part sank out of sight. It was a staggering sight to see those towering masts with their steel yards come tumbling and crashing down —the old ship literally disintegrating before our eyes. The fourth sea brought the Mainmast down, and almost immediately afterwards, the Foremast. When morning broke, the only vestige left was the bare bows, and, although weighing hundreds of tons, they were tossed up, high and dry, on the rocks, like a battered shell,—all that remained of that once proud ship, the old *Holt Hill*.

No doubt St. Paul's island in prehistoric times rose out of the sea, as the result of some titanic submarine volcanic disturbance, and there is no disguising the fact, a volcanic horror it has remained ever since. No waving palms, coral reefs, and silver sands on St. Paul's; just a bleak, bare, barren, and, for the most part, inaccessible island. Cold and raw, with the ever present threat of going up in the air at any moment.

Peep of day next morning saw us scrambling up the cliffs aiming for the top of the island. As we got up a bit, we found the cliff side consisted of nothing better than loose rubble, cinders, and lots of loose rocks. The result, and residue of the last volcanic effort. It didn't help the climbing, for whenever we got hold of a rock, in all probability it was just stuck in the rubble, and promptly came away, leaving one balanced, half in mid air, and half hanging on to the rock. "Stand clear below," was the caution, and then, let go!

That rock would start another, until there was a full fledged avalanche careering down the cliff side, making it altogether a fairly exciting climb, but not by any means the easiest part was dodging other people's rocks!

By the time we did get to the top, the sun was up. Did we not revel and roll in the dry grass? What a treat to feel warmth once more.

CHAPTER NINE — *A DESERT ISLAND*

As we were lords of all we surveyed, and at perfect liberty to go where we wished—without the slightest fear of trespassing—three of us set a course, as it turned out, right straight across the island. Frequently we had to work our way round huge gaps in the ground, from which came sulphurous fumes, in a kind of steamy smoke. Admitted there are a few goats on the island, but they are like the proverbial Chinaman who can live on the smell of an oil rag. Whatever they do live on, certainly does not detract from their activity. "Now you see me, now you don't"; a glimpse on the skyline, and gone again. Certainly before one could have got within rifle range—if we had possessed such a thing. No doubt these goats, also the rabbits, of which there are a fair quantity, have been put on the island by ships, in times past. The rabbits and goats, unfortunately, find their living on top of the island; whilst any unfortunate human beings must always keep to the sea level, in order to get water.

We continued on our way, and the going was somewhat like walking up a fairly steep hill. Up this slope we trudged. No signs of either water or life. No trees; not even a bush. I suppose we had been working our way along for the best part of a couple of hours, up and still up, looking more at our feet, than to our front. Suddenly I stopped, for we seemed to have come to the edge of the world. There, lying like a panorama, over two thousand feet below us, was a wonderful lagoon, absolutely circular, with cliffs all round, except just where the sea had broken in on the far side. There, the cliffs ran down to two shingle spits with a 16 foot channel between them, giving entrance to the lagoon. One chap with us who had eyes like the proverbial hawk, said he could see huts. I had good eyesight too, but perched up there I could see nothing resembling house or hut. As a matter of fact, as it turned out, there were five huts, and when we did get down we found the one he could only just see, was actually large enough to hold the whole forty-two of us, at one end.

As there was nothing to be gained by staying perched up there, we started to look for a break in the face of the cliff, which was pretty nearly perpendicular, but overgrown with long rank grass, any three or four blades of which it was almost impossible to break. We soon found a place where we could negotiate the overhanging lip, and with a very creditable imitation of monkeys, we commenced to swing, toboggan and bump our way down.

We found that the whole of the cliff side was honeycombed with caves, and we frequently discovered ourselves dangling bodily over one of these openings.

I am convinced, and I always have been, that if a thorough search should be made of these caves, hoards of pirates' treasure would most certainly be unearthed, but the first step towards anything like that would have to be the burning away of all this rank grass.

Everywhere there are indications showing that the island has been used for many purposes. Traces of old whalers, and sealers, and evidences of occupation long before that. There were boats, of a build unknown to the oldest sailor amongst us, the planking and timbers, although inches thick, crumbled away in one's hand. Old time anchors, with their wooden stocks rotted out;

in fact there was actually a built slip, where a small vessel could be hauled up, scraped and painted. The huts must have been in existence for over a hundred years, and there were many other indications that immediately jump to a sailor's eye as evidence that it had been used as a base for some seafaring enterprise.

What more ideal place to catch an unwary East Indiaman, after running his Easting down and ready to turn north? Very likely he would be trying to sight the island to correct his position. In bad weather a schooner could lie in the lagoon, happily, and in perfect safety. No matter what sea running outside, the lagoon is always like a millpond. A lookout on the top of the island would soon spot one of the lumbering old timers in the distance. Then the schooner could be warped and towed out, just hiding in the entrance, till the time was judged ripe to make the attack, and that, we can imagine, would be both sharp, and short. Then back with their booty to the lair, leaving no track or trace. Even wreckage would not stand one chance in a thousand of ever being sighted in those latitudes. The caves lent themselves as perfect hiding places for the plunder and, in my firm opinion, there it remains to this day, for it is notorious that pirates never lived to enjoy their ill-gotten gains.

There is treasure hidden all over the world, but in my humble opinion St. Paul's holds the long sought secret of many a pirate's hoard.

It has always been,—and still is,—my ambition to search these caves, and sometime, with a bit of luck, I will.

There are all sorts of good reasons why St. Paul's has never yet been searched. One very good reason is that there are a few thousand bleak miles of sea to negotiate; eternal gales to contend with, a crew to pay, and provisions to find. Furthermore, you must take water with you, or content yourself with condensed water. Another item on the catalogue of wants would be the wherewithal to burn off the grass that at present very successfully and completely hides the openings to every one of the caves.

Why didn't we search whilst we were there? For the simple reason that we were far too busy keeping body and soul from parting company. In later years I did get one expedition together, and it was only by the slimmest chance that it fell through. We had the ship, and we had the very necessary capital (which is of some importance). Like many other dreams, it didn't materialise, but I still in my dreams see that smart little schooner anchored in that lagoon, loading up with gold, jewels, and all imaginable treasures, that forever live in the mind of the treasure hunter.

Having got down to the edge of the water, we started in to work our way round towards the huts, which, by now, we could see quite clearly. Here and there we came across boiling springs, amongst the rocks, which showed that something down under was still alive and warm.

Bill, my cousin, tried the water in the springs, and said it was fresh. I just took his word for it, as it was a bit too hot for my taste, and in any case, up until then, I was too excited to be particularly thirsty—though that added joy was to come, and pretty soon.

Arrived at the huts, the first cry from the fellows already there was, "Have you found water?" I said, "Yes," and was asked to show them where it was. So off back I went; but I suppose half an hour had elapsed between times. Anyhow, we journeyed off for the springs, climbing over the rocks from pool to pool; but they were all salt; salt as Lot's wife.

What had happened, I found out later, was, that between the time of our coming round the lagoon, and taking these other chaps back again, the tide had risen and flowed into the pools.

Others said they had found water on top of the island —a small well.

By next day most of us had become pretty desperate, and it behoved us to call up a volunteer party, to shin up those two thousand odd feet with oilskins, sea boots, and any other receptacles that would hold water. Fortunately, the north point had a gradual ascent, and afforded some decent foothold.

The water party was led by an able seaman, named Bartle Macintyre, one of the finest sailors I have ever met, and one that nothing ever daunted. Actually, he made the party climb that cliff, with only six short intervals of rest. Arriving at the top, I, for one, was just about all-in. But after one last spell, we started the tramp to find this well. The going now was not too bad, and we made good time, though, as far as I was concerned, things were getting hazier and hazier, and I was rapidly losing interest. I could see the fellows walking ahead, but they seemed a mighty way off. I was long past speaking; in fact my tongue was just completely dried up, and my lips were split in two or three pieces. I remembered quite well, one of the chaps coming back and relieving me of the pair of oilskin pants which I was carrying, tied at the bottom to fill up with water.

I pointed to a slight depression I had noticed, and two or three of us went down to see if, by chance, there was any water, and found the ground fairly moist. They called the others back. We tore up the damp ground squeezing the mud into the palms of our hands and drinking it. Although it was just mud, and barely wet enough to moisten our lips, it was as nectar to our parched throats. Very soon we all took the trail again.

I knew, quite well, why they had taken these oilskins from me, and I realized that once I stumbled and fell down (which seemed quite likely) I should not get up again. I was conscious, clearly conscious, and remembered every incident; how the fellows gradually faded away into the distance, finally, I saw them no more. But I still kept trudging on and on, determined to keep up on end as long as I could. After a time I suddenly brought up with a start, for in front of me, I saw a pool of beautifully clear water.

"Ha," I thought, "now, this is a mirage. Now in what books have I read about mirages?" and I stood there trying to recollect a book, or the name of an author that had dealt with these mirages, for I was fully convinced that that was what I saw. Then, as I gazed at this pool of water, which also seemed to be getting a bit hazy, I imagined I could see men lying down around it, and, in an inconsequent way, I considered that just another strange phenomenon. Then I further noticed they seemed to be actually drinking. "Well," I thought, "I have read about a mirage, where you could see water, but never where you could actually observe men going through all the motions of drinking." Still I gazed, making no effort whatever to reach the water, for I was stone wall sure that it was absolutely nothing but a mirage. Then it seemed as if I could even recognise some of the faces. "Why, that is Bartle Macintyre," I thought. Then, at last, it struck me. Can it be real? and I bent down to try and touch the water. Sure enough, it was a real pool of pure clear crystal water. Instantly I tried to scoop it up in my hands and drink, but I might as well have tried to lift the water with a sponge; my hands just absorbed it. Then I remembered a quart bottle in my pocket, which had been overlooked when they relieved me of my precious oilskin pants. I plunged this into the water, filled it and drank it; filled it again and drank it. Three times in all.

I suppose after drinking like that, nothing but an ostrich like constitution saved me, though perhaps the saving grace was that we all laid down without moving, and went fast asleep.

Later we woke, filled every single receptacle to its utmost capacity and started on our way, back to the lagoon.

We took a slightly different course returning, which carried us through some high coarse grass, and here we retrieved the Captain, who, despite all our persuasion, and in fact, some threats of force, had steadfastly refused to leave the scene of the wreck. The loss of the ship seemed to have preyed very heavily on his mind, and certainly he was never the same man again, and never took another command, although at the Board of Trade Enquiry he was to all intents and purposes, exonerated from blame.

We happened to see his head appear at one time above the long grass, and then he disappeared, having, as it proved, fallen down, and it is doubtful if he would ever have got on his feet again had we not found him. We gave him a good drink, and partly carrying him, managed to get him away.

Before our party left the huts in search of water, several boats had already been found—in various stages of decay—and we had launched one, in slightly better condition than the rest, with the idea of having it meet us at the edge of the lagoon on our return with water.

Knowing the conditions of the fellows when we left, we should not have been surprised if an attempt were to be made to rush the water containers. So the strongest formed a sort of bodyguard, whilst we youngsters became the carriers. Much to our surprise, the fellows in the boat took very little notice of us, and at first we thought that this was perhaps part of a rather deep game to catch us unawares, and so get hold of the water. It should be borne in mind that before we started, many of them were half crazy through drinking salt water.

About half way across the lagoon we got rather tired of sitting tight, protecting our precious water bags, and asked them if they didn't want a drink. To our amazement they replied, quite indifferently, "Oh, no, we found water just after you left!"

So we had had our little jaunt for nothing.

Actually what they had discovered was the selfsame springs that we had found on our first journey round the lagoon, only it so happened that in their search they had come across them again, just at dead low water, which, as it turned out, was the only time when the water could be obtained in any other condition than salt. I say in any other condition, for there was really little to choose after all, either salt or fresh. The taste was utterly vile. They were just some sort of mineral springs from which the water had to be collected while still boiling hot, and then allowed to cool down, but the taste was somewhat similar to what one associates with, say, a mixture of chalk and antiquated egg! We drank it simply because we must quench our thirst, but even though years have passed I can still taste the beastly stuff. However, that was our drink, and we could take it or leave it, just as we liked.

The menu card included penguins, crayfish, Cape salmon and eggs. The least said about the latter, the better. Had we only arrived a few weeks earlier they might have been possible, but at that time, most of them that still remained eggs were in a very advanced state of incubation. The penguins were slightly better. Half fish and half bird, they seemed to have acquired all the bad qualities of both. The fish, unfortunately, took after the water, and tasted, if anything, worse. Crayfish formed the staple diet, when we could get them, which was only when the tide was rising, and not always then. Outside the lagoon, there were stacks of perfectly good and eatable Cape salmon. So there were in British Columbia! Lacking the wherewithal to catch them, they were as useful to us, in our position, as were the others. The old relics on the island that *would* actually float, were not equal to sea work; and after the first couple of days there were mighty few of us anyway with strength left to row a boat across the lagoon, let alone outside the shingle spits, in the open sea.

Everything on the island seemed poisonous. Some of the fellows took penguins' skins to wrap round their feet in lieu of boots, but if they had the slightest scratch they very soon had to discard the skins, as their feet just swelled up and festered.

Our faith had to be pinned to crayfish, which we caught by attaching the innards of a penguin to the end of a line; throwing it out into the deep water, and then, drawing it slowly in, the crayfish following. But this could only be done on an incoming tide, as that was the only time the crayfish seemed to rise. They were pretty hefty chaps and could easily nip a finger off between the serrated edges of their tails!

CHAPTER TEN *A FIGHT WITH ALBATROSSES*

SEVERAL expeditions were made overland across to the wreck, in the hopes of getting something from the old ship, but all we ever secured was about a dozen pounds of pork,—this had evidently been washed out of one of the harness casks, on deck, and drifted ashore; a bit of canvas, and about a fathom of rope. Out of the rope we made our fishing lines.

The party returning from the wreck, on the occasion when they had retrieved the pork, had the good luck to catch three rabbits, and eventually made their way down the broken north end of the cliff, which we had found easiest to negotiate. The only drawback, as this returning party soon found to their cost, was the fact that it led down close past an albatross rookery.

It is a well-known fact that to a man fallen overboard an albatross is almost as bad as a shark. The latter attacks the man from below the water, but an albatross can, and will, drive his beak clean through a man's skull whilst swooping past in the air, which very likely accounts for the Ancient Mariner grabbing one by the neck and hanging on—I don't blame him.

When the albatrosses scented the pork and the rabbits, they rose in a cloud to share a cheap meal. The party of humans had no alternative but to back up against the cliff, put the pork and the rabbits to the rear, and do their best to beat off the birds. Someone who was working on the beach down below heard their SOS, and raised the alarm. Arming ourselves with sticks, staves, or anything we could lay hands on, we dashed up the cliff (as well as we could do any dashing by this time) to the rescue of the party who were making a valiant fight to retain their precious pork and rabbits. Arriving there, we handed out sticks. Those that had knives used a stick in one hand and a knife in the other; and for the next half an hour it was just a battle royal with these huge birds, measuring anything from fifteen to twenty feet from tip to tip of their wings. Finding that their grabs at the grub were ineffectual, they varied operations by swooping down, and making a dive at one's face or eyes as they planed past. We, of course, retaliated, first with a stick, giving them a crack over the head, and then, as they fell, driving a knife in between their shoulders, which we found the best way of settling them, otherwise, they simply rose and went for us again.

Beyond some pretty severe gashes, we came out of it quite well, still hanging on to our pork and rabbits.

What a meal that was! All boiled down in a huge cauldron, mixed in with a few fish, some grass, and thistles. It formed about the one and only decent meal during our occupation of the island.

There are very few albatross rookeries to be found in the world. These birds do come ashore to breed, but otherwise they seem to live on the wing, and if they do sleep, they also certainly sleep on the wing, for you meet with them thousands of miles from land, in gales of wind, when they couldn't possibly sleep on the water. They have absolutely no fear, and will hover, with the tip of their wing almost touching the bridge of even a steamer, and stare the officer of the watch straight in the face with their little, black, beady eyes. They fall an easy prey to a little bit of pork, and one of the easiest methods of catching them from a ship, is to get a piece of tin cut into a triangle, with the sides half an inch wide, tie some strips of pork on to the tin, and let it drop astern on the end of a line. At the point of an albatross' beak, is a hook, almost exactly resembling a lion's claw. When they make a dab to catch the pork, the point of their beak goes into the centre of the triangle, and is drawn to the apex, where it jams, and, providing he will rise in the air, proves an easy capture. Unless the line is slacked off he can never get his beak out. On the other hand, if he determines to resist, and puts his feet and wings in the water, it is good-bye to line, bait and all.

I have seen one caught measuring thirty feet from tip to tip of its wings.

The rookery on St. Paul's consisted of a number of ledges where it seemed as though the fathers and mothers of all albatrosses came to spend their last days. Some two or three hundred feet below at the base of the cliff was a mound of bones covering nearly half an acre of ground, fully a hundred feet high, and must have weighed scores of tons. It was nothing but the bones of ancient albatrosses, that from time immemorial had gone there to die, eventually tumbling off the ledges from old age, to add to the bones below. Some of the beaks we picked up were over a foot in length, and the birds they had been attached to must certainly have had well over a thirty foot spread.

On nearly all these outlying islands there is a cache of provisions, supposed to be maintained by the Government of the country to whom the island belongs, but in point of fact, this job is usually carried out by British ships. We searched everywhere as long as our strength held out for this cache, which we knew must be there, but never found it. Some twelve years later, when I was on my first voyage out to Australia in the White

Star Line, I happened to be reading a book of sailing directions, which described the situation of these various caches, and the one on St. Paul's was referred to as being "marked by a cairn of stones on the South spit." I knew it at once. The cairn of stones had been there all the time, but painted on the side was "Mrs. Smith and child, wife of Captain Smith, died such-and-such a date."

Naturally, we thought it marked her grave, and that being so we would not touch it. Yet tobacco, potatoes, tinned provisions of all kinds, were there beside us all the time and to be had for the taking—and last, but not least, matches also. Amongst the forty-two of us there had been only one dry match, and with that we made a fire, which we had to keep going night and day, the whole time we were on the island.

We seem to have been slightly worse off than other ships that at odd times had left their bones there; that is, in the way of getting provisions.

In the entrance to the lagoon the wreck of H.M.S. *Megæra* is still visible, although she was run ashore there as long since as 1874. Bound from Simon's Bay, East Africa, with a crew, and relief crews, numbering 375, she sprung a leak the first week out. She was only 1,400 tons, and heavily rigged for sailing, although she had 350 h.p. engines down below. She sprung a leak under the bunkers, in the sheathing, where a rivet came out, and when the engineers attacked it, with a view to securing a supporting plate, they found that the ship's bottom in places was the thickness of a sixpenny piece, and to attempt to do anything would undoubtedly have been fatal. They were already running before the usual heavy westerly gale, and mountainous seas, and it seemed hopeless to turn her about and try the Vanderdecken touch and beat back to the Cape.

There is no sea in the world equal to that which one meets down in those south latitudes, it comes literally swinging round the world, with no land to break or intercept it.

One moment you are riding right up on the back, getting the full force of the gale, and the next you are down in the trough, with only the upper yards on the mast visible to anyone around. Even a twelve thousand ton ship, on the side of one of these seas, is like nothing better than a fly on the wall. The saving grace is that they are so big that they seldom break. Woe betide the ship that is running before it, and one of these seas does break! I saw it once, and it was nothing short of a miracle that anyone lived to tell the tale.

The choice the Captain of the *Megæra* had put before him was a mighty bitter one. A short beat back to the Cape, or a three thousand mile run to the nearest land, and that land was only the islands of St. Paul's and Amsterdam. He took the wiser course; in fact, the only course, and ran with every stitch of canvas towards St. Paul's. The pumps were continually getting choked with weed, and to make matters worse, the straining of the ship caused other rivets to loosen up.

Ultimately, every man jack on board, including officers, was bailing with anything, and everything, to keep her afloat. Stoke-hold fires had been put out very early on, sails were passed under her bottom, and held in place with lashings of rope, but proved to be of very little use. She was making a good eleven knots under sails alone, and of course these patchwork quilts were simply washed away. After many days of intense anxiety, they at last sighted St. Paul's, and finally came to anchor at the mouth of the lagoon.

They got the ship pumped out, and then fires going, divers down, and the holes plugged.

They then went to work and tried to put a supporting plate on the outside, when, with hardly a moment's warning, the whole original plate gave way.

They had just time to slip their anchors, and run her as hard as they could for the beach. She grounded between the shingle spits in sixteen feet of water, and in the process ripped nearly the whole of the bottom out of her; and there her bones still lie to this day.

Fortunately, whilst still afloat, all provisions, sails and stores had been landed, and they had actually on the island food for all hands for one month. But, as there was every likelihood of their spending several months there, they had to go on short rations forthwith; just enough to keep them alive; and well it was they took this drastic action, for it was four months before they were eventually taken off.

They were more fortunate than we were in the fact that they possessed their own boats, thoroughly seaworthy, and could work outside the harbour where ample fish could be caught. In fact, as an officer of that ill-fated ship told me, he caught no less than 1,100 pounds of fine Cape salmon within a few hours, with only his boat's crew, and this only just outside the shingle spits.

Several ships came in sight but never near enough to make out their distress signals. Eventually, with one of their lifeboats, an officer was able to board a passing ship, bound for Surabaya, but before anything could be done in the way of rescue, the usual gale sprang up, and she was driven away.

However, they made port with this officer and his boat's crew on board, who got in touch with the naval authorities at Hong Kong, and the P. & O. s.s. *Malacca* was despatched at once to take them off. Beyond some casualties through scalding when the boilers burst at the time she was run ashore, there were no losses.

Some of the tales that are left written on St. Paul's have not that happy ending; and with the crew of more than one ship, it has been the last survivor who has finally scratched his message on a piece of wood or stone, to be read by those who came after. Just a silent record of a few of the risks that have to be taken by those who "go down to the sea in ships."

It is bad enough to be stuck on an island with little hope of rescue, but it is worse when, after many days, a ship heaves in sight and deliberately leaves the castaways. In all the time we had been there not one single ship had been sighted, till the early morning of the day we were taken off. That morning, the first man out of the hut rubbed his eyes to make sure he was really awake, for there, lying becalmed, close in to the island, lay a full rigged ship under all sail. The next second everyone was awake and dashing out of the hut in response to his roar of "Sail-ho!"

We had only one boat that made any pretence at floating, and this, with her crew, was detailed for fishing. The tide served that morning at daybreak, as the best time for catching crayfish, with the result that the boat was right over the other side of the lagoon, and the ship was hidden from the boat by the south cliff. We yelled, and hailed, and only after a long, heartbreaking delay, got the boat from under the cliffs.

As soon as they were in a position to see the ship, they pulled as hard as their strength would let them, out of the harbour, and were actually half way between the island and the ship, when a slight breeze sprang up. It is hard to believe but down went that ship's helm, she went about, and deliberately stood off from the land.

On shore we had a huge fire burning, sending up columns of smoke, and everyone of us that could stand was waving his shirt. We could even see the men on her deck.

It was a rank impossibility for those on board not to have seen the column of smoke, or our boat, and yet, away she went, and that is the tragedy that so frequently happens in these cases.

One of the most glaring instances was that in which the *Volturno* on fire in mid-Atlantic, in fine weather, was passed by a big steamship, without her taking the slightest notice. It was fine, clear weather, and the dense column of smoke rising from the burning oil could have been seen twenty-five or thirty miles away, and yet, a ship not five miles off, passes and takes no notice. Again, in the case of the *Titanic*, which I am going to tell about later, we were using every modern method, visible and invisible, to call the attention of a ship actually in sight, yet, there she lay, making no attempt at rescue, whilst some fifteen hundred people patiently waited and were finally drowned with that ship's lights still in sight.

In our case on the island of St. Paul's, the boat had no alternative but to return. We did not even get the name of the ship, as there was no name on her stern. If there had been, the Second Mate could easily have read it; and yet, where will you find a ship without her name and port of registry on her stern? Some have said, "Oh, it must have been a phantom ship, the outcome of some delirious imagination. You were starving you know." They might just as well have put it down to the "morning after the night before,"—only unfortunately, we lacked the wherewithal.

She was not seen by one, or half a dozen, but by all of us, and you can't mesmerize forty-two men. Anyhow, it just about knocked the bottom out of what spirits we had left, and they were mighty few. We had been there eight days, and it would take less than another eight to finish the lot.

Anyhow, we weren't going to be caught napping another time, so we instituted a day and night look-out, on a hill top above the camp, where a good view could be obtained all round, northward and westward. The same hill where many other ships' crews have kept their sometimes fruitless vigil, others to watch for their welcome rescuer, and where the *Megaera* managed to mount a twelve-pounder gun.

The boat we had for general purposes, including fishing, was now detailed to stand by, to intercept any other ship that might come along, and the crew, although allowed to fish, were forbidden to be out of hail. We launched another boat for a fishing party; she floated, and that is about all that could be said for her. She was nearly as broad as she was long; in fact, it would be interesting to know what kind of ship ever brought her to the island. Then we settled down for another wait, though, as it turned out, not for long.

CHAPTER ELEVEN
A TIMELY RESCUE

LATER on, that same afternoon, to our joy and amazement, we again heard that welcome cry of "Sail-o!" from the look-out. At once, the fire on the look-out hill was lit, a piece of canvas hoisted up on the flag staff, which we had also rigged, and the boat was instantly manned and shoved off out of the harbour. It was not long before all those who could were up on the look-out hill; and, sure enough, there was a little barque which had just rounded the point, sailing along the western side of the island, with just a light breeze, all sails set. She did look a picture; in fact, speaking for myself, there has never been a more welcome picture in my life.

Our vital consideration now was as to whether or not she would see us or our signal; or if our boat would float long enough to be able to intercept her. We waited, and waited, as she slowly drew along the land, then, at last, we knew that she had actually seen us. Down came her t'gallant sails and staysails; up went her mainsail and foresail, and she definitely hauled in towards land. Joy! oh, joy, never was there a more welcome sight. And, furthermore, she had also seen our boat, which we watched go alongside, and the Second Mate jump on board.

These then were the questions from Captain Hayward:

"What ship?"

"*Holt Hill*, sir."

"What happened?"

"Wreck, and total loss."

"How many more of you on the Island?"

"Only thirty-seven, sir."

"My God! I can't take all of you, I'm already short of provisions for my own crew of six."

Then, after a few moments anxious thought:

"I will take half of you."

Mowatt replied, "Well, sir, I'm afraid it will mean certain death for those left behind."

"Is it as bad as all that," asked Captain Hayward. Then flinging caution to the wind, "well, all right, tell them *all* to come along then. We'll manage somehow."

Mowatt was just a bit wise in his generation, and said. "My men are played out, sir. Do you think you could send four of your men in the boat?"

Our boat's crew *was* played out, even with that short pull, but Mowatt figured that with four of our chaps on board, weak though they were, there would be no likelihood of a repetition of what had happened that same morning, and it would be all the more certain if he could persuade the Captain to let some of his own men go away with orders for the rest to come aboard. He asked Captain Hayward to stand in as close as he could to the mouth of the lagoon, so that the *Coorong*, would not need to put a boat out, and we could come off in the contraption we had floating inside the harbour.

Our boat came ashore, manned by the *Coorong's* crew, and told us to get aboard our own boat and come off. The thirty seven of us tumbled into that old galliot, and with makeshift paddles and oars and got her through the entrance. Fortunately, it was one of those rare days when there was practically no sea, and very little wind. The moment we got into her the seams started to open, and the water commenced to pour in. We baled desperately, with everything we had, and it was the toss of a button, whether we would fetch the *Coorong* by boat or by swimming. We were even tearing our shirts, and stuffing the rags into the seams, in the endeavour to make her float a few minutes more. We got alongside, and the last man was hardly out of her, before she filled and and sank, like a stone. But we were on board with the welcome feel of a ship under our feet once again.

"Well, boys," said Captain Hayward, "I'm glad to have you on board, and I've put out on the hatch there, all the biscuits and butter I've got. Help yourselves, you might as well have one square meal. I really ought not to take you all, but it seems that if I leave you, you may all be dead before the next ship comes along. I'm just trusting to sighting a ship, and getting provisions. I'm part loaded with sugar, from Mauritius to Adelaide, and you can help yourselves to that, for what it's worth."

How she came to stand out of her course from Mauritius to Adelaide was food for quite a bit of thought.

She had a fair wind, and being short of provisions Captain Hayward was particularly anxious to make the best of a fair wind; yet, for some unknown reason, as he relates himself, "I couldn't get St. Paul's out of my mind, and when I went below that afternoon (the one previous to picking us up) I could not sleep. The question as to whether there was anybody on St. Paul's would not leave my mind, partly due, perhaps, to the fact, that I *had* once taken a crew off there. Finally, in desperation, I came on deck, and gave orders to alter the course for St. Paul's, and I went below, and had my nap, without any further trouble. Up on deck, later on, of course, came the thought 'what a pity to be losing this fine fair wind,' for by standing away south to St. Paul's, it meant a serious loss of time. Well I changed my mind, and put her back on her course again for Cape Leeuwin."

"That night, when I went below, it was just a repetition of the afternoon's efforts to sleep, and, to make a long story short, I simply had to get up on deck, and alter the course, back again for St. Paul's."

"Of course, this chopping and changing had got the whole crew on their toes, and when finally we did sight the island, nearly everyone was on the look-out."

"It was from a man working on the foretopsail yard," continued Captain Hayward, "that we got the first inkling, when he hailed the deck, saying he could see a signal flying. In a few minutes we saw your fire, and finally, the boat, and well, here you are and I'm very glad to have you."

It was well that Captain Hayward put us on drastic rations from the very first, for we never sighted a ship from there to Adelaide, twenty-two days. Half a pound of bread, half a pound of meat, and as much pure unadulterated raw sugar as we cared to eat.

Before that, if anybody had asked me at the age of sixteen, if I could live on sugar, I should undoubtedly have said "Give me the chance," but as we soon found out, it can't be done.

We arrived in Adelaide a regular pack of scarecrows; thoroughbred ringbolt chasers, which means in ship's parlance, that we were capable of reeving ourselves through any fair-sized ringbolt in the deck.

From the Semaphore our fame had spread before us, and when the *Coorong* docked, the wharfside was packed solid with crowds of those hospitable Australians who, during our stay, did their level best to burst us with good cheer. So the skin and bones brigade mustered on the wharf, and gave three hearty cheers for Captain Hayward. Three more for his crew. Then, from him, "Three cheers for the crew she's fetched."

There we said good-bye to our jolly old rescuer, each going his various ways; soon to have the world between us; yet, how small a world.

Ten years later I anchored off Adelaide, fourth Officer of the White Star liner *Medic* then inaugurating the new White Star Australian service. Off watch, and strolling round the decks I happened to meet the pilot who had brought us up to our anchorage. With the usual ship's camaraderie we got yarning about the ship, and Australia. The Pilot's friend asked, "Have you ever been to Australia before?" "Yes," I said, "and Adelaide at that, but many years ago."

"On what ship?" he asked.

"Well, I wasn't exactly on a ship bound here, I was brought here after being wrecked on St. Paul's Island in the South Indian Ocean."

"Was that ship by any chance the *Holt Hill?*" he asked, rather eagerly, and followed this question up by asking if I remembered the name of the ship that rescued us, and brought us to Adelaide. I replied:

"Yes, perfectly. The ship was the *Coorong*, belonging to Adelaide, and her Captain was Captain Hayward."

He quickly stepped forward, held out his hand and said:

"Glad to meet you again, I'm Captain Hayward."

CHAPTER TWELVE — *HOME IN A TEA CLIPPER*

I SAMPLED Australian life for three good and hospitable months. Sometimes up in the Bush on a station, at other times in the town sharing a happy-go-lucky life with those impulsive, lovable, carefree people. Picnics that could be planned with safety weeks ahead. Glorious sunshine and three good meals a day—what more could a healthy lad of sixteen want? Welcome everywhere as a survivor of a wreck that echoed round the world, and which was common knowledge with every man, woman and child of that island nation.

All good things must end, and the time at last came when I must tear myself away from the everlasting attractions "Down under," if I was to keep to the sea as a career, and I had no intention of parting company with her, as yet. Despite all the hours of buffeting, I never hesitated in my allegiance to that hard-boiled mistress; harsh and bitter as she can be at times, at others, full of captivating smiles and surprises. A hundred years at sea couldn't wholly unfold all she has to show you. Things that would make a landsman's eyes pop out of his head. But you must laugh in her face, when she hits you hardest, and, above all, never fear her; she will let you out, and make up for it in the end.

Our crew had all shipped off home, except another boy and myself. This was before the days of D.B.S. (Distressed British Seamen), when all you have to do is to walk into the nearest British Consul's Office, and be forwarded on to your port of hail.

Another curious law of the sea that still exists is, that a man's pay stops from the time his ship is wrecked. In these days of steam and quick passages, it does not cut so hard, but in the case of the *Holt Hill* it caught out some of the crew pretty badly, particularly the Mates, who must work their way back to England, before they could hope to pick up their proper rank, and pay again, and you could safely reckon on say 125 days to the Lizard. Even when you got home there was still the ship to find.

However, these problems didn't worry Archer and myself, and I don't suppose we should have broken away when we did, had it not been for the Agents, impressing on us the necessity. They told us, when we used to go round on a Saturday for our pocket money that the Company was worrying them to send us home. Eventually they said they would have to stop our allowance if we didn't get a move on, and get a ship. They had been awfully decent to us; so had everyone for that matter, so much so that when we did finally get a ship, we very nearly deserted—which would have completely torn our Indentures, and put a finish to our budding career.

We had shipped on Board the *Duke of Abercorn*, one of the old time tea clippers; towed down from Adelaide and anchored off the Semaphore, waiting for a breeze. That night, Archer and I had the 8 to 12 watch. It was a real Australian summer night, soft as silk, and full of magic. I can't just describe it, but it gets you in a weak spot. It did with us, sitting there on the rail looking at the shore lights twinkling and beckoning. Thinking of all the jolly fine times we had had there these three months past; reflecting on one or two very nice folk (we'll call them folk anyway) who would be tickled to death to see us back ashore again. I suppose it was through talking there that the urge at last got too strong,

HOME IN A TEA CLIPPER

and we suddenly determined to chuck our hands in, and get ashore again; a perfectly crazy idea, but what of it.

We couldn't lower a boat; too much noise, and anyway it would be sure to be seen.

There was a long wooden ladder, and a big wooden refuse shoot; they would float. So forthwith we proceeded to launch the first part of our rickety craft. The fact that it was a good three miles to the beach, and rotten with sharks, didn't enter into our calculations. We had got the ladder overboard, when fate, and our good fortune intervened, in the shape of a light breeze.

Quickly orders were being bellowed along the decks. "All hands on deck. Man the windlass. Heave short. Loose all sail." Then, to the clank, clank, of the pawls of the windlass rose the words of that good old shanty "Rolling Home." It's a wonder if we didn't make some of them turn over in their sleep, particularly when it came to the line, "To Australia's charming daughters, we must bid a long good-bye." However, it was soon all over, and within an hour, the old timer was heeling over to a steady breeze on her first clip for the Cape.

. . . . .

Less than a month, with an extraordinary good slant of easterly winds, saw us within a couple of days of the Cape. Then the wind banged round out of the westward, and became a dead muzzler.

For fourteen solid days we tried to beat up those few miles tack and tack. Like Vanderdecken of old, it seemed as though we should never make Table Bay, till at last, in desperation, we reached away south, and picked up a slant which carried us round.

It was almost in sight of the Cape that I got my first view of a huge Sea Bat.

For the last couple of days we had been shortened down, and I was up loosing the fore royal, when I spotted my fish, lying apparently asleep, on the surface of the water. Even at that height he looked monstrous. I could easily gauge his span, by comparing him with the fore yard, which was immediately under me, and measured exactly 90 feet from yardarm to yardarm. I could see he was a fraction less, 10 feet perhaps. We were almost on top of him, before he sounded; in fact, it looked as though we were going to hit him. Then, with just a couple of flaps of those gigantic wings, and he was down and out of sight. Since then, I have seen two others, but smaller.

The *Duke* was a real old timer. Built long before the days of steel and iron, she had raced with such redoutable ships as the *Red Jacket*, *Thermopylae* and *Cutty Sark*. In those days she carried more of a crew than the crack Atlantic liner has on deck to-day. Nineteen knots, day after day, she had to her credit, in her old logs, but these hair-raising races from China, are no more.

We rounded the Cape, stretched up through the Tropics and Trades, through the Roaring Forties, and finally reached Falmouth for orders, and a few days later made fast in the East India dock, after being away just on eighteen months.

I had to go through the hoop with Messrs. William Price and Co., the owners of the old *Holt Hill*, in Liverpool for staying so long in Adelaide. Other delinquencies, mainly to do with practical jokes in foreign ports, were also on the list of the "Please explains." Unfortunately, other nations don't appreciate the Britisher's love of a skylark, particularly when played by a set of boys, whose reputation was rather too well-known.

It was to find the ringleader, that Archer and I were called up and hauled over the coals.

I always think it was a good thing, that the half deck crowd of the *Holt Hill* was broken up, and scattered amongst other ships of the Line; I think, as a combination—not forgetting Old Jock who loved a lark as well as any of us—we were just a bit too hot for our own welfare.

CHAPTER THIRTEEN *SEA FIGHTS AND CYCLONES*

I soon got my marching orders, and joined up again, with a happy half deck crowd in the old *Primrose Hill*. We were particularly cheery, and, for the very good reason, we were bound for the Cape, and not for that monotonous nitrate coast where 50 per cent of sailing ships were now making their way. Steamers were quickly nobbling all the decent trades and ports. Cape Town was one of the few left, and that only till the docks and breakwater were finished.

We got away from England in September, which meant we should dodge the winter in the north and pick up the spring and summer again down south.

It always seems as though a ship on leaving port would never get clear of the accumulated muck, and dirt, and we were no exception. Scrubbing decks, washing paintwork, and reeving new running gear till again she was all spick and span.

I was now in my fourth year and was expected to be able to get through any job that came my way, with all the despatch, accuracy, and neatness of a fully fledged A.B. No longer one of the "skysail yarders." Anything up there was for first and second voyagers; nothing above a Royal for me now. As a matter of fact I was working just below the Royal yard one day, when I saw staged, a fight to a finish between a full grown bull-whale, a sword fish, and a thrasher. In point of fact, the latter two do the attacking, and the whale does the running, or tries to, but it's not once in ten times that the poor devil escapes. Sometimes he does by sounding, and going down so deep that the sword fish cannot follow. But if the sword fish once gets in a position under the whale's tail, there's very little chance for that manœuvre, as every time he attempts to sound, the sword fish drives home that vicious 4 ft. bone snout, and sends the whale scuttling to the surface.

The thrasher (grampus of old) can only attack from above. He has two enormous fins, anything up to five feet long. One projecting from his back, and one from underneath, a short chopped off body, and no tail. When the sword fish attacks and drives the whale to the surface, the thrasher then leaps out of the water, and lands on the whale's back, driving deep, one of those knife-like fins.

We had a ring side seat, and watched the fight from start to finish. It's not enough to say it was thrilling, which does not convey much; it was more than that, it was terrific, and almost unheard of. Even the watch on deck knocked off to the sight. It did not last long, but it was terrible while it did last, to see that fifty ton whale thrashing the water into foam, in a vain endeavour to land one or the other attacker with its flail-like flukes. At other times flinging its whole huge bulk right up in the air, and coming down on the water with a report like a 12 inch gun. Again, tearing round in circles, leaving a trail of blood and foam.

Then, as suddenly as it started, it was over, and the old bull whale was dead, and then, from every quarter, came the scavengers of the sea, sharks, barracuta and so forth.

We were lying becalmed on a sea like glass, and nothing would have given some of us greater pleasure than to shove off and go to the assistance of the bull; but there is a trite saying from across the pond, "Don't monkey with a buzz saw."

The trip down to the Cape was the same routine as with most any ship bound south. Across the one and only Bay, down past the Western Isles, through the Roaring Forties and into the Trades. Then the pulley-hauling of the yards, working her through the Doldrums and across the Line. More Doldrums, plenty of fish, and torrents of rain till we picked up the S.E. Trades, and started to stretch away for the Cape in earnest.

Eventually we lifted the renowned Table Mountain above the horizon and finally came to anchor in Table Bay.

At this time the notorious breakwater was still under construction, and, although representing a cool million, cost the Colony little or nothing, as it was almost wholly built of convict labour.

It was a cheery gang that laboured there. "So many months," or "so many years on the breakwater," was a common saying, and quickly applied to anyone who was apt to sail a bit too close to the wind. Many proved I.D.B.'s—and many that were *not* proved—subscribed their little quota to that breakwater; in fact, culprits of petty crimes, which in the ordinary way would have been met with a small fine, were joyfully consigned to carry out Cape Town's ambitious scheme, of protecting the bay with that huge rampart of granite and stone. There is no doubt it was needed, for many and many a ship's bones lie rotting on the beach in Table Bay through lack of protection from the dreaded nor'wester.

First comes the "table cloth" on the mountain. Then the notorious south-easter, which literally brings fine stones and gravel skeltering down from the heights above. That is all right for the ships in the harbour; they are sheltered, but the fun commences when the wind swings round and comes screeching out of the nor'-west. Then the sea and the wind drive right straight into the harbour, and in those days it was a common sight to see a dozen or more sailing ships riding stretched out to their anchors.

On the occasion of which I am speaking in the *Primrose Hill*, when we rode out a black nor'wester, we paid out 120 fathoms on each anchor, and that is the limit of the cable carried. On to each cable we bent the end of a thirteen inch coir hawser (thirteen inches in diameter); this was laid along the decks, and made fast to the mooring bits.

These preparations were, necessarily, carried out before the wind shifted round. Once the sea came into the harbour it was impossible to get forward along the decks.

Ships then are to be seen diving into huge seas, in far worse condition than when out at sea under shortened canvas. Shipping them green over the bows, and everybody hoping against hope that the ground tackle will hold. It sometimes happens that one anchor, or even the coir spring, on some ship will carry away. Then the trouble starts. That particular cable parts, the second anchor will not hold her, she then drifts down and fouls another ship. One or other either sink where they lie, or both part their cables and drive on shore. Once they hit the beach there is not a chance in a thousand of a single soul being saved. Shore lifeboats are called away, and render all the assistance they can, but with that gigantic sea running, accompanied by a terrific gale, there is barely time to get the shore lifeboat afloat before one, two and sometimes even three ships will go crashing up on the beach in a jumbled mass, to be pounded to matchwood in a very few minutes.

Perhaps, if the warning is sufficient, a ship will prefer to get up her anchors, and get under way, and out of the harbour before the dreaded shift to the N.W.

comes about. Every sailor prefers deep water and plenty of sea room to monkeying around in conditions like those that used to prevail in Table Bay.

Now, of course, the breakwater is completed, and one can lie in comfort behind it, and watch the seas doing their worst. They still come right over, but their force is broken.

Leaving Cape Town behind, we ran our Easting down before the usual old greybeards. Not an uncommon procedure running before an exceptionally heavy sea, is to erect a canvas screen so that the helmsman simply can't look astern at the sea which every moment threatens to come over the poop.

It often happens that the gale increases from hour to hour very slowly, very steadily, and the temptation to continue running, whilst making an excellent passage, has often proved too great, and the undoing of more than one good skipper. The hope is always there that the gale has reached its maximum. The glass has, perhaps, steadied a little, temporarily; may even show a tendency to rise. The seas grow and grow, until the term "mountainous" becomes a literal and actual fact. Then the psychological time comes, when the choice must be made. Heave to, or run it out; either bring her up to the wind under shortened canvas, making no progress whatever towards your destination, but riding in safety, or continue to run with ever-increasing risk. In the latter event, the opportunity for carrying out the manœuvre of heaving to, with any degree of safety passes; in fact, from safety it quickly becomes a risk, then a heavy risk, and finally an impossibility.

No choice then remains. Run you must, and hope for the best; but if one of those mountainous seas of water should bank up astern and break, then every man must seize some immovable object and hang on to it like grim death, hoping against hope that she will lift to it and ride. If, on the other hand, it breaks over her, and she is what is termed "pooped," the chances are just about a hundred to one that this is the finish. Apart from sweeping everything before it, smashing up everything that it doesn't wash overboard, she is filled up rail and rail, and before she can shake the water off, the next sea is on her. Fortunately, one is not held in suspense. About ten minutes has seen the finish of many a good ship, and the "gone to glory" of every man jack of her crew.

We got through all right, and after sighting St. Paul's, this time in safety, turned north for the sea of fragrant smells. Up through the Indian Ocean and past the Andaman Islands, where the scent of spice spreads over the sea like a glorified chemist's shop. It's round here one can realise the origin of the tale of the sea serpent, but in point of fact, they are conger eels, and abound in this sea, but can only be seen when lying becalmed in a sailing ship. They may not encircle the earth, but they are quite big enough to encircle a good sized sailing ship—not that there is any danger of their ever doing that; in fact, such are the conditions of the menu on board ship, that they would be welcomed.

It was in the Indian Ocean that we got mixed up with my one and only cyclone. A hair raiser of the first water. There is, as a rule, plenty of warning when a cyclone is cruising about, and no excuse for anyone to be caught out. For instance, long before there are visible indications from the weather, the barometer will give ample notice, as it did in this case.

Twenty-four hours later, it commenced to bank up to the south east, a big rolling sea got more and more confused, for no apparent reason. Little or no wind, but huge masses of clouds. As these rose, the underpart turned a bilious green and later on, as the edges were torn away, we saw flecks of lightning, vicious, and threatening.

Long before this, the ship had been snugged down to the shortest possible canvas; in our case three lower topsails. It is not only the canvas that is on her, but that which is actually furled, which has to be taken care of; for the wind, when it comes, will rip a sail out of the gaskets, just as easily as it will blow away a paper bag. All hands must get aloft, literally marling the sails down to the yards; not a corner the size of a pocket handkerchief must be left for the wind to get hold of. Once a full cyclone has struck, no man can even hold on to the rigging, much less secure any sails that are started out of their gaskets.

We were lucky. We lost a couple of staysails, and a couple of flying kites ripped out of their gaskets, and one lower topsail blown clean out of the bolt ropes. This went with a report like a six-inch gun.

That would not have happened, only through some miscalculation we let the centre pass over us.

A cyclone, as is well known, is a revolving circular storm, with the centre a flat calm. It was proverbial in the old days, and before the tonnage of ships reached four figures—that no ship could pass through the centre of a cyclone and live. The seas simply pounded over from all sides, filling her up rail and rail, so that she was literally swamped. With the high bulwarks and big washports, we proved that it is possible to pass through; and in the circumstances with not a great amount of damage. Apart from what happened to the ship, there were three broken ribs and a broken arm, to add to our total casualties. This happened whilst the centre was passing over. At all costs we had to get the yards round on the other tack to meet the change of wind, and in order to save ourselves and the ship, this had to be done during the time we were actually in the terrific maelstrom in the centre, with the seas leaping straight up in the air and thundering on board from all sides.

However, we managed it, and the yards were hauled round before the wind struck us again, instantly and with full force, in diametrically the opposite direction from which it had been before. It was at that moment that the mizzen topsail, with a cannon-like report, went sailing away out of the bolt ropes.

Having drawn clear of the cyclone, and the wind settled down to an honest gale, all hands were set about clearing up the wreck. Even yet, occasional seas came thundering on board, and a man caught unawares is quickly apt to lose the number of his mess—in other words, be washed overboard. Hundreds and hundreds of fathoms of rope to be hauled in through the wash deck ports, and scuppers, disentangled from round spars; ripped sails to unbend, and fresh ones to be sent aloft. Everybody on deck, and not a thought of sleep or rest; hot food, of course, is out of the question. A cyclone always seems a treacherous sort of beast compared with a good straightforward blow, that one gets with mountainous but regular seas, off Cape Horn, or running one's Easting Down, or even in the Western Ocean, where it can be notoriously spiteful and vicious.

CHAPTER FOURTEEN *"SHARKS"*

A FORM of sport that always finds favour in a sailing ship, is carrying on the eternal warfare with the sailor's hereditary enemy, old John Shark. The ideal condition is a calm day, with the ship riding on a sea, probably like glass; just a lazy motion, sufficient to send the sails slatting gently backwards and forwards up against the mast. Even from the deck, in these circumstances, the slightest ripple on the surface of the water is clearly visible and, to the man aloft, the sea an open page for many miles round. The result is that when John Shark slips his fin above the water, he is spotted at once.

Directly that sinister black triangle, is seen cutting through the clear water, then, immediately one hears the cry from some sharp eyed boy around the crosstrees, "Shark on the weather beam" or "shark ahead" as the case may be.

In the discipline of a sailing ship—which is as strict as that of a man-o'-war—no other word or indication is permitted; but this cry conveys all the information required to the watch below, which is all that is intended. A couple of hands will tumble out with their shark hook and line, harpoon and grains.

Personally, I never favoured the recognised shark hook, a massive great thing, with a lump of chain attached; in fact, in all my time at sea, although I have caught scores of sharks, I never caught one with the recognised shark hook.

What I much preferred was a dolphin hook, three-sixteenth metal and three inches between barb and shank. The whole of this you can almost hold in the palm of your hand.

About three feet of stranded wire, seized on to the shank, and a great hank of boat lacing, or codline, as it is sometimes called—not a great deal thicker than heavy brown string, was my full equipment.

The hook, buried in a nice chunk of fat white pork about the size of one's fist, trailed out astern, made a most attractive bait, with no sign of hook or line. The next thing was to throw out a few scraps of pork, to draw him and his pilot fish close up towards it.

A shark has very poor sight, but he makes up for it with instinct, which, on occasions, I have seen used with terrible exactitude. His pilot fish, a bit bigger than a mackerel, and striped like a zebra, will go up and nose round, but for some reason will never touch the bait. It is not certain what, if any, message they convey to the shark, but the fact remains, if they do not approve of the morsel, the shark will hardly ever touch it. It is by no means every shark that is accompanied by pilot fish. In any case, he will snap up the odd outlying bits, and head up for the bigger lump, which he takes in his stride.

A shark's mouth is right underneath, but that does not compel him to turn on his back to everything. More often than not, he will just slide his nose over it, or, at the most, turn on his side. God knows, they can do enough damage without turning over, and I have seen a man's leg go, like snapping a carrot; the whole thing done with such horrible quickness, the man hardly knew it was gone. This seems barely conceivable, but it must be realised that a shark's tooth is sharper than an ordinary razor, and has a cutting surface that can only be believed when experimented with. The edges consist of extremely fine serrations, which easily wear down, but though the shark wears out one set of teeth, that in no way bothers him, for he quickly grows another row, and you can catch them with three, five, and even seven or more rows. I have taken one shark tooth between my fingers, and drawn it firmly and quickly down a *Strand Magazine* and cut clean through seven pages. This will give some idea of what our friend can do, when backed up by the enormous muscles, attached to his tremendously powerful jaws.

However, to go back to the catching of our old enemy. Having gathered up the outlying bits, if you have not aroused his suspicions, he will come along and quickly take the baited hook in his mouth. It is just here, that fisherman versus shark is put to the test. If you let him swallow the bait, he will snap your wire; if you only let him get the bait between his lips, and hold it there, as he often will, when you strike you will either pull the bait out, or your hook will go through the flesh, which easily tears away.

You must let him get it down to the corner of his mouth, where it hooks into the gristly portion of the muscles at the joint of his jaws, and then you have got him for a certainty. At the first jerk he commences to dive, but he never goes down far, and you have just got to get that strain on this small line—regardless of the burns it causes through running out through your fingers—until you can bring him up again, and his nose above the water. Having got him there, and the stern of the ship (from where all shark fishing takes place) not rising and falling too heavily, it is not a difficult matter then to hold his nose up and drown him. Most species are not only cowards, but are extraordinarily easily drowned by lifting and dropping their heads, and so forcing the water in through their gills.

If you want a downright good tussle, where you are

pretty certain to leave lots of skin on the line, hook a 15 ft. tiger shark. He will give you all the fun you want. I still carry marks on my hand, left by the teeth of one of this breed—even after he had been landed on deck, and his head cut off.

He was the Captain's catch, and to make doubly sure had had a harpoon driven home; otherwise I don't think we could possibly have got him on board. He fought like a fiend, and as he came over the rail amidships, lashing and snapping, his first accomplishment was to take a piece out of the Captain's arm. Admittedly it was not a very big piece, but it was sufficient to be uncomfortable for many days to come. He landed on deck with a crash, and immediately sunk his teeth into a spare topmast, lying on deck. The carpenter was standing by with his axe; as, the first job, when you get one of these fighters, is to lop off his tail. After dancing round for about fifteen minutes, Chips at last managed to get his tail where he wanted it, and off it came. It was not a difficult matter then to get him steadied down, and have his head off.

One chap went to turn the head over with his foot, and immediately the jaws closed on it. Fortunately, his boot was unlaced, and he was able to kick it off and so save his toes.

One foolish first voyager drew his sheath-knife, and, before anyone could stop him—in an act of joking bravado said, "You!" and attempted to drive his knife into the shark's body. An ordinary knife will not penetrate shark skin, so the result was, the blade of the knife stopped, and his hand continued down, severing all the sinews of the first three fingers of his hand.

That made two for the hospital, and I made the third, for whilst getting hold of the head, and standing it on end, I'm hanged if the jaw didn't snap, and catch my fingers, and it was some time before we could prise the mouth open, and release them.

There is really only one safe thing to do when getting one of these warriors on deck and that is to dislocate his jaws at once—which we had foolishly omitted to do.

It is no child's play catching sharks, particularly when carried out on the slippery decks of a ship, but such is the feeling between sailor and shark that a man will always willingly lose his watch below to terminate the existence of one of these wretched beasts.

The tales that one could tell of the horrors of men falling overboard, sometimes unthinkingly dangling their legs in the water from a stage, sometimes taking a chance and going for a swim, when to all intents and purposes it seems impossible for a shark to be within miles; even on the beaches, children paddling, have been taken. Incidents of this kind could be multiplied indefinitely, but it is doubtful if it would make good reading.

Frequently, these sharks are so ferocious that when hungry they will fight, and often tear each other to pieces. I have caught them with huge gashes, and the scars of old wounds, inflicted in one of these furious fights.

CHAPTER FIFTEEN — *I GET MY "TICKET"*

Soon after our arrival in Calcutta four of us were "out of our time," or apprenticeship, and fully qualified, as far as sea service went, to face the terrors of the examination room for our second mate's certificate.

Through the two or three previous years we were supposed to have swatted up mathematics, navigation, nautical astronomy, seamanship, Rule of the Road, and all sorts of stuff that the Board of Trade have concocted to prove the square-rigged, deep-sea mate. By far and away the majority of which, once the coveted blue paper that entitles you to the eventual certificate, has been obtained, is stored away, or forgotten, until the next examination looms up on the mental horizon.

Calcutta used to have a name for ease in getting through, but when we faced the music, the new examiner, Captain Jenny, was trying to work off the "easy" name, and that in no unmeasured manner. In fact, he made a well-known boast that he would fail three out of every four that came up for examination, and, in our case, made good his boast. Curiously enough, although I was the duffer of the party, I was the one to get through. Although I had no particular objection to mathematics and navigation, I was certainly no adept, whereas one of our chaps, Austin by name, who went up with me, used to work the ship's position every day, and, with the cussedness of fate, he was the first to be chucked out. No second chances then.

When the head examiner (Jenny) came in looking at some of the papers, and I heard him say, "Oh, this won't do," I actually laid down my pen, making sure that I was going to be the next one to close the door from the outside, but it was Dale that took the count.

However, to make a long story short, Whitney or Rivetts as he was called, weathered the storm that day, but went down the next, leaving me the sole occupant of the examination room, and no one was filled with more amazement. Furthermore, I may say, there was some amazement on board—not all complimentary—when it was found that *I*, of all people, had stuck it out and got through.

Officers were scarce in those days, so, with my chest thrown out like a man, and a real deep sea roll, I went on board a big four-master bound for New York, as a fully fledged Second Mate.

I will pass over the awful blunders I made before I gained any sort of confidence, and I also will not dwell on the perfectly poisonous time I experienced that passage. We had a particularly dirty bit of work as a skipper, and for this reason I am neither going to mention his name nor the ship's; suffice to say, that the instant she made fast in New York I hopped ashore, and never saw either him or his ship again. As a matter of fact, she was lost next voyage with all hands, and I'm not surprised for although an accomplished bully, he was only a "fine weather" sailor.

It was getting on for Christmas, so I wanted to get home, but I also wanted to see New York, as I had heard so much about it. Fortunately, I was wise enough to visit a post office first, and send my money, such as it was, home, keeping just sufficient—as I thought—to see me through.

I got in tow with a chap putting up at the same hotel,

who had been sailing out of New York for many years, and what he didn't know about the under life there, was not worth knowing.

Of course, all this undertow was well known to the police, likewise it was common property that you could buy almost anyone in the force or out of it, from the highest to the lowest. They used to call the places "dives," and, believe me, entering one of these night haunts, was a dive, morally, intellectually, and physically. In one place I remember the *pièce de resistance* was a butting match between a goat and a negro. Each was placed on his own side of a ring, the negro on all fours, facing the goat (very like a dog fight is staged) and the goat induced to attack the negro. At a word, the billy goat was released, and each bounded towards the other, to meet in the middle of the ring. The goat broke his neck, and the negro fell unconscious to the ground; to the thunderous cheers and shouts of approval from the onlookers.

Knives, pistols and knuckle dusters, were in common use, and applied on the impulse, any moment; or in staged incidents,—which are best left to the imagination.

I very soon got heartily sick of it all.

After the clean breath of the sea, where everything is open and above board, where men settle their differences in their bare feet, on a white deck, with a perfectly good pair of fists, all this gouging, twisting, and bone breaking, left me thoroughly disgusted with the so called "high spots" of New York. Anyway, I soon found myself without money, as I had, to a certain extent, financed my initiator.

For two days I managed to survive on ten cents, the last of my wealth.

I had friends in New Jersey, who, having heard that I was putting up in Brooklyn, had sent me a cordial invitation, but I, little fool that I was, wanted to see the high lights, so made some half-baked excuses, which let me out. However, I ate humble pie later on, when, having expended my last two nickels, on two free lunches, I was left completely broke. Then I just had to write to these friends and ask them for a loan.

Previous to this, I had had my marching orders from my hotel, and only saved the situation there by realising that there were such things as pawnbrokers. In a few minutes I had deposited a very precious telescope with "uncle," and with the proceeds I laid in one enormous dinner.

My friends, of course, sent me money at once, but by this time I was completely fed up with New York, and everything connected with it, so I returned the loan, picked up my bag, walked on board the first British ship I could see, and, with amazing cheek, asked the Captain to take me home.

He was certainly amused, and pointed out that in the first place he was not a passenger ship, and in the second, I didn't look like a passenger!

I said "No, I wanted to work my passage home in time for Christmas."

He talked to me very kindly, and we had a long yarn about where I had been, and what I had been doing and I also told him on what ship I had been Second Mate. He said he knew both the ship and her Captain's reputation, and in the end he got up, said nothing, and walked away, leaving me standing in the middle of the deck. I thought, "Now, what does that mean?" and then it dawned on me that it was a clear invitation to go and bury myself away, in some nook or corner until the ship got to sea. I seized my bag, and made the best time down to the fo'c'sle; rolled myself up in a corner; shoved the bag up in front of me, and hoped for the best.

I must have gone to sleep, for the next thing I remembered was a voice roaring down the hatchway, "All hands on deck."

Joy. Oh Joy! that did *not* include me, and I went to sleep again. Next thing I heard a voice saying "that chap must have gone ashore. He's left a lot of stuff here, what are we going to do with it?" I stuck my head out and replied, "You are not going to do anything with it. You are going to be very nice and leave it all alone."

"Hullo! young fellow, you'll be in for it now. You'd better go and report yourself."

Along many decks. Up many ladders. At last I found myself standing stiffly to attention in front of the Captain who looked very stern and unsympathetic. "This young man has stowed himself away, sir," said the Chief Officer. Glowering at me from under his bushy eyebrows, the Captain barked: "Well, what have you got to say for yourself?"

Not by the flicker of an eyelid did he admit recognition, and, of course, I played up. Told my little tale of being paid off in New York, and going broke; my anxiety to get home and so forth. Then, when the Captain realised that I was going to make no reference to our meeting and subsequent long yarn of yesterday, I saw a friendly glint appear in his eye.

Much to the Chief's astonishment, the Captain's tone moderated noticeably, as he said, in a resigned sort of voice, "Oh, well, I suppose we shall have to take him."

We were bound for Glasgow, and that trip was my first taste of "Steam." Frankly, I didn't like it. Good times; good food. Always sure of your watch below. Yet I loathed the smoke and the smell, and longed for the towering tiers of bellying canvas, the sound of the water rushing past the scupper holes; in place of the monotonous clank and bang of machinery. I sadly missed the feel of something living under my feet. This ship seemed wooden in comparison. Still, I was not going to grumble on that account. She did me a good turn—a very good turn—and fourteen days later saw us docked in Glasgow. Without a cent to my name, there was nothing for it but to sink my pride and borrow half a crown from my friendly skipper, and send a telegram home asking for money for my railway fare. This, after an eighteen months' voyage! Such is life at sea. Still, I had a few pounds tucked away safely in the Post Office at home, but with a sailor, money is merely earned to spend, and as long as one gets a reasonable amount of clean enjoyment out of it, what better use can it be put to?

CHAPTER
SIXTEEN *FIRE AT SEA*

NEXT voyage saw me Third Mate of the last of Greenshield, Cowie and Company's sailing ships. Another big four masted barque, the *Knight of St. Michael*. Like so many other firms, they were being forced into steam.

In the early 'nineties, when a sailing ship arrived at her home port, it was still an event, but with the advent of the steamboats it became merely an incident.

I still retained a good deal of the square-rigged man's contempt for the steamboat sailor, though, as it proved, it wasn't going to be so long before I was one myself.

We sailed from England in the March of '93, and plunged into a series of gales that became notorious, even for that month of evil repute. In three weeks, no less than eleven sailing ships had gone to their last account, between the Scillies and Dungeness, and we should have added one to their number if we had not been a particularly well found ship. As it was, I blame the three weeks of battling about in the Western Ocean for our later troubles.

We were loaded with an unromantic cargo of coal, and with the everlasting working of the ship, there had evidently been just sufficient friction to cause it to heat up, and eventually catch fire. When we did get wind of what was going on down below, it was only after we had been thoroughly smashed on deck. Bulwarks stove in, boats nearly all gone, and a head wind to beat up to the land.

Had we possessed boats to carry us all it would not have been so bad, but, situated as we were, if she did go up, there wasn't the ghost of a chance for a quarter of us. Our one remaining boat, the pinnace, would just about take twelve, with any reasonable degree of safety, and that only in a smooth sea. Then, the rest would have to make out as best they could on the cumbersome raft we had put together, out of spare spars. No doubt it would float all right, but the question of hanging on to it in a breeze was a horse of quite a different colour.

Then again the pinnace could not stand by the raft. She must shove off and try to make the land, and find something that would come out and search for the raft —and a fine search it would be. No, look at it anyway you liked, we'd about as much chance of surviving as the sailors' proverbial snowball in the lower regions.

The next long drawn out couple of weeks gave us lots of time to argue it out. It was the only subject we could discuss with any degree of naturalness. We tried singsongs; but what was the use of trying to forget it, when, instead of joining in the chorus, a fellow would casually stroll over, and put his hands on the deck above the fire. Of course, the singing at once petered out, whilst someone would call out, "Any hotter, Bill?"

"Aye," the casual reply would be, "just a bit."

Did we jump to those braces to trim the yards to each little variation of the wind? Did we not! And let me say, not only the watch on deck, but the watch below as well—in fact there was no watch below. Neither was there much likelihood of rest during the day, or sleep at night, with a potential volcano immediately underneath one, and level betting that if you did sleep the chances were you'd wake to find yourself rising on the rim, getting a good start heavenward.

During the last few days the boys nearly grew corns through sitting on the fore sky sail yard looking for the land, whilst the decks grew ever hotter and hotter. If it had lasted much longer we should have been able to dispense with the galley fire altogether. Then, one Sunday morning, bright and fine, a good stiff and steady breeze came away from the S.E. sending her through the water at a ten knot clip. But, would it hold, without hauling into another head wind and the consequent tack and tack?

Forty-eight hours more and we should sight the land. Every sail was tended with a care never even lavished on a prospective cup winner! Tighten up a halyard here. Another pull on a sheet there, till the most critical eye was satisfied, and we were getting the very last ounce of speed out of her.

Then Monday evening, just on the edge of twilight, when we had almost given up all hope of seeing anything that night, came the glad cry, "Land-o!" and our troubles were nearly over; at least, the chances of being frizzled or starved were. No more need for a look out aloft. If she could stick it for another few hours, we should be able to make the shore even with our precious raft.

As the darkness shut down we judged we were close enough in, seeing that we had no chart of that coast, and the water was shoaling quickly. Finally, "Stand by, halyards and sheets." Then the welcome order, "Lower away and clew up," and down went the anchor. Nothing mattered now. We could nearly swim ashore. Much too cold for sharks. All the same we couldn't see a sign of a town though Bahia Blanca was marked on the chart as being right on the coast. The only chart we had was merely one of the South Atlantic, where a spider could spread its legs over a hundred miles.

There was nothing for it but to take the pinnace. Though I tried to cheer them up by pointing out that if the ship did go up what fun they could have, running through the surf on the old raft!

As it turned out later, there was a joke on all of us, for just where we were anchored—if a S.W. gale came up—there was nothing but breakers, that would have extinguished the fire, the ship, and ourselves included. However, the S.W. gale held off, and we got ashore through what surf there was, without smashing up the boat. Having pulled her up high and dry, the Captain and I went off prospecting.

As a result of beaching her in the surf I had got pretty well soaked, so I discarded shoes and socks, as the country seemed to consist of limitless sand and nothing but sand. Not hillocks, or the ordinary decent sand hills, but sheer precipices of sand with sides like walls. It made the going rather bad, but we managed to forge ahead till, eventually, we came across a sharp line of demarcation between sand and vegetation. "Oh!" we thought, "this was fine. Vegetation, now we'll strike something soon." We did, or rather I did —prickles! Prickles an inch long, in fact the first one I trod on felt six inches. I tried picking my way, but it was no go. I had to sit down and nurse my feet, picking out the spikes. Then I got the Captain's handkerchief and my own wrapped round one foot, and a heavy weather cap round the other, and away we went again. Every now and then in the cussedness of things, either the cap or the hankies would slip, and I'd do a hurried squat.

So it went on. At any rate we weren't sitting on our tame volcano! and that was some blessing. We could see the ship every time we mounted a precipice. Then we both cheered as we sighted some horses, and

FIRE AT SEA

made up our minds, there and then, that we were going to have a ride until we found habitation, and chance being shot for horse thieves. Having picked out a likely couple of nags, the Skipper approached his, whilst I stalked mine. I don't know what aroused my suspicions; perhaps I had got to recognise a potential volcano when I saw one. Be that as it may, I felt quite contented to look over my horse's back from the near side, and at the Skipper and his mount on my off side. Incidentally, I kept my hands to myself. He clicked his tongue, and cheerily walked up and put his hand on its withers, stroked and patted it. That was all right, but he couldn't see what I saw. Apart from abruptly ceasing his browsing, a distinctly saucy little look became apparent in that gee gee's eye—a look I've seen before, and sometimes suffered through not having seen.

"Come on, man," shouted our noble Captain, at the same time planting his six foot two on the horse's back. That did it—sort of put the match where it was wanted—and up he went. You might call it a graceful curve; it didn't look it! and the thud with which he landed on his back fairly shook the ground. I could not have stopped laughing to save my soul. When the Captain did get his wind, and could speak, he just grinned and said, "Let's walk."

About an hour later we walked up to a hut full of about the most cheerful looking cut-throats you could meet in any Chamber of Horrors. Fortunately the Skipper was in uniform, and, as the British Consul said later, it was that, and that alone, which saved us both, and quite possibly the ship. They got the idea he was a one time big feller, and best left alone. Incidentally, he did not improve his chances by hauling out a handful of sovereigns and giving an old dame, who evidently shared the hut, a couple. Then the blokes that were going to pilot him to Bahia Blanca wanted some, and he cheerily gave them a few. They were so utterly flabbergasted—and I was—that they never thought of knifing him, and taking the lot. At any rate they didn't, marvellous to relate.

Off he went, on his sixty mile ride to Bahia, whilst I pushed off back to the boat. I had only to do about ten miles on the back of the hacksaw they lent me, but that was enough, and to spare. I wasn't a bit surprised to learn later, that on arriving in Bahia, Captain Dodd fell off in a dead faint. I should have split up the middle long before.

I was given half a sheep, as a sort of peace token I suppose. It had been killed on the spot and was still bleeding profusely. This I had slung across in front of me, and accompanied by three most choice villains, set off on the return journey to the boat.

These horses are evidently born to walk, my old sawbones seemed so anyway; though I will say, the way they could take those precipices of sand, beat creation, and came very near beating me, and would have done, most likely, if I hadn't just leaned back and unhesitatingly seized the beast by the tail. Let 'em laugh, thought I, it's better than getting mixed up with bleeding sheep, and both going over his nose. When we arrived on the beach, what with digging him in the ribs with my bare heels, and whooping and yelling like a Red Indian, I managed to get up a gait, something of a cross between a trot and a canter. Whatever the hybrid motion was, the effect was awful, for every time I came down, he was sure to be in the act of coming up. This, in conjunction with his serrated vertebrae did not improve matters. Fortunately I hadn't far to go to fetch the boat. The combined effect of the fellows lying under her lee was grand.

FIRE AT SEA

The picture, from their standpoint, was me, bare-back on a horse, with the bleeding remains of the Skipper hung in front, bawling and yelling for assistance, whilst being viciously pursued by three perfectly typical cut-throats.

One could hardly blame them for seizing boat hooks and stretchers to hold off the attack. I think the old pirates astern of me were registering astonishment too, but their surprise and amusement was, that anyone should *want* a horse to run.

Though we could not speak a word of their lingo, they knew we were mad Englishmen, and that, I suppose, covered everything. We were soon very good friends. Seeing the way they had been received, and that in any case there was nothing worth stealing, they eventually returned to their respective hutments, whilst we tried to find the soft side of the perishing cold sand, and so spent the night with one man keeping a bright look out in case our friends of the sombreros should change their minds!

In the morning, when we got back to the ship, we found the mate had taken the bull by the horns, and after rigging all the hoses and buckets available, had whipped off the hatches, and with improvised smoke helmets, attacked the fire at its base, and got it out; if not exactly out, at any rate sufficiently under control for all hands to get to work, and dig down night and day, until they had got a trunk way clean through to the lower hold. Also, we hammered up the ends of several lengths of three inch iron piping, after drilling it full of holes. These we drove down into the coal in different places, and then tucked in the business end of a fire hose. By the time Captain Dodd arrived with a steam launch—or as they called it a tug—the fire wasn't worrying us a bit. It wasn't out, but we'd definitely got it where we wanted.

With the "tug" also came a pilot who gave us the cheery news that if a S.W. gale had by chance sprung up, the whole area where we'd chosen to anchor would have become a mass of breakers.

The next order was to "Man the windlass and loose all sail." We didn't need any hurrying either. The "tug," bless its little heart, took the tow rope, and promptly got it round her propeller.

Some cheery soul suggested we should hoist her in the davits to clear it. Meanwhile, instead of towing us we did the towing, whilst they cleared the rope, and before that came about we'd fetched the narrow part of the channel, close hauled. We went about, but before we could get way on her to go about again, she stuck her nose into the opposite bank, fortunately mud.

With blessings pouring from aloft, we furled all sail, and in case the reader has forgotten, I'll say again that she was a four masted barque.

We decided that the function of our little matey, with the smoke and stink, should in future be confined to just pulling our head round each time we went about. That seemed a fairly simple proposition, but again it proved too much.

After getting our nose out of the mud, and once again responding to the order "set all sail" (which in the ordinary way, comes once a passage, and that once is quite enough) we stood over to the opposite bank, and, of course, rammed that. I'll just say we again furled all sail, and leave it at that. Later, we once again "set all sail." We had steam on deck by now to the winches and windlass, otherwise the order would have been futile. The spirit was willing all right, but there is even a limit with old shellbacks, though you would not perhaps think it, to watch them. Anyway, we'd reached that limit, so when she inevitably took the mud again, and we'd got the canvas stowed once more, we decided she could stay there, till the tide rose, and lifted her off. That would be in the morning, so we hailed our little chum, and told him to come and tie up alongside. Whether he didn't like being out all night or not, I don't know, but anyway the agent who was on board the little hooker, hailed us, and with a very ultra Oxford accent, imparted the information that they'd "sprung a leak, and couldn't pump, unless the main engines were going." (I heard one of our chaps say, that he didn't know until then that she had any, and if those were the main engines probably the auxiliary would be a foot pump.)

Whether the yarn was rigged on the spur of the moment it is hard to say, they didn't wait to argue, but hiked off up the river as hard as they could go. Neither did they show up again, so we remained at anchor as it was hopeless to attempt to beat up a narrow channel with a ship of that size.

Later the following day the wind came away light from the S.W. This was a fair wind, so we up anchor, and under six topsails and foresail picked our own way, with what ought to have been the help of the pilot, but it wasn't and he soon stuck us in the mud again. After that we decided to dispense with *all* local help and rely on our own instinct, and a couple of good lead lines, with the result she was soon anchored within some ten miles of Bahia. That was as far as we dare go, till we could get hold of a real live tug. Meantime we must do the journey, when required, in the one remaining boat. I wasn't sorry as it gave me a real good excuse for rigging the pinnace up with mast, sails, and false keel, all complete. I was always crazy on boat sailing anyway.

One day, coming off with a Mr. Jones, Lloyds Surveyor, the Skipper addressed me by name. Lloyds Surveyor pricked up his ears and said, "What's your name, Lightoller?" I could tell by the easy way it slipped off his tongue that he'd said it many times before.

Now some ten years previously a relation of mine, one Charles Lightoller, had left England (no, not necessarily for the country's good, though I will admit he was hot stuff) and no track or trace of him remained. That branch of the family had tried for years to get some authentic news of whether he was alive or dead; but the United States had seemingly swallowed him up, when he went in at New York. I asked the Surveyor whom he had known of that name. Of course, it was Charles, all right, and not only that but he had died whilst actually a partner with Jones, in that out of the way little spot in the Argentine of South America (and once again, how small, etc.).

After six days swinging to an anchor, with always an eye on our slumbering friend down below, giving him an occasional sousing with the hoses, along came the s.s. *Toro* from Buenos Ayres. A full blown tug, with no doubt about what he could and would do. He just kicked up his heels, and stretched out that thirteen inch coir hawser of ours, till it looked like a fishing line. We could now send the sails down, and did, gladly. Another couple of hours, and we were moored alongside the one and only wharf the place possessed. A rickety contraption at its best. As a precaution we dropped a couple of anchors just in case we should wake up some bright morning, and find ourselves bound down river with wharf attached.

There is over thirty feet of a rise and fall in the tide, at Bahia, and as we broke the end of our precious teakwood companion ladder the first night, to say nothing of a couple of mooring ropes, I, as Third Mate, took on the night watch. The broken gangway was one reason, and another was that being a pretty fair shot I was able to keep the ship supplied with game. I wasn't asked how I managed to stay awake night and day, so long as no more gangways were broken. Most nights, after everyone was in the hay, I piped down on the galley seat. First, I led a line from one of the wharf piles, in through the scupper holes in the ship's side, through the scupper hole in the galley, and made the end fast to a pile of kids (double handed tin dishes the food is carried in). As the ship rose to the level of the wharf, so the line tightened up and eventually landed all the kids with a mighty crash on the deck. As an additional precaution, I tied the bare end to my foot, so I was pretty sure to wake up—at any rate before I went through the scupper hole. The noise of the kids was enough to waken the dead, and it always worked.

Then, after slacking up the moorings, and tending the gangway, I was free again. In this way I scrounged a good few hours' unofficial shut eye. After breakfast, instead of turning in, I made for the Saldero, where I was certain of a mount and a dog from one of the Directors—a Major Dicks. Then, with a gun I had purchased, I hit the trail for the foot of a low range of hills, where there was heaps of game. Partridges, also a kind of grouse, and, best of all, a Martinet; about the size of a Buff Orpington hen, white flesh, and good eating. I was always sure of enough for at least two good meals for all hands—officers and crew. This was good luck for everyone, including the skipper, for although he lived ashore, it eased his hand in providing meat.

Ships' allowances for food in foreign ports those days were notoriously low. I suppose owners thought all we had to do was to slip ashore and pick peaches, bananas, and oranges, to our heart's content. I expect they also thought that wild pigs came to the foot of the gangway, or perhaps the galley door.

One day I bagged a wild cat, though it should have bagged me by rights! I'd got tired of the level plain at the foot of the hills, and started in one day to explore the hills themselves. Mostly pretty sheer cliffs. Climbing round a particularly awkward bit, I just got footing on a very small plateau, when, at the same time, my long whiskered friend decided to come out of her lair to see what the row was about. She put her belly to the ground, and waved her wand in an unmistakable manner. It was a case of who's going to be first; well, I was, by a split second—which I believe is the shortest measurement of time. She got both barrels as she rose, and before she could rise again, the contents of a Derringer I had, by luck, in my pocket. Dicks fixed the skin up for me at the Saldero, and I think someone in England still has it.

One night before leaving Bahia Blanca, whilst cruising around the shore with some of the other chaps, I had the distinction of being jailed for murder. Just how it came about in the first instance, is rather difficult to say. We were on the pampas or open plain, and I, somehow or other, lost touch with the other chaps; I suppose I must have been taking a short cut, and I'm afraid my short cuts are rather notorious. Be that as it may, the fact remains, that I got completely lost, and to make touch with the others again, as evidently shouting seemed ineffective, I blew my whistle, the ordinary whistle that every officer on board ship carries. They answered, and we came together all right.

We were journeying along in the dark, quite cheerfully, when we suddenly found ourselves surrounded by gendarmes. What *they* said we didn't know, and for what *we* were saying they didn't seem to care. They went through us each individually, and pretty effectively, until they came across my whistle; gave a slight blow on it, gurgled with what might have been anger or delight—and about three of them seized me by various portions of my anatomy and shuffled me off, just as hard as they could go. Our other fellows naturally thought, "Here, this won't do," when they saw me vanishing into the dark, and several of the gendarmes very soon found themselves sprawling on the ground. This added to the fun, and also fuel to the fire, for more gendarmes seemed to spring up out of the ground. In any case, they were on us like a shot. We got a downright sound whacking, with the flat of their swords, and I was pushed into a tin tabernacle they called the jail. It behoved one not to be too violent, or, judging from appearances, and the way it swayed, the whole thing would come clattering down.

There were two or three drunks sharing the cell, and I passed an interesting hour or so until the other chaps routed out the British Consul, who gave me back my whistle and my freedom. The only fact that I could sort out from a jumbled up story was that a man that night had committed a murder, and he had a whistle. Heaven help the whistlers on a night like that!

CHAPTER SEVENTEEN *THE NITRATE COAST*

It was in Bahia I got promotion, and once again found myself second mate of a three skysail yarder. It happened through the appointed second mate going on a terrific binge. He was an awfully good chap, and a splendid sailor, but a bit wet.

Scores come a cropper the same way, though in the aggregate they consume less alcohol than their prototype ashore.

The fact is, that through months of enforced abstinence, a sailor becomes very susceptible to the effects of drink and if he has any weakness that way, he is fairly sure to come a cropper in the long run.

Having discharged part of the cargo and completely extinguished the fire, we eventually battened down the hatches again, towed down river and, with the remainder of the cargo sailed for Iquiqui on the Nitrate Coast.

It was a grand feeling, and one I thoroughly enjoyed, having once again a big ship with her mountains of towering canvas under my sole charge during my watch. One never tires of the bright moonlight nights such as one experiences in the tropics. So bright that it is dangerous to sleep in the full glare of the moon without shelter of some kind. The phosphorus in the water is sometimes dazzling as the ship cuts her way; so bright in fact, that I have actually read a piece of newspaper by the light of the phosphorus alone, stirred up by the rudder. Of course, by moonlight such as I speak of, in the tropics, it is quite easy to see to read; every rope and every rope yarn is picked out like a clear sharp etching. The truck, although over 200 ft. away, can be seen with absolute distinctness, waving in lines across a sky literally smothered in stars. Here and there the deep vast purple between the constellations is only made the deeper by their particular brightness.

To watch such a star as Sirius setting, is almost like looking through a kaleidoscope of boyhood memories. It resembles nothing better than a huge lamp, changing colour second by second through every hue, purple, crimson, blue, red. But it must be seen to be appreciated, and then only in the tropics. I've known many an old shell wax poetic over the glories of one of these tropical nights.

We made our way once again round the Horn and up to Iquiqui, where tier on tier of ships were loading nitrate for Home and the Continent. The nitrate is brought off in lighters, loaded with sacks, each weighing exactly two hundredweight. These are hoisted on board by a dolly-winch manned by half a dozen men, or, if the ship sports the luxury, a steam winch. A platform is built down below, and the whole of the ship is loaded by a single native Chilean, from this platform, which must be adjusted to this man's height to an inch. These huge sacks, after being hove up and landed on the platform, are placed on this man's back and dropped by him in tiers in the hold, and once dropped, never touched again. Of course nitrate is a terrific weight, and a ship cannot be anything like filled with it. In fact, both in the lower hold, and 'tween decks, there are just a couple of pyramids. It is terribly hard on the ship, and causes the sides to buckle in, with the result that all rigging has to be taken up when loading, and eased out when discharging. The man's back that carries these sacks is like a piece of leather, and after handling that dolly-winch for a couple of months, one's hands become likewise.

One meets every type and description of ship, and of all nationalities, loading nitrate, and one notorious Yankee hard-case ship, the *Frederick K. Billings* lay next to us. They lived like fighting cocks, as far as food goes, and made our British ships resemble second rate soup kitchens, but oh! they did have to work for their living. It was a common rumour that many of her crew had definitely decided they would not sail in her, but to the ordinary mind, it seemed as though they had no alternative. The inhospitable bleak cliffs of that nitrate coast could afford little shelter to a goat, let alone a ship's crew. However, they solved the problem and in a pretty drastic manner.

On gala nights the custom is to set fire to a 2 cwt. bag of saltpetre on the beach, and the light from this will illuminate the whole harbour, the heat generated being simply terrific. Imagine then the *Frederick K. Billings* when, after making all preparations to take to the boats, one of the crew dropped a paraffin lamp down the fore hatch. The ensuing blaze beggars description. In precisely sixteen minutes, that ship was burnt to the water's edge (decks, masts, yards, sails, and rigging), and had sunk to the bottom; but not before she had burnt every vestige of paint off that side of the ships immediately adjacent to her, ruined all their running gear, and reduced them to a piebald wreck. The crew of the burning ship had just time to leap overboard and swim for it. Most of them were picked up, and in the ordinary run of things, handed over to the authorities— a proceeding they considered infinitely preferable to sailing under their bucko Yankee mates.

This happened in Iquiqui, which also has the distinction of having produced an island from the sea in one night, and in consequence is named Iquiqui Island.

Unfortunately it rose under a ship at anchor, and her remains are still visible, and will remain visible for many years to come.

A little further up the coast, at the Port of Pisagua, the operation was reversed, and one can now sail in a small boat over the houses of the old town, which quietly subsided into the sea one night, also as the result of one of the frequent earthquakes.

Although we had to work like niggers all the week, Sunday, as often as not would see us away in one of the ship's boats fishing and shooting, in fact it *had* to be a busman's holiday for there was little or nothing else to do, certainly not in the town, and less outside of it. It is a bleak, barren coast all right; where trees don't grow, and the rain never rains—in fact it is a common saying that a good tropical shower would do more damage than a fire.

Anyhow, a good boat and a good crew, complete with harpoon, grains and rifles, was more in our line. Bar seals, all was fish that came to our nets, whether herrings, rock cod, sharks or the occasional sword fish— and he is a fighter of the first water.

Half a stick of dynamite was the best negotiator for rock cod. Herrings often come in in shoals so thick that the top layers are pushed completely out of the water. Then you bale 'em up with a bucket. If they are running deep, then you send a charge of dynamite well down. If they are only just a couple of fathoms down, a good method is to tie a piece of stick on to one end of, say, three fathoms of twine (and don't forget for a moment that a fathom is six good feet), then tie the stick of dynamite on to the other end.

To prepare the charge, you push a hole down the stick of dynamite with a pencil. Then take a detonator, and insert the end of the fuze. Carefully nip the sides of the detonator with your teeth, at the same time bearing in mind that if the detonator does go off it will blow the top of your head off. Then with the fuze, push the detonator into the dynamite, and hope for the best. Light the fuze, throw it overboard and stand by, but don't do like the Mate of the *Thistle*, stand with one foot on the twine, or, as in his case, the charge will naturally jerk back on board. Like a sportsman, he grabbed the dynamite again, despite the spluttering fuze, and tried another shot, but this time he had got a complete turn round his ankle, and when he got that clear he was only just able to put the skylight between him and the charge, before there was a neat hole blown clean through the deck, and every scrap of crockery and glass in the pantry underneath was shattered to fragments. What the steward had to say when he realised that the top of his head might have been just where the hole appeared, is not printable. When this occurred the *Thistle* was lying in the next tier to us.

So much for herrings.

This Sunday in particular, we were after bigger fry, and hooked a tartar. We'd sailed well clear of what goes by the name of a harbour (only really there isn't any) when we saw a fin above the water, and at once jumped to the conclusion that it was our old enemy John Shark. Everyone laid back to their oars, and we rapidly closed on the fin, which my subconscious mind already told me, was attached to no shark.

However, it was a fin, and a big one, and that was good enough. As we drew closer I gave the order "Way enough; lay in the bow oar." The bow oarsman then took his stand in the eyes of the boat, with the harpoon in his hand, and the rest laid on their oars. With the way we had on the boat, she ran close up, and then the bow oarsman let fly making an excellent shot, burying the harpoon just abaft the fin. We knew instantly that we had tackled something tough, for although a shark at times will put up a pretty good fight, it was nothing compared with the fuss this chap made. Out flew the line and down he went, in fact it was some time before we could snub up enough and make him tow us. He made straight out to sea, at the rate of knots. After ten minutes or so he eased up, and came to the surface. Then we could see it was no shark indeed, but a fifteen foot swordfish. Carefully hauling on the line we managed to get a rifle shot in, and away he went for another stretch, but it was soon evident that the bullet, by luck, had done the trick.

Now a sword fish, in its last throes, has a nasty habit of coming up right under a boat. We were aware of this, and a couple of us were peering over the side down into the water. We saw him coming but couldn't stop him, and he drove his sword right through the bottom of the boat, actually grazing the back of the stroke oarsman. We were then in a nice mess, some ten miles away from the ship, and a 15 ft. swordfish securely attached to the bottom of the boat.

There was nothing for it but to lash mats and oars together, in the form of a raft, take the plug out of the boat and let her fill. Then get over the side and dive down, and make a line fast round his tail. Taking this line over the raft of mast and oars, we pulled his tail up to the surface, and at the same time turned the boat on her side. With the help of the boat's axe, we hacked the sword short off at the snout; righted and baled out the boat. Well satisfied with the trophy, for our trouble, despite the ten mile pull back.

Eventually the great day comes when the cargo is all stowed and the ship is down to her marks. An age old custom on the Nitrate Coast before breaking moorings, is to cheer each ship in the harbour. A spokesman is chosen who usually has a voice like a full-toned foghorn. He faces the ship hailed and calls "Three cheers for such and such ship." The crew let go like one man, and the ship cheered must reply, though she may be the best part of a mile away, and woe betide her if she does not pick up her name, and reply in time; for all the ships round about, that have spotted this lack of attention, join in raising loud groans, and to hear the weird reverberating echo—particularly noticeable at night time—of a dozen or more ships' crews groaning, is a thing never to be forgotten. The ship "groaned" never forgets it either. Once "groaned" it is then too late for her to answer the cheers of the hailing ship; she has just to grin and bear it, and to stand the chaff for evermore. It is looked on as a terrible disgrace, and years afterwards some of the crew, in some outlying port of the world, will mention the ship they are from, and somebody will at once say, "Oh yes, you were 'groaned' in Iquiqui, on such and such a date."

Finished loading, then comes the great affair of breaking moorings, for here one is moored fore and aft. Each ship in the harbour sends over a few men, and it is a whole day's job to get up the stern moorings, get the cable forward, shackled on again and hove in. Every bit of the work has to be done by hand, and when it is taken into consideration that every link of the chain, of which there may be fifty or sixty fathoms, weighs anything up to ten or fourteen pounds, it will be realised that it is no joy ride. At last it is completed, sail is set, and the ship quickly slips over the horizon.

CHAPTER EIGHTEEN — *DERELICTS*

As it turned out, this was to be my last voyage in sail, and will always stand out as being the very worst. The passage out consisted of a series of gales topped off with a fire. Whilst on the homeward voyage we never had the skysails in once, except as a matter of form off the Horn; 165 days from Iquiqui to the Lizard (Cornwall). Six weeks in the Doldrums where it rained so incessantly that we had the oil completely washed off our oilskins. Five times we crossed the line, to-day a mile or two north, to-morrow we had drifted south again; next day further south, then north again and so on, till we were like jellyfish. Bad weather may be bad, but too much so-called good weather, is I think, worse. Particularly when it means, as in the Doldrums, hauling and pulley hauling the yards round day after day, and night after night, till, as in our case, the crew got absolutely exhausted. However, all good things must have an end, as ours did with a flicker of wind from the N.E. Round came the yards once again and, for the hundredth time, the hope that it might be the true N.E. Trades, and this time, it was. Why I say true Trades is because one often picks up the false N.E. Trades even south of the Line, and again you'd get the Portuguese Trades sometimes 35° and even 40° north of the Line, which *may* develop into the true Trades of the Tropics and good old flying fish weather. As a matter of fact, they remained only too true, and in consequence, worked us away to the westward, so that we were well over to the Gulf of Mexico.

On this voyage I caught what I firmly believe to be the first specimen ever known of a fish with hands and feet. The head winds had forced us over towards the Gulf, until we were well within the region of the well-known "Gulf Weed" almost identical in appearance with mistletoe. This weed flows out of the Sargasso Sea, and originated the old tale of ships which become embedded in acres and acres of this weed, to turn slowly round, and be steadily, but surely, drawn to the centre of the much feared sea, until at last, with provisions and water all gone, they become derelicts, continuing their everlasting circling through the ages. One almost regrets that the steamer has torn that theory all to pieces, as they crossed and recrossed the dreaded Sargasso Sea without ever sighting any legendary and seaweedy island.

In point of fact derelict ships never remain stationary, either in the Sargasso or any other sea. There is a continual flow, mainly due to the currents set up by the revolution of the earth, and the retarding action of the water. The earth, moving round to the eastwards, tends to leave the water behind it, and promptly sets up what is called the Equatorial Current, which has its origin around the Line on the Coast of Africa. This flows to the westward, increasing in momentum till it strikes the north coast of South America, and flows north into the Carribean or Sargasso Sea, through the Gulf of Mexico, circling round and flowing out through the Straits of Florida; thus forming the Florida and Counter-Equatorial Current, and flowing back again to the eastward, and bringing into existence the great Gulf Stream, which strikes the coast of England, and to which we owe our much maligned climate. A split in the Gulf Stream takes place off the Coast of Ireland, one part going south, forming the Reynolds Current—

one of the most erratic in the world. The other branch goes north, making the Arctic Current and coming down the Coast of Newfoundland in the guise of the Labrador Current, bringing with it thousands upon thousands of icebergs. In fact, one theory regarding the formation of the great Banks of Newfoundland, is that they have been caused by the deposit from icebergs, which were originally glaciers, and brought with them, through the countless ages millions of tons of earth. The icebergs, on striking the warm water, are alleged to melt, and deposit their material at the bottom of the sea. Whatever the truth, the Banks are certainly very much in evidence, and form a happy hunting ground for cod, fog and icebergs.

The smaller currents are unfortunately the most erratic, and don't help matters when trying to make a decent landfall. About the worst culprit is the Reynolds Current, which flows across the mouth of the English Channel. A heavy south-westerly gale in the Bay of Biscay will set this chap running like a mill race in the wrong direction. One of our crack Atlantic Liners (I won't mention names) coming home from New York; instead of being well south of the Scillies, found herself north of these islands, and sighted the Seven Stones Lightship. This, despite the fact that the Captain was one of the most able and careful navigators on the North Atlantic. A glance at the map will show what a narrow shave she had.

Apart from icebergs, another inducement for the sailor to keep his eyes skinned is derelicts, that have been known to drift about the world for years, covering thousands of miles. Individually, they are a worse danger than icebergs. Often they are nothing but waterlogged and dismasted old Nova Scotia schooners, loaded with timber, just floating awash, and utterly impossible to sink, but able to rip the bottom out of any unwary liner. It is by no means uncommon for the hull of a dismasted ship to float, for weeks and even months, with the remains of her crew, unmanageable, and unnavigable, with limited provisions and no means of communication. If she has been dismasted anywhere near the Line, she is fairly sure to find her way into the Great Carribean Sea, or the Gulf of Mexico, where she may circle and circle indefinitely. On the other hand she may, with luck, come out on the Florida Current, but long ere this happens, only a few pitiful skeletons remain to tell the story.

But to get back to my walking fish.

I had succeeded in collecting a good many specimens from the floating Gulf Weed when one of the watch below, lying around on the hot decks, pointed out a fish I had missed lying hidden under the fluke of the starboard anchor. I picked it up and popped it in my aquarium, which consisted of an old five gallon kerosene tin. After a time, the peculiar action of the fish, caught my eye. It sort of sidled up alongside a piece of weed, and remained stationary, or went to the bottom of the tin, and there also remained stationary, without moving its fins. My curiosity was aroused, so I got the cap off the end of a telescope and filled it with water, and examined the little beggar closely with a magnifying glass. Sure enough, it had tiny, but fully developed hands and feet. Actually, the fish was slightly flat, and swam on its edge. The arms out of each side consisted of a transparent fin-like substance. This formed the lower part of an arm and ended in a perfect little hand with five fingers. Little flat legs of a similar nature, but just from the knees down—folded up underneath the body, when swimming, as the arms also folded into the sides. When it went to the bottom of the tin the legs came down and it stood on its feet, or it would rise alongside a branch of weed, and deliberately grip hold of it with its hands, and hang on.

It dawned on me that this must be a very rare specimen, and I set out to try and find some methylated spirit or anything else in which to pickle it.

None to be got. "Try whisky," said one humorist, and I even had the temerity to suggest to the Captain that he should give me some whisky, as there was no methylated spirits, but I, with the fish, was consigned to places even hotter than the Gulf of Mexico. "Fish with hands and feet," snorted the autocrat of the sea. "Get out of this, or I'll pickle *you*." I fled back to my precious fish, to find that some crabs had solved the difficulty by eating it!

For many years I stood the jeers of all and sundry that listened to this fish yarn, but I got my own back when, in the usual scare headlines of a New York paper, they informed the world, that the "First known specimen of fish with hands and feet had been discovered and brought home by the Captain of a steamer." As far as I know the "only specimen" is still swimming round quite happily in the New York aquarium.

Within a hundred miles of the spot where I got my fish I also saw what is believed to be the biggest shark in the world.

I had the forenoon trick at the wheel. She was steering easy "By the wind," just moving through the water.

I momentarily dropped my eyes from watching the weather leech of the mizzen royal, and glanced over the rail to leeward, and saw, what at first I took to be a blackfish. Still I knew it couldn't be that from the fin, and the colour, and then it dawned on me it was a shark. But, my godfathers, what a shark! I let out a yell, "Shark on the lee beam."

The Captain was on the weather side of the poop at the time, and ran over to leeward and saw it.

There was certainly no shark hook or line in the whole wide world that would hold this chap, so the Captain dashed into the chart room for a rifle, and, snatching one out of the rack, slipped in a cartridge, came out on deck and fired. I doubt if the bullet took any effect, but before he could reload, Tiger Jim had disappeared.

I believe to this day that it was Tiger Jim, a well-known shark that had been sighted by sailing ships again and again in those waters, and he never leaves them. He is nearly as well known as Pelorus Jack, the porpoise (and the only fish individually protected by Government!) that used to pilot ships through the Cook Straits.

Reports as to Tiger Jim's size vary. Some went up as far as thirty-six feet but, as luck would have it we got a first class opportunity of measuring him. When I saw him, and recovered from the shock, his tail was just abreast of the wheel. When the Captain ran across the forward end of the poop Tiger Jim's nose was just level with the forward 'thwartship rail. In this manner we arrived at a very accurate estimate, and it came out at exactly thirty-one feet, and he could have taken a full grown calf at a mouthful!

On our long passage home—165 days from land to land—I came to seriously consider the advantages and disadvantages of "sail."

If one ever could tear away from the never-ending glamour and romance, the ever close and intimate association with those utterly absorbing revelations of the deep sea, then common sense said "steam." But the soul of any square rigged sailor in the 'nineties revolted at the prosaic monotony one coupled with a steamboat. Still, anyone with an inch of foresight, knew well that sail was on the wane. Steam had come and come to stay.

One might as well make up one's mind to stow away the hard-learned lore of sailing ship days and let it become just a treasured memory, and turn to the machinery of modern times.

It was a bitter pill, but I swallowed it with the best grace I could find and became a "steamboat sailor," so that frequent term of ineffable contempt, would now apply to me! However, I stuck to my guns and said good-bye to the good old windjammers that I loved.

CHAPTER NINETEEN "*BULLY*" *WATERS*

I SOON found myself third mate of a Western Ocean Packet, bound across the Pond. No more watching every vagary of the wind, no more luffing up to a squall and easing her away as she would bear it. Never again to hear the music of that gurgling hiss, as the water skirls in the scupper holes. How one was to miss that straining heel, as she laid her lee rail down to the water, with the welcome sound of ropes surging and cracking, or even the well-known cry as the strain increases, "Stand by the royal halyards."

Now, three watches, and, when a squall is in the offing, "Quartermaster, pull the dodger up, please." Nothing to do but keep a sharp look-out. All the driving done for one by the stokehold gang below. Just the steady plug and thud of the engines; into one sea and through the next. No quick, downward flick of the wheel, as she lifts her head to crash down into the trough, like the way one nursed a sailing ship. I tried it on a steamer, but it hadn't the slightest effect; the only way with a steamer is to ease her engines. In fact, one seems wholly dependent on the engines.

We were bound up the St. Lawrence, and in those days ten knots was considered quite a good speed. In many places in the St. Lawrence, such as the Racine Rapids, and even up at Montreal, before the revetment was built, I have seen the ship doing her ten knots and barely making headway. Even alongside at Montreal, the engines had to be kept going at very nearly full speed whilst the ship was made fast, with the result that owing to the huge head of steam, the moment the engines were stopped, the safety valves lifted, and the row for the next half an hour or so was simply deafening.

I soon began to see that steam had its good points —lots of them. Better time, better food, better pay, and one did not lose touch so completely with the world.

Had I been of a steady disposition and stayed in Elder Dempsters, where I started in steam, no doubt I should have got to the top of the tree very quickly, but for one thing I was not steady, and for another, it was only the tallest tree that would satisfy me. Time and again I took to the beach on some hair-brained stunt or other, just wasting time; spending months shooting or fishing, until funds petered out. Then off to the sea again in the first company that would take me. Get through an examination, and then have another glorious binge—not a boozing binge—for I've a wholehearted contempt for the chap who takes more than he can hold.

It was after one of these little breaks that I found myself in the African Royal Mail s.s. *Niagara*, bound down the Coast of West Africa, under that notorious and well-known Captain who glorified in the name of Bully Waters, a man of such exceeding unpopularity that his life would not have been worth a minute's purchase in the streets of Liverpool. To even cross the town he invariably took a cab for safety—and I'll admit he needed it. He made an open boast that he had killed two men, though in point of fact, of course, he didn't actually kill them, but, owing to his perpetual bullying and driving, he was the moral cause of one man committing suicide, while the other chap just died, and though malaria went down in the log, that wasn't the real cause.

When one takes into consideration the enervating climate, the terrific heat, heavy work, unquenchable thirst, and withal a skipper who could literally wear the sole off a sea boot, it is easy to understand a man lacking a bit perhaps in courage and strength of character, just cracking up completely. Bully Waters seemed to have the natural born ability to taunt and torment men to the limit of their endurance; as a rule just stopping short of the point where a man loses control. Why no one ever brained the beast puzzles me.

A double crew is carried on these boats, one part white to work the ship, the second part of negroes to work the cargo. These latter are trained to handle the cargo peculiar to the West Coast, both discharging and loading. Work commences about 5 a.m. and Waters, on principle, would visit every hatch, quarrel, annoy and thoroughly put every officer on edge, and then, having set everybody by the ears, retire happily to his cabin, have a drink and go off to sleep again.

On one of these occasions we were part loaded with about twenty tons of explosives, mainly gunpowder. This had to be discharged at a place called Borutu, and it happened to be at my end of the ship, stowed in a specially built-in magazine. Embarking this cargo at Liverpool, every possible precaution is taken as a matter of form, such as men wearing rubber boots, every particle of iron work carefully covered up, and the kegs handled gingerly from man to man, until they eventually arrive, and are stowed away in the magazine; whilst, at the masthead, high above all, the powder flag flies. When we arrived at the port of discharge, although we did not trouble to cover up the iron, nor adopt rubber boots, still powder is powder, and has to be treated with a certain amount of respect. Our "boys" passed it up by hand, via wooden stages, and placed it on the deck, whilst it was taken from overside by a company of West African Housas (one of the finest fighting races in Africa). The latter had a stage rigged which brought them from the shore to the ship and breast high with our deck. These men are born scrappers, and it was only by using the utmost tact that peace was kept between the Sierra Leone boys, belonging to the ship, and the Housas belonging to the shore. At any time the slightest carelessness on the part of one of our boys, say dropping a keg on one of a Housa's toes, would, as likely as not, end up in a free for all tribal fight, which would take the whole of the white men on board to put a stop to, and that only after some few had been knocked out.

We were already labouring under these conditions, when Bully Waters must come along and raise Cain about the "slowness" with which the explosives were being discharged. These early morning efforts invariably ended in a wordy war, for I could cuss just as long and loud as he could—and did. Work was going on all right, and skipper or no skipper I was not going to be bullied by him or anyone else. A very effective method I found for dealing with him was to deliberately stop all work, and give him my whole attention. Not edifying, it's true, but it used to do the trick and did on this occasion. When he had finally retired, Massey, the fourth officer, and I put our heads together and decided to give him all he was asking for. So a half ton iron tub was procured from forward, and every scrap of care just thrown to the wind. The boys were worked up—as it is always possible to work up any of these West African tribes by telling off one boy to beat a tom-tom, until they were just dancing in a frenzy of excitement. The half ton tub was loaded up, by simply hurling in kegs of powder until it would hold no more; many hitting the lip of the tub, and bursting scattered powder everywhere. Up went the tub, off with the catch, crash came the whole half ton of powder kegs on deck, to be simply torn away in bulk, and almost thrown at the Housas who were waiting overside. These Housa boys also soon got wound up to the dancing stage of excitement. Powder above, powder below, powder everywhere. It was not long before everybody connected with the ship found a reasonable excuse to park themselves on shore, as far away from the ship as they could get.

A certain amount of zest was added, by the fact that the s.s. *Matade's* bows were even then visible in the Bush, as a result of discharging a similar cargo in the same place, when, even though infinite care was taken, luck was against them, and up she went.

I got a certain amount of cussed contentment out of the knowledge that even Bully Waters dare not come to my end of the ship and show the white feather by calling a halt, nor, on the other hand, dare he funk, and go on shore. However, she did not blow up, and he gave me a rest after that, so it was worth it.

I did one more voyage with him and was not so lucky. Due to his everlasting bully-ragging, I succeeded in drowning three boys and a quarter-master, and incidentally nearly drowning myself.

CHAPTER TWENTY   *A SURFBOAT TRAGEDY*

WE had arrived off Grand Bassam to take in mahogany logs, but it happened to be a "surf day," and as a result there was no communication by boat between ship and shore, and no logs could be floated off to the ship for loading. The question to be settled was, should we stay in hopes of the weather moderating, or should we push on homeward.

Waters gave the Chief orders to go in with the surf boat, and get in touch with the shore and find out if they proposed to ship off any logs. This the Chief proceeded to do; anchoring and trying to signal to the shore when he was as close to the surf as he could get, with any degree of safety. Grand Bassam is open to the full force of an Atlantic swell, and if there is, or has been, a good westerly gale within a few hundred miles, the sea banks up, with the shoaling water, curling over as it rushes in, to finally crash down the beach, throwing up sheer volcanoes of surf. To be caught in one of these mountainous breakers, even in a surf boat (double-ended like a lifeboat) is almost sure to be fatal, unless every member of that surf boat's crew is trained to the last hair, and even then, the chances are odds on being capsized. Our boys were quite good in the surf boat, but not by a long shot equal to tackling anything like the sea running that day. Waters sent for me and asked, "Why the hell can't the Chief get in touch with the beach? He's too far out." As a matter of fact, from where we were it did seem as if he might get closer in. I replied that "although he seemed well clear of the breakers, it was impossible to form an opinion, unless one were to take a boat and see for oneself." He gallingly sneered, "I don't know what the blazes you fellows are afraid of." This jeer was calculated to a nicety, knowing full well that it held just the right sting to make me carry out any crazy attempt to make touch with the shore. Naturally my reply was pointed and pungent. "All right," said he, with biting contempt, "take the gig and let's see what *you* can do."

Like a fool I took the gig, a boat with a square stern, the very worst type of boat for the work in hand; called away a crew, and off we went, in full view of the first and second class passengers, many of whom were witnesses both to the "dare" and the disastrous results. They gave their opinions in no measured terms a little later on, for it all happened within a mile or so of the ship.

The Captain's last instructions were "take a lead line, sound in, and see how far I can bring the ship." This called for a Quartermaster.

We sounded in as far as was necessary, and then coiled the lead line down in the stern sheets, and went on to make touch with the Chief. When we got alongside of him, we found he was riding right on the edge of the breakers, one instant shooting skyward on the lip of a sea, and the next, dropping like a stone into the trough. He certainly couldn't get in any closer. I said I would pull a little way up the coast and see if I could make contact further along.

Nursing the gig up to the seas, I worked her along the coast line. One minute we were pulling like mad up the face of a curler, and the next buried away down out of sight of everything in the trough, and, all the

A SURFBOAT TRAGEDY

time, right on the edge of the breakers. Every wave had an ugly lip to it, and threatened to smash down on us.

With the Quartermaster I tried to signal the shore. This was no easy matter whilst at the same time keeping just out of the clutches of the breaking seas. Every now and then, we had to pull her head sharply round, and work her over a comber that had just reached breaking point.

What exactly happened in the next few moments I don't know. Either my attention was drawn too much to the beach, or one sea, out of pure cussedness, determined to break further out than the others, but turning my head seaward, I was just in time to look up at a gigantic comber on the point of crashing down right on top of us. It was literally over us, and I could see the pale sickly green light of the sun filtering through the overhanging water, some fifteen feet above us.

I gave the order sharply to "pull port, back starboard," but although I got her head up to the sea, before I could get way on her, the sea broke, right square into the boat; filled us up, and drove us right down to the bottom under the weight of tons of water. I felt the heel of the boat actually hit the sand, and, marvellous to relate, we all came to the surface with the boat, and still sitting in our places.

Even then, I believe I could have got her through, if I had had a white crew, or if these negro boat boys, though born and brought up to the surf, had not lost their heads. They looked round, and, seeing the next big curler just preparing to break, they cowered over their oars in funk, instead of pulling to meet it as it rushed at us. This time the boat was rolled over and over, and I went to the bottom with the infernal lead line wound round my feet.

I had not noticed that I had been sitting with my feet in the middle of the coil.

After disentangling this mess under water, I came up to find the boat bottom up, and a man's hands flapping helplessly above the water, close by. That was the Quartermaster, and he was drowning. There was no time for any recognised life saving methods, I grabbed him by the back of the wrist, gave him a sharp jerk towards the keel of the boat and put his hand on the keel before he had time to grab me. Instinctively, he pulled himself up on to the boat, only to be washed off a moment later by the next sea. I got him up *again*, but it was no use; there was nothing in the smooth planking of the boat for him to hang on to. By the third time, I was getting done up myself, so I took some of the gratings and oars that were floating about, and shoved them under his arms. That was the last we ever saw of him.

To make matters worse for myself, I was wearing a very thin blue serge uniform; although anything but white ducks is almost unheard of as wearing apparel in this climate, yet for some unknown reason that morning I had donned this wretched thing.

When I made up my mind to swim for the shore I discarded the coat, and released a spring belt I was wearing to rid myself of my pants, but only added to my difficulties through my pants jamming round my ankles.

With a thundering crash would come the sea and down I would go, literally rolling over and over in the sand on the bottom, coming up with my lungs bursting. Barely on the surface with hardly time to catch a breath, then down again.

This was drowning.

One hears about the panorama of one's past life passing in a sort of mental review during those memorable moments.

Nothing of the kind. I was worried because I had always told my chum sister that I would never be drowned.

She fussed a lot over me at times, so I used to say to her:

"Don't you bother, the sea is not wet enough to drown me. I'll *never* be drowned," and that was on my mind and making me feel really mad. I kept saying to myself, "Here am I, after what I've said, being drowned after all."

The pounding I was getting must have knocked me stupid, or I would never have let it go on. I came to the surface on one such occasion, to see a sea already bearing down on me, just curling over and falling, and here was I sort of crouching away, hating the damn thing; when it suddenly dawned on me, "swim into it, you fool." This, of course, is the only way to get the better of a surf; get on its back; whatever you do don't get under. A couple of strokes, and I drove right straight into the hollow under the crest that was already falling. Almost immediately I was whipped up on the back of the breaker and carried at race-horse speed for the shore. In riding a surf, all one need do is to keep in a certain position on its back; the knowledge of this particular spot can only be gained through surf riding experience—which fortunately I had had at odd times in different parts of the world.

I was swept up on the beach, but it was far too steep to get a foothold, and in consequence I was carried back with the next backwash out into the surf again. Rolled over a few times, then up on the crest of the next; a lightning sweep to the shore, crash on the beach, and back once again with the undertow.

This had gone on just about long enough when I saw some negroes running along the shore joining hands, with the evident intention of forming a human chain into the breakers, and I remembered no more. When I regained consciousness, I was trying to disentangle my pants from my feet, and drag the former up to respectability round my waist. Eventually, I succeeded. As there was no one to be seen, I got rid of some of the sea and headed for the nearest habitation, which happened to be one of Swanzi's Factories.

The negroes had gone to the French Authorities post haste, to inform them of the defunct. They will not touch a dead white body and would not have pulled me out only they had seen that I was still alive.

I was now supposed to be dead, and the French authorities came down to view the corpse, but by this time the corpse was in the said Swanzi's Factory absorbing whisky.

Three boys and a Quartermaster were drowned, and Bully Waters learned the lesson of his life—and earned a dandy dressing down when he got home.

Never again did he dare an officer, just to serve his own purpose, and I gained the unsolicited honour of being the only white man to have swum through the surf at Grand Bassam.

I might say that the Chief's difficulties were by no means imaginary. Under such conditions, even a trained crew could hardly have made the beach, and certainly not without the help of a surf man on shore. For one thing, the psychological moment for running on the back of a breaker can never be detected from the sea. There is a man on shore who has probably done nothing else all his life but signal the surf boats when to "run." He has a long bamboo staff in his hand, on the end of which is a flag, which he keeps at the "dip" until he sees the opportunity. Meantime the surf boat, with or without a cargo, has approached the edge of the breakers, and there it stays, alternately shooting in the air and dropping into the trough.

Four surf boys aside, each with his paddle poised ready for the signal. The big toe of his right or left foot, according to which side he is on, tucked into a rope becket, made fast to a rib of the boat. The coxswain holds her stern steady on to the seas, as they come rolling along; with the boys quietly back paddling to keep her in position.

This may go on for ten, twenty minutes, or even half an hour, until at last the man on shore sees the chance. Up goes his staff, and he races backwards and forwards along the beach waving his flag, for it must be remembered that the boat may be anything up to half a mile off shore. Instantly they see the flag, placing complete reliance in this man's judgment, they dig in their paddles and drive like fury for the beach, shouting with all their native excitement at the top of their voices. If the man ashore has judged aright, and he rarely makes a mistake, the boat is picked up on the back of a huge comber and rushed for the beach at simply race-horse speed. They must just keep on the forward edge of the crest, but not too far ahead or the stern will kick up, the nose go down, and the boat be flung end over end. Not too far back, or the drag will get them, and holding them back at the mercy of the next breaker to come crashing down into the boat, when the chances are that no one will get ashore.

There are many days after a westerly gale that it is impossible to get any boat whatever to and from the beach. This had unluckily happened to be one of them. All the way home, Bully Waters was a sadder, wiser, and quieter man. It was peace, perfect peace. Nevertheless I, for one, had had enough of Bully Waters.

Another thing that helped me make my decision was the fact that on the passage home I had a whole-time dose of malaria. This in itself was not so bad, but unfortunately we had a doctor—thorough good scout —who said he believed in allowing patients any amount of latitude, to follow their own inclinations. Whether it was because I made a particularly bad patient, I don't know, but the fact remains that he allowed me to have iced drinks, lie in my pyjamas, and have my boy fan me; take cold baths—in fact, do everything I ought not to have done. The ultimate result of this was my temperature soared to 106.2°. Down the coast 105° is usually fatal, and on this day in particular, one of the crew passed out at 105°.

I was lying under a punkah, and some of the chaps kept coming down; in fact, nearly all the officers, on one pretext or another, came along to say a few words, and sort of give me a pat on the shoulder and say "Cheerio old boy." I little thought it was the long cheerio they were wishing me, as, in their opinion, I could not last the night. However, later on, that same night, to their surprise, I showed a slight improvement, and some of them put their heads together and decided to take the law in their own hands and see if they could not induce a sweat. Forthwith three or four of them armed themselves with hot bottles and hot blankets, in which they rolled me like a mummy, using sheer brute force, with the result that they broke the fever on the spot, and I eventually recovered. But it had given me the shaking up that was necessary to make up my mind to give up the West Coast with all its attractions—and they are many.

CHAPTER TWENTY-ONE

TRAIL OF '98

WHAT put the Canadian North-West into my head was the fact, that on a previous voyage homeward bound, amongst the passengers we had two splendid fellows named Matchett and Green, who had been prospecting up the interior, from the West Coast of Africa. We became great friends, and first of all they tried to persuade me to chuck the sea, and go out again to Africa with them, which I would have done, except for the rotten malaria and blackwater fevers. "Well, then, would I go out gold prospecting with them to Australia?" That did not appeal to me either, as there's no room for any but experts. Placer mining was finished in Australia and anyway I knew nothing about either placer or quartz.

Ultimately we compromised by deciding to go treasure hunting on St. Paul's—that had a tremendous pull, but although we actually got to the very point of buying a little brig, which we were to turn into a schooner, the scheme, to the sorrow of us all, fell through.

Finally, we agreed to meet the next spring twelvemonth, in Vancouver B.C., and push up into what was then the Great Unknown, and we left it at that.

Up to this time Klondyke had not been heard of, but both Green and Matchett, with the true miner's instinct, were determined that the British North-West was the coming country for the gold prospector.

At home one day some weeks after leaving the *Niagara*, Bully Waters and malaria, I happened on an advertisement of cheap fares to Vancouver. Here, I thought, was the very chance, to get out there twelve months ahead of Dick and Matchett, and learn a bit about gold prospecting. Furthermore I should then be able to pull my weight with the others. Five minutes earlier I had no idea of going, but just on the impulse of the moment, I said to myself "I'm off."

Putting the paper down, I strolled out of the room and with a touch of the dramatic, informed my people that I was going out to the Klondyke. (The rush by this time had started.)

Opinions were somewhat varied, but only to the extent of what particular degree of a fool I was! However I was sufficiently pig-headed and self-confident to ignore the opinions of people, who certainly knew what was good for me far better than I knew myself—at least, so it has sometimes appeared in the light of later days. But, on the whole I have never regretted the decision that took me out to the Canadian North-West, nor one single experience with which the days were filled. I certainly did not make a fortune; in fact, not only made nothing but lost all I had. But I had a grand time.

The idea had been to go out and work on the Cariboo Mines, learning what gold was, in order that I might meet Matchett and Green the following spring, and be able to do my bit along with the experts. Man proposes, but the facts of that hard bitten country, disposed and bust up all my well laid plans.

In the first place, work on the Cariboo Mines was shut out with Chinamen. This upset my calculations from the start, and, as often happens, the king pin removed, all the rest went wrong. So we had to look for some other hunting ground.

As one got deeper and deeper into the country one learnt that the reports which had been blazoned forth in England, had that element of truth which made them worse than a pack of lies. The object was to get men into the country. They got them in their thousands, and hundreds of thousands, and there they were, left stranded, to settle, or find their way out, as best they could.

With a kindred spirit (also of the sea), with whom I had made friends on the way out to Canada, we made up our minds to stay east of the mountains and work north to the Slave Lakes. But we were to discover that the bubble of this district had also been burst. One place after another we heard of "finds," only to learn later that they were purely a figment of the imagination, a mirage, that promptly faded on closer approach. We were not going to be beaten on that account however, and since all places we heard of as likely from a prospector's point of view became no good, and not worth while, we decided to make for rail head which at that time was Edmonton, and to strike a trail of our own, west-north-west, for the mountains, and then north.

All we lacked was someone with some sense and some knowledge of the North-West. We were to find that out later when experience should have at last overcome our abysmal ignorance of the "Trail."

Gold we found in plenty, but never in paying quantities. It is all float gold east of the mountains, and this we learned through bitter experience.

The generally accepted theory is that the range of Rocky Mountains rose, throwing the sea back on either side. On the west, into its native ocean, but on the east it was trapped by the land, and results in endless muskegs, swamps and lakes, which infest that part of Canada. We lived in a state of moisture and the only wonder is that we didn't grow webs to our toes.

Time and again we thought we had struck rich, only to find, on applying the test, that it was worthless. Right down on the banks of the Saskatchewan, in Edmonton, a man could "wash" a dollar and a half a day. The further north, and the richer it gets, but the more the cost of transport. Up on the MacCleod, Athabaska, and Smoky River it pans out at times, almost all a man's heart could desire, but owing to the configuration of the country, it invariably peters out, and pay dirt in any reasonable quantity is never forthcoming.

We, of course, were just tenderfeet, my chum and myself and two others, but, as Matchett and Green used to tell me, "having been a sailor the trail will never worry you" and they were right. We remained in camp in Edmonton with a temperature anything down to 40° below Zero, or 72° below freezing point, whilst we gathered together an outfit of stores and horses. Many a chuckle I had over the thought "if only some of my shipmates saw me now."

Soon we had things licked into shape—or what we considered shape, and launched ourselves out into that wild Nor'-West mid-winter, rivers still frozen and bearing. We struck away with lots of confidence and little sense, over muskegs and jamb piles; no tenderfeet us! we would cut our own way. The only wonder is that we did not break our horses' legs, and our own necks before we had gone a score of miles. Horses up to their bellies in snow, stumbling over fallen trees, making a bare mile an hour. This went on for three days until, by sheer accident, we stumbled on a perfectly good road, which had been running parallel with us, all the way to Prince Albert, and along which we might have comfortably journeyed had we not been so pig-headed in our determination to make our own trail and not admit our ignorance.

The party, as I have said, consisted of four, my chum and myself, and two fellows from the Black Hills. My chum was also a sailor, and by this time we had come to the conclusion that as far as wood-craft in the Canadian North-West went, our feet were very tender indeed.

Not so the other two chaps, who, like so many others from the great U.S.A., were never willing to admit their limitations; in fact, a frequent expression of these two otherwise splendid fellows was "We're from the Black Hills; we ain't no dog gone tenderfeet." That might have been quite true, but it is a solid fact, which we were very soon to find out, that their experience did not run on all fours with their self-confidence; in fact, it was amusing at times to see how quickly their views changed, and with child-like simplicity they would say "what in hell do we do now?" If it was a river, they were perfectly frank, that they had not the first idea how to get across, but even in the depths of our first three days' trek, when we became tied up between two chains of lakes, it was really comical at times to see how jumpy these two would be "old timers" from the Black Hills, became.

On one occasion we were all startled by a steady thump or beat; with the closest resemblance imaginable to a pit-head pump, a sort of steady thud, thud, thud and then a pause, like the usual gas engine. Our Black Hills companions were the first to give voice to the general uneasiness by an abrupt enquiry, "Say, bo, what in hell's that?"

As a matter of fact, I had heard it for some time and was turning over in my mind the possibility of a pit engine or quartz stamp within the limits of hearing. At the same time one had to take into consideration the way in which sound carries in the vast trackless regions of the North-West.

One speaks, rather loosely, of "perfect silence." The Canadian Nor'-West, in winter, is one of the few places where one can experience it; where the snap of a bough, bursting through frost, a common enough occurrence in a temperature 40° below, echoes like a pistol shot, and carries for three or four miles. It is easy to be deceived both as regards sound and sight, where the silence is so absolute and the visibility so perfect.

Days went on, and at odd times we could hear this mysterious thudding. One day, after it had been particularly noticeable, our Black Hills pals suggested a night watch, in view of the possibility of Indians. (I firmly believe they thought it was Indians signalling.) My chum and I were quite in agreement with them as to the possibility, in view of the number of tepee poles, and evidence of wigwams we came across. At the same time, Bill and I were quite resigned to the fact that we were tenderfeet and would, therefore, stand little chance of anticipating the approach of Indians, whether asleep or awake. All the questionable joys of standing a night watch, after a day's work, were only too familiar to both of us, and frankly, we preferred to take the chance and have the blankets. On this point at least, Bill was luridly emphatic, so that ended all talk of keeping watch. Our Black Hills boys were none too pleased, but they did not see the fun of staying awake all night since Bill told them they could keep the first two watches, and give us a call if they liked, and then turn in. "Yes, but are you going to turn out," they asked. Bill replied, in the most convincing language that we were not.

The thudding was still going on at intervals, and we were certainly very mystified by it; until one day, whilst leading the trail, I suddenly heard the sound quite close on my left. Throwing an arm up for the whole pack train to stop, I dropped the lariat to the ground, which would stop the leader in his tracks, then throwing my rifle from my shoulder, where one carries it at all times, by the sling, I dropped on my stomach, and commenced to worm my way towards the sound. When the sound stopped I stopped; when it went on I went on, until, after scuffling along for twenty or thirty yards, I poked my head into an open glade and peered around. There I stayed for some little time, every now and then hearing the drumming. Then suddenly I saw the cause of all our uneasiness. Sitting on a fallen tree was an old cock partridge, drumming with his wings, calling to his mate! We put the cause of all our anxious hours into the pot, and cooked him for the next meal!

That sound must at times have carried for miles with absolute distinctness. After that, any circumstances we could not explain was always classified as "another partridge," for the benefit of our U.S.A. boys. They certainly never suggested another night watch.

The natural difficulties of the country come under the headings of muskegs, jamb-piles and rivers. The former are just swamps without bottom. You have your pack train plodding steadily along, the ground commences to get moist, then damp, then wet, and finally soft. The horses commence to pick their way from tuft to tuft, at last one slips, and down he goes, right up to the belly in pure swamp. This means timber has to be cut and laid alongside of him, whilst a couple of chaps sit astride the logs, unload the 250 lb. pack from the saddle and pass it back piecemeal to the dry land. Having done this, one fore leg is pulled out of the mire and rested on a log, then the other fore leg ditto. Next his tail is seized, and then, with a terrific yell, and altogether, with a sucking squelch he comes out. (That is if the horse does his part, otherwise you try again.) This operation a dozen times a day, wet through and covered with mud, is included in the joys of gold prospecting in the north-west.

Then rivers. Such rivers! When they do break in Spring, it's a sight to be remembered. Crossing them is easy enough up to this point, but after they break, then, apart from the cold, one has to contend with literal icebergs tearing down out of the mountains with a torrent of melted snow, grinding and crashing together with thousands of tons of pressure behind them. Of course, you've got to realise that after the rivers break the crossing in the first instance has to be made with a horse, and by sheer good hard swimming. At the same time a line must be taken, and the drag from it always feels like a ton weight in the water; with a river only just broken this is of course quite impossible.

First you must travel up stream, until a suitable spot is found for taking off, and, what is more important still, a suitable spot is located lower down on the opposite side, where a landing can be made. If you don't make your landing, it's a thousand to one you cannot get back again.

A rope long enough to reach at least twice across is coiled down clear on the bank, and on no account must that rope be checked as it runs out, otherwise you immediately check the swimmer. The first river we came to was the Pembinaw, and I had made three shots before I found the bright Alecs on the bank (again our Western States men) thought the rope was running out too quickly and in consequence were checking it under their feet!

As a matter of fact there were rapids just below us and unless I was well over in the first few hundred yards I had perforce to let go the end of the rope altogether and get back as quickly as possible in order to avoid being swept into the rapids. Eventually, I found out where the trouble lay and on the fourth attempt succeeded.

In water of this temperature a suit of underclothes and a belt does not offer much protection. I really don't know why one always wears a suit of underclothes; it must be that the thick wool helps when one comes out of the water; however it seems the usual practice up there to wear a suit of wool underclothes. Having once got the line across all is plain sailing. A few well-seasoned logs are pinned together with green willow pegs to make a raft, which is towed back and forth.

CHAPTER TWENTY-TWO *CROSSING THE ATHABASKA*

ONE river we struck as we got up to the mountains, seemed the father of all rivers, the Athabaska, broken up into rapids and nearly three miles across. We arrived on the banks one evening, and set out to get over as it is always better to have dry clothes and the river behind you in the morning. We forded a considerable distance, and arrived on an island in the middle, where, in the end, we had to camp for the night. Next morning we set out to find a ford. There wasn't one, and, what was of added interest, we found that the river was rising.

A couple of days before, we had chummed up with another party of three heading the same way, so we joined forces in the hope that many heads might help. I can't say that they did, but fortunately for all of us, the assurances we had received from old timers that sailors take naturally to the trail, proved quite true and of inestimable value, though parked in the middle of the Athabaska, with a rising river in front and behind us, it did not seem as if all our sailoring experience was going to help much; and it didn't, despite seven attempts to find a ford. There seemed nothing for it but to take the bull by the horns, get on a horse, get into the water, and hope for the best.

The opposite bank, another island, was only a matter of a hundred yards, but the sides were sheer, with the exception of two places where the bank had broken away. There seemed practically no hope of fetching the break higher up the river, but the lower one was just possible. So I determined, that night, that unless the river went down I was going to have a shot at it, particularly as there was every unpleasant indication that the river frequently submerged the whole island. Bill would go anywhere where any one else would lead. He certainly had no fear, and he was the only one of the party who would face water. His horse was none too good though, just a bundle of nerves; whereas mine, that I had chosen out of a corral of fifty or sixty, could and would do anything but talk. This was to be the one and only occasion on which I ever saw him baulk at water, and that night, when I tried to get him to face this flood—which was nothing but white water, coming tearing and foaming down out of the mountains—he certainly didn't like it. In fact it is no exaggeration to say he just hated it. Bill *would* come, but unfortunately he had never ridden a horse in his life, much less swam one. I cautioned him, "Now mind, as soon as he loses his feet, get off his back and hang on to his withers," and in we went, Rufus step by step, and every step a snort. He certainly did not like it a bit, and, speaking generally, a man is a fool to force one of those intelligent pack horses when he baulks. But this was an exception. So with a pat and an urge, he went on, step by step, with the water foaming between his legs, till at last he lost his feet, got a dose of funk, and tried to fling back. Fortunately, his head came round my way, and I was able to give him a hearty smack on the nose, and head him off again in the right direction. Then he stretched himself out and went through the water like a harbour launch.

Having settled him on his course I looked round for Bill who had followed me in. All that was visible at that moment were the four legs of a horse, sticking up above the water, and just in the act of rolling over.

Bill must have lost his head and tried to stick on his horse's back, both of them rolling over in consequence.

Amazing though it seemed, I struck the higher break in the opposite bank, an accomplishment I had thought utterly impossible. I'll say that horse could swim! The moment old Rufus touched the ground with his feet he tore out of the water like one possessed, snorting like a grampus, thoroughly wound up, and shaking like a leaf with excitement. Throwing a leg over him as he came out, I kept him going and galloped down to the lower end of the island as hard as we could coiling the lariat up in my hands at the same time. Bill had one chance as he swept by, and one only. If he missed the end of that lariat, he was bound down to where the river humped itself up in a canyon, a few miles below, in which no canoe, let alone a man, could live for a minute.

Arriving at the lower end of the island, I drove Rufus down the spit until he was as deep in the water as I dare go and still retain good foothold, and then waited until Bill came past. It was a critical moment, for I knew I should only get that one throw, and that to pretty well the full extent of the rope. I must land the end of the lariat somewhere near him, where he could either swim to it—in which case he would lose his horse—or, if I was fortunate enough, get so near that he could secure the end, and still hang on to the horse's halter.

Actually, what happened, I made my throw, and, with unlimited luck, landed the end right alongside of him. I yelled to him to hang on to his horse, while he took a quick seamanlike turn round his wrist, and with the other hand gripped the halter. My end was round my waist, slacking and easing away to the strain whilst Bill and his horse, swung round into the eddy where we were standing, and got their feet on firm ground again.

No one ever had a closer call, though Bill didn't seem to worry.

We spent that night turning ourselves round, like a roast of beef on a spit, trying to warm one side and then the other, lying in nothing but our underclothes, in front of a roaring fire we had built up out of driftwood.

The whole of the next day we were alternately fording, swimming, and freezing, whilst we made our way to the mainland, where we eventually located an Indian canoe. This we brought down to where the others were marooned, and eventually succeeded in ferrying the rest of the party over. The river was by then within a few inches of the surface of the island and they had made all preparations for taking to the trees. That would have been all right, but, unfortunately horses can't climb.

It is undoubtedly a great game crossing rapids in a canoe. You tow up stream so far, until you find an eddy or little bay, causing a bit of slack water. Probably just a cut of a few feet into the bank will do. Then a bit lower down on the opposite side, another convenient eddy must be found. Then load the canoe, and don't forget to put the paddle on top of everything, ready to hand. Give her a push, leap in, and land in the bottom on your knees, sitting on your feet—if you are lucky. It needs a bit of practice but fortunately I had had plenty of opportunity for that in the dug-outs of Rio de Janeiro, in which you surely do have to part your hair in the middle. I had won many a race in Rio, and compared with a Dug-out, the Canadian birchbark is easy. Having landed in the bottom of the canoe you seize your paddle, and dig like fury. The water fairly curls up at the bow, and you simply tear across the river at the rate of knots. Head her straight for the opposite eddy as though you were going to ram the bank at full speed. Actually what happens is, the stem touches the dead water, and the river, sweeping down, swings the stern round, bringing the canoe to a standstill, riding motionless alongside the bank all in one movement. It is thrilling all right—particularly with rapids just below you—but tiring when you have to keep it up all day, as we had to, to get clear of the island before it disappeared.

All throughout this long trek, swimming rivers, getting through jamb-piles, over muskegs; hail, rain, blow and snow, my old banjo survived. It had, as a matter of fact been a good companion and helped cheer us up and pass many a weary hour, right from the start of the voyage on board ship, also on the slow going train bound west, and even, at times, on the trail.

Bill was a particularly good step dancer and singer, which had, as a rule packed our car on the way across country. Many an evening we passed away singing old popular songs. On the trail the banjo was brought out when we were not too dog tired, after a terrific day's struggle—times when it needed all one's powers of self-control to prevent quarrelling with anybody, or everybody who came near. There was the amusing side too, such as up in the mountains, when Indians squatted on their haunches all round us. They rarely speak, nor do they ask for food, but it is always the custom to pass them a dish of beans, which, of course, is the staple diet. After we had finished our meal, and put on our pipes, the smoke of the fires slowly blowing across, sometimes, partly for a lark, we would start up the banjo, and Bill his song and dance. It was worth while, just to see the looks on those Indians' faces. Their features always seem carved out of stone, and it is considered the worst form for them to register any surprise, but to hear the sound coming out of that banjo usually beat them, and, immediately it was put down, they would gather round and peer into it, to see where the sound came from.

How that old banjo survived beats me. It always seemed to come up smiling even after swimming a river or working through a forest.

One follows the old buffalo trails which almost invariably lead to a ford, also wherever buffalo could go between the trees, so also could a pack horse pass between them. I have, on more than one occasion, seen the banjo athwart two trees, and old Rufus gently putting pressure on it, wondering, I expect, what sort of a fool I was to make up his pack so badly that he couldn't get through. As a matter of fact, the banjo was always just lightly placed on top of the pack, and was apt to swing across. However, nothing was ever broken, all credit to the old boy.

For days and days we would be plodding on through forests, hardly ever seeing the sun. Then, just like walking out of a door, you walk out from amongst the trees, with nothing but the prairie in front of you, without even a shrub in sight; nothing but the limitless snow.

On one occasion, after being several days in the open, we arrived at the edge of one of these forests, and camped for our midday meal before diving in. It was obvious to even the most inexperienced that something very special in the way of storms was brewing. A heavy bank was coming up as black as night, but, full of beans (literally and metaphorically), we would be hard cases and allow nothing in the way of weather to stop us. We still had to learn that, above all, discretion is the watchword, in that hard country. So, having finished our meal, we once again hit the trail. It was not long before snow, in the powdery dusty form which it always takes in the interior of Canada, was sweeping through the trees, growing thicker and thicker, every minute. It never snows in flakes; always this fine dust, which on the open prairie will suffocate a man in a few minutes. We stuck to the trail for a couple of hours until it completely disappeared under the snow. We realised we had lost the trail when one of the horses went over the edge of the cliff and rolled to the bottom. By the time we got him and his pack up again we decided we had had enough, and finding a suitable spot, went into camp. The first thing was to get a fire going, and in that country one always carries a bit of birch bark. This will burn and burn brightly under almost any conditions; very nearly under water. With this, and a few pine branches, it is always possible to start up a good blaze, and if one can get hold of willow then you can have all the heat you want, and no smoke. We were glad to get any fire whatever, so just dropped jackpines across it, and as it burned up, so cut down bigger and bigger trees, until we had one gigantic bonfire going, throwing out a tremendous and mighty welcome warmth for some dozen or two yards all round. It was the only way to hope to hold off the snow and get any degree of comfort.

A weird sight, in the middle of this Canadian forest. Sitting around a gigantic fire, the horses' tails to wind, nothing but an impenetrable canopy of snow all round, but so great was the heat from the fire, and so fine the snow, that it actually melted and evaporated before it could touch the ground. The upper part of the trees, in fact trees twenty yards from us, were out of sight in the snow, and yet where we were, within the snow walls, was warm and dry. Soon we had the billy going, and a pan full of pork and beans on a fire. Wet clothes and wet blankets, which had been under the pack saddles, hanging up to dry. Even the crashing of an occasional tree could not keep us awake. We slept and dreamt of the gold we were surely going to find some time soon.

A few days later we did actually make our strike. It came about when we had been choosing our camp for the night. In this choice there are two essential factors, food and water for the horses. It may be a swamp—it frequently was; and in that case you can cut yourself some perfectly good boughs of jackpines and make out as comfortably as you can; but grass there must be. On this occasion, where we were prospecting, was on a creek, and next morning while some of the party went off with their rifles, others, of whom I was one, went down to the creek with gold pan and shovel to "wash."

This washing out, on bars and banks, had just about become a rite by this time. As a matter of course one shouldered gold pan and shovel, and trudged off whenever a river showed up. To a certain extent, it had become perfunctory, although there was always the suspense and the latent thrill as to whether "colours" *would* show up. You take a shovel of pay dirt, throw it into a pan of water, and commence by giving it a heaving circular motion, which sends the water swirling round, stirring up all solid matter in the pan. The lighter earth, smaller shingle and gravel, quickly flow over the edge as dip after dip of water is taken, until, finally, there is nothing left but black sand, and in this resides the float gold, which is separated and collected by introducing about a teaspoonful of mercury to which the gold adheres. Then, squeezing the mercury through chamois leather, you have a little nugget of gold left behind—if you are lucky.

I forget whose pan it was that first got down to the black sand, but there was a yell, "We've found." Everybody dropped everything and dashed over to see what it was. Sure enough, there were the colours shining bright and clear, as the pan with the residue of black sand and a little water, was given that final scientific twirl which throws the black sand forward and leaves trailing out behind the glittering specks of gold.

There is then only the last test; viz., application of muriatic acid. If it is gold it only shines the brighter, but if it is false, maybe mica, it will at once turn black, and disappear.

Our next call was for the acid, which could not be found. Evidently it was stowed away in some chap's pack who, at that moment, was off with his rifle trying to pick up a stew for the pot. Nowhere could we discover the muriatic, but we had some acetic acid, and with this we decided to give it a try-out, until we could make the proper test.

The effect was, that the gold only gleamed the brighter, and we jubilantly assured ourselves we had "found." At once, everyone started planning out the camp, the sluice boxes, and all the necessary paraphernalia connected with placer mining. More pay dirt was washed out, and still more colours found—and wealth and affluence were assuredly ours for the taking! All that remained was to gather up the gold that was lying at our feet, and trek back to civilisation.

About this time the fellow with the gun, gameless as usual, arrived back in camp. Of course the good news was told, and, quite as a matter of form, merely to confirm what we were convinced was already a fact, we suggested the muriatic test. He got the acid out of his pack, and over we went to the gold pan; gave it a little swing, and on the glittering contents poured the muriatic. Result, complete, absolute and utter black out. It was mica. Down went all our hopes and with them our spirits.

However, these disappointments soon wear off, and one is ready again to strike the trail with that buoyant confidence that forever lies in the prospector's heart. Good pay dirt he is confident is only a little further on.

To be well bitten with the gold bug is a glorious sensation—always on the verge of the great discovery. The sun is never up early enough, and sets too soon. There would be nothing to beat it, if one only had plenty to eat. Even the scenery alone up in these mountains, almost compensates for the hardships. Everything is wonderful and seems so amazingly near. Even the snow caps of the Rockies, towering thousands of feet above, look as if one could leave the sunshine and be tobogganing within an hour, so rarefied and wonderfully clear is the atmosphere. Look up a draw (an opening between the mountains). "Oh, yes," you'll say, "we'll fetch that to-morrow night," but maybe it will be three days before you reach it; a spot which seemed at most some ten or fifteen miles away.

A grand country, but a hungry one. At that time, even the Indians themselves were starving, and burning out the forests for game. These mountain Indians are the only tribe left that are not treaty-bound; though, nevertheless, they have a wholesome respect for that magnificent body of men, the Canadian Mounted.

Naturally, one keeps one's eyes peeled, and a rifle close to hand night and day, but there was never an occasion, or even the remotest approach to a necessity to use it. They are a friendly lot—wonderful, both at hunting and on the trail. Their powers of endurance are almost beyond belief, on foot and on horseback. I have known a trained Indian runner, to go for three days and three nights, without let or pause, and without food, other than what he was carrying with him. I'll admit he was making his way with a very urgent message;

but for endurance they are mighty hard to beat. They keep up a glide, or lope, doing a steady four miles an hour the whole day through. Their pack horses are trained to walk, and never break into a trot or a canter, but the distances they can cover, with this little short step, would be utterly beyond the power of the horses commonly met with in civilisation. Of course, this applies to the pack horse, and should not be confused with the ordinary cayuse, which is the boon companion of other Indian tribes such as Blackfeet, Crows, and Sioux—who are not exactly the chaps to have with one on a pack train. On the other hand *they* can perform marvels of horsemanship also.

One evening in North Edmonton, there was an argument between a half breed Blackfoot and some white men as to whether a certain tribe of Blackfeet had or had not been wiped out by the Crows, on the banks of the River Saskatchewan near by. There is a place close to the banks of the Saskatchewan known as the Hudson Bay Flats, where an old Hudson Bay Fort used to stand. A flat piece of land extending over perhaps, fifty or sixty acres. It was claimed, that in a fight between the two tribes, the latter drove the former over the edge of the cliff, into the river and drowned the lot of them. This half-breed Blackfoot maintained that his tribe were neither drowned nor annihilated, but that they went down the cliff on their horses and swam the river. Almost everybody smiled at his claim, for although the cliff consisted of earth, yet it was so utterly sheer, that it seemed impossible for a man to get down, with any degree of safety, let alone a man and a horse. Furthermore, taking into consideration that the Blackfeet rode at it, full tilt, with the Crows in pursuit, one could imagine nothing but sheer annihilation.

To me the smile certainly seemed justified.

Then this half-breed got shirty and said he would ride at that cliff himself for a bottle of whisky, and he was not long in finding a man who would put up the bottle, if he would do it. The next day we all turned up on the flats, and this chap mounted his cayuse, bare back, a good quarter of a mile away from the edge of the cliff, and without pause or hesitation rode straight at it, over the edge, and down the odd hundred feet and into the river. All I can say is, he simply went over and down into the river, and swam back. How he managed it, or why both horse and man didn't go head over heels, is simply beyond me, but the fact remains that he never left his horse's back, although he laid full length along it, with his head resting on its rump. I have certainly never seen, and could never have imagined, such an amazing feat—but I'll say he won that whisky.

These fellows are now all Treaty Indians, but whether with either the Crows or the Sioux, there is now very little to fear. The Canadian Mounted Police have brought it home to these tribes (likewise renegade whites) that there is going to be law and order, and they know, for a stonewall certainty, that any break away from this, and somebody will pay the penalty.

The same applies to the white man. There's none of the wild and woolly West business in Canada. If a man drew a gun he'd probably get his stern kicked, good and hard.

In the past it was the custom for one of the Canadian Mounted to be detailed off to track down and arrest any man who had committed a crime, whether small or great, and the powers of endurance exhibited by the tracker were never less than those of the man he was tracking down. Day after day, and week after week, he would follow his man, and eventually track him down. Of course, if the crime had been such as murder, the man had to be brought back alive, or with very clear evidence of his death. There was a recognised procedure in the latter instance which gave evidence enough when dealing with Indians, the details of which there is no need to go into too closely. In any case, there are lots of really good writers who have written up the Canadian Mounted—though the romance has been somewhat dimmed since they mounted them on motor-bikes.

CHAPTER TWENTY-THREE *NO GAME... NO GOLD*

We had hit the trail out of Edmonton with little or no meat, and what we had was mainly bacon. We lived in the full expectation of finding lashings of game through the country. The sum total of all we saw, was a moose, a bear, and a porcupine. The moose my chum got, the bear we didn't get, the porky I got. How Bill got the moose was proof again that his guardian angel was forever alert. The moose is an ugly customer to wound, and has some very nasty habits of kneading a man to death, when sufficiently annoyed. A 44–56 bullet in the stomach, certainly provides an inducement for all the trouble one may be looking for. Bill was a rotten shot at the best of times. I saw this big bull moose—evidently disturbed by some of our would-be hunters, come flashing through the trees, and at the same instant Bill also saw it and raised his rifle. I thought, "Now we're for it," but it was too late to shout at him. He let drive. In my heart of hearts, I half hoped he had missed it altogether, but, to my utter amazement, the beast dropped in his tracks—stone dead—shot through the heart. And I have seen Bill miss a target as big as a haystack!

The bear was my misfortune. Following the trail along the hillside we had come across a jamb pile. This was a whole forest of trees on the side of a hill, fallen down flat years and years ago, and now become thoroughly seasoned timber. Once we had to cut through a jamb pile owing to one of the horses having driven a willow stake through its chest, and in consequence being unable to lift its near foreleg, but one never attempts to cut through timber of this description, from choice. Although the hill resembled the roof of a house, it was going to be better to make the climb up, rather than to try and cut our way through.

Old Rufus was easily the best pack horse, and, almost invariably, led the trail, as he was doing at this time. All the same, it seemed almost impossible for a horse to climb up that hill light, let alone with 250 lb. on his back. Whilst we were discussing the best plan, Rufus settled the matter by suddenly starting off up on his own, just as if he wanted to show what he could do when he wanted. I had no choice but to follow him, as I held his lariat in my hands, which if I had dropped it, would have been bound to foul his feet. He went up that fifty or sixty feet like a lamplighter, and arrived on a little plateau, with me puffing and blowing at his side.

This little effort had been carried out in silence, and I suppose Mr. Bruin's first intimation of anyone in the vicinity, was our arriving just outside his front door. Probably it was sheer curiosity that made him stick his head out within six feet of Rufus' nose on the off side. I, being on the near side, could, of course, see nothing. The old chap made up his mind to go down again even more quickly than he had decided to come up. He just let out a squeal of indignant surprise, and swung round, smiting me a mighty crack on the side of the head with his nose, which laid me sprawling, whilst he sat on his hams, and slid down that hill, 250 lb. and all, with his tail streaming out behind. A more ridiculous sight I have never seen, and, despite the nearness of the bear, I had to roar with laughter. The hill was so steep that his hind legs were almost between the forelegs, as he tobogganed down the hillside. My rifle, which I had been carrying in the sling as usual, over my back, had been flung clear in the tumble, and long before I could get hold of it, our one and only bear had vanished.

The porcupine I met whilst trying to find a draw out of the mountains.

All old timers warn tenderfeet "not to lose heart in the mountains." I suppose it is the amazing solitude, the immensity of the spaces, and the seemingly utter futility of man that engenders the spirit of funk, when, buried in these appalling masses and precipices of granite, known as the Rocky Mountains. I think there was more than a little evidence of funk in our camp, in fact it had even been suggested by someone that we should turn back. Not one of our original party, I am glad to say, but the poisonous suggestion was there, there could be no doubt. It was the mountains that had got everyone, so the best plan as far as we could see, was to get out of them. I was making my way along in glorious sunshine on a well fed animal, happy with the world, and confident of finding a way out for the party, then all would be well. At this juncture I saw an animal fifty yards in front of me, crossing my trail. It looked like nothing on earth; certainly nothing that I could recognise, never having seen a porcupine like this in my life before. It was truly the father of all porcupines; and looked as big as many a young donkey. Of course in the tall grass he was anything but clearly defined. However, I judged as best I could where the head of the beast should be, and where probably his fore-shoulder would come, and let drive. He sank down out of sight in the grass. I circled round, still on horseback, until I located him, and pumped in a couple more 44–56's.

He was dead all right so I proceeded to skin him. Having completed this task, the next thing was to get him clear up off the ground, and out of reach of the coyotes. It was quite impossible to lift him, so I had to slip the lariat on to a hind leg, lead it over the bough of a tree, and hitch it on to the cinch of my horse. In this manner I hoisted him up and made him fast. I then cut off a fore-quarter, and took it with me, intending to cook it for a meal that night. I did, but I might as well have tried to feast off a cut of rhino hide; there was just about as much chance of getting my teeth in. I picked him up on my return and took him back to camp, where we boiled him three times a day for seven solid days before we could even get our teeth into him. I will admit that through lack of solid food, our teeth had become somewhat loose, but believe me, they hardened up before we had finished with our friend the porcupine. We remained in camp for several days, undecided whether to go ahead or go back. Meantime fierce arguments arose on the advisability of pushing on. By far the majority were in favour of going back.

It was undoubtedly a fact that we could only push on at a tremendous risk, as our supply of food would shortly give out for a certainty, and we should be compelled to depend on the country alone, which up to the present had proved a mighty poor source of supply. The point settled itself in the end, however, and it happened this way.

Bill and I would not saddle up to turn back, and the others could not cross the rivers without our help, so it was a sort of stalemate. Every day some of us went out prospecting to see what hopes there were of getting colours or finding a draw out of the mountains. On one occasion we came across a creek, though it would be termed a small river in England. It looked as though this river passed between two fair sized ledges of cliff a little further on, and then struck open country.

In this case we knew there must be a bar, and on this bar we should find proof as to whether with this particular creek the water flowed at any time through a gold bearing area, by the colours obtained, also we might find a way out of the mountains.

We soon knocked a raft together, by cutting dry timber into lengths, boring holes with a one and a half inch auger, and pegging with green willow, the pegs going through one log and well into the next. Immediately the wood takes the water, it swells, and binds the whole far firmer than any rope could do, every bit as strong as if it were lashed with good stout wire. Not only that, but owing to the resiliency and bendability of the willow, a raft of this kind can go bumping over rocks, without any danger of coming to pieces. In fact, it becomes literally impossible to separate the logs, without either drying them out, or cutting through the willow pegs with a saw. We launched our craft, and with gold pans and shovels, a day's provisions—or what we had in our straitened circumstances to allow ourselves for a day's food—took to the river. We paddled out towards the centre, and let the current do the rest, which it did in short order and very effectively. She soon shot past the ledges we had seen, and then, instead of the ravine opening out as we fondly expected, the river took a sharp turn to the right (for which we had not bargained) and literally dived down between two solid walls of rock.

There was nothing for it but to hang on, and wait for whatever was going to happen. Everything was well secured to the raft, and this proved fortunate, for as the river narrowed down it humped up so that quite reasonable sized breakers formed, curling up against the race of the stream. We had just time to fling ourselves flat on the raft and hang on for dear life, while the thing plunged madly down the rapids. Steering was out of the question. We had to chance hitting a rock and being shot off. Fortunately, the passage was short, and sharp, but by no means sweet. Still, one could not help noticing the difference between being struck with these freshwater breakers, and similar seas of salt water. You can knock a man down with a bucket of salt water, but not so by any means with fresh water. Every time we rushed at a breaker, each would yell to the other, "Hang on, Jack," "Hang on, Bill," and we would crash through the breaking water comparatively easily compared with meeting a similar breaker at sea.

I suppose we were some five or ten minutes making the passage, although it seemed more like as many hours. We came out with the raft into open water and paddled with our shovels to the side, soaking wet through, although that condition was more or less normal. Mackintoshes and umbrellas are not exactly part of an outfit. When it rains you get wet, and when the sun shines you get dry, and you are lucky if you are dry when you go to bed. Yet such a thing as rheumatics or illness is unknown.

Having landed, we automatically started on the usual procedure with gold pan and shovel. Colours as usual —quite good colours, but not good enough to justify packing food from Edmonton. As we couldn't get back that night we prospected a bit further down on the opposite bank, but, with the same result. The raft would have to be abandoned, likewise, everything else except bare necessities, for the climb back.

Peep of day next morning we were off, up and up, colder and colder, as hour after hour of steady climbing took us up higher and higher and at last into the snow line. Then down the other side, with always the sporting chance of making a slip and starting a non-stop slide to eternity; or even meeting a grizzly. The result would be the same in both cases! There are not many grizzlies left, any more than there are buffaloes, but there are still quite a few, and a grizzly is about the most cussed customer that one can run across, in all the Nor'-West. As a rule he'll attack on sight, and nothing short of a 45-90 has the slightest effect, and even then it has got to be planted carefully, in exactly the right spot and followed up quickly, or you are going out. Once a grizzly gets its paws on a man, he has far less chance than with a lion, and that's little enough, by all accounts. Admittedly they have not the speed of a lion, but whereas a lion is not difficult as a rule to bring down, a grizzly seems to have about ten times more vitality. We should have been a sorry pair if we had met one, for all we had was our shovels. We thought, when we launched our craft, that we were only going a couple of miles there and back on the river, so we had not even taken our usual inseparable friend, the rifle.

When, at long last, we did get back to the camp, we found the pros and cons of advance or retreat, had been definitely settled by the rest of the chaps packing their traps and clearing out. They had left us, what at any rate they considered was our share of the grub—a tent, our horses, rifles, and blankets.

Well, we had each other to swear at, and that was something; although, as a matter of fact, when we did hit the camp we were far too hungry and played out to consider the merits of the other chaps', shall we say, desertion, or even our own loneliness. That came later. It was a fair taste of just what it must be like to be absolutely alone in these mountains. One could well believe all the tales one heard about chaps who, from one cause or another, have been left on their own, going stark, staring mad. There is sound advice in that caution, "Don't lose heart in the mountains."

The actual loneliness didn't worry us a great deal, our sea training took care of that, but it was the fact of turning back.

To turn back spelt utter failure of the whole expedition. Going on, no matter how slowly, was to break fresh ground, with always the possibility of making a strike. If we did decide to go on then we must make up our minds to kill one horse and smoke the meat; that would have to be done and we were both just as enthusiastic on that programme as we should have been over a suggestion to kill either of ourselves. Your horse becomes your pal, and treats you as such, and he expects the same treatment from you. He will nose round you on the trail, and stand around when you are cooking, in the hopes of getting a lick at the gold pan for salt remaining, when you have finished baking.

No, we didn't enthuse over the idea one bit, yet there was no alternative that we could see, if we were to make the Smokey River, get in a satisfactory prospect along the course, and finally fetch Peace River Landing. Even supposing for one instant that we could bring ourselves to kill one of our old pals, apart from feeling like murderers, and something far worse when we sat down to grub, the chances of ever making the Landing with a cumbersome raft, were about a thousand to one against. However, some decision had to be made, and that right quickly, for the share left us consisted of less than a week's supply. It seemed as though the others must have had it in their minds, that after taking perhaps a day to make a decision—which is exactly what we did—it might take four or five days to catch them up, and we should have food for just that time.

To make a long story short, we stacked our packs, cached our tools, and hit the trail back with three days' grub between us.

CHAPTER TWENTY-FOUR *THE RETURN TRAIL*

WE'D no worry about catching up with the others. We knew only too well that the first river would bring their outfit up all standing. They were all downright good fellows, but never cut out for this sort of thing.

Sure enough, there they all were, sitting on the banks of the Athabaska, contemplating that uninviting flood. They looked a bit sheepish, but it was no use grousing, the only thing to do was to make the best of a bad job and get on, so we scouted up river until we found a canoe, which we brought down and started the ferrying. A hundred pounds at a time was the maximum load when shooting these rapids.

We had found a very suitable spot, where the canoe would lie snugly under the bank whilst we loaded her up, and a nice little bay lower down on the opposite side for an eddy. It was a bad spot as far as the river went, for it was in full flood, but it was an excellent shoving off place, and a good spot for landing. Furthermore, there was a level bank, without tree or scrub, for towing the canoe up river on the far side ready for the shoot back.

Having got half the provisions over, and two or three of the chaps, I thought now was the moment to strike a bargain for provisions. Somehow, I did not feel quite the same towards these fellows, and I determined to get my whack out of them, so that Bill and I could pull out on our own. I told them, quite frankly, when I got half of them parked on one side, and half on the other side of the river, that they could have the canoe and welcome, but in view of the few provisions they had left us two, I did not feel obliged to waste any more time ferrying them back. (I still think I took rather a mean advantage.) Anyhow it was soon happily settled —as far as I was concerned. We got our fair whack of grub, and they got safely over the worst river in the Nor'-West in one of its worst moods.

To take a man over, he had to lie in the bottom of the canoe, underneath the little wooden spreaders. The whole canoe is as light as a feather, built of bark, and stitched with hide. Even with only one man lying in the bottom and the other on his knees paddling, she is pretty deeply loaded, and needs careful handling.

After the provisions and horses were all over, two fellows were left. To save a journey I told them both to get into the canoe, and we would make the final shoot. It was a ticklish job, and as I required every inch of room I had unwisely put the paddle on the bank, until they settled themselves in the bottom. "Being in all respects ready for sea," or, as in this case, for the river, having her nicely, if somewhat deeply trimmed, I turned her bow off with a hand on each gunwhale at the stern, ready, as she took the fast water, to vault in—and it is a bit of a job vaulting into one of these tiny craft, particularly as at the same moment you strike white water. A shove, a jump, and I was in, at the same instant reaching down for the paddle, which, to my horror, was not there. *I had left it on the bank.* How it was managed, I really don't know, but I was over the side in about half a split second, and gave the canoe a terrific tug that stopped her way, and actually, by some miracle, brought her back out of the rapids and into the eddy. The chaps lying in the bottom did not realise what had happened, until I told them. They both looked a bit green, and I'll say it gave me some jar. In any case, I decided to take more time, and more care, so I left one on the beach, and made two journeys of it, this time with safety.

Next morning, the other party struck the trail, but something had happened to Bill's feet, and he was two days before he could get his boots on, and, as we had to eat something every day our provisions again became perilously low. However, when we did catch the other party up, they had been sitting a corresponding number of days on the bank of the next river. Perhaps the saying "We're from the Black Hills, we ain't no tenderfeet" did get rubbed in a bit. That was in return for all the hot air Bill and I had to put up with when away from water, and I must admit I got a certain amount of fun out of pulling their legs, anyway.

For the last week, before striking civilisation, provisions completely petered out, and we lived on the inner bark of jack pines and sourdocks. This inner bark is mainly resin, and as none of us had used a razor since we had started the trail, we all had pretty good healthy beards, which, when mixed up with this resin, turned them into useful doormats. Still, we were not bothering about our outward appearance, so much as our inward feelings, and great were the rejoicings when we met an outward bound outfit, on the same quest as that from which we were returning. We were able to trade a rifle, and ammunition, for some good old sow-belly, beans and tea and had our first square meal for a month.

Bill and I actually arrived back in Edmonton with our horses, a rifle, half a cup of rice, and three cents between us. At that time Edmonton was full of returned prospectors as a result of the great disaster which had befallen the overland trail. It was a saying in those parts that you could find your way from Edmonton to the Klondyke, via the overland trail, by the bones of men and horses that had died by the way. Very little was heard of it outside the country, in fact, the north is notorious for its silence, both of nature and man. A more silent man than the Hudson Bay trapper and trader, and the old time prospector, it would be hard to find.

Many many outfits set out from Edmonton on this terrible overland trail, with little or no idea of what they were going to run up against.

One amazing ass started on a bicycle, with bottles of Bovril strapped on behind.

The trouble commenced in the earlier days, when they got away insufficiently "grub staked." Having gone so far and taken such an appalling time to cover the distance, which on paper, of course, looked trifling —they found themselves with insufficient provisions to complete the journey. Many would push on and on, in the vain hopes of the trail improving and their being able to make better time; also, in the fond hope of finding game. Very nearly everybody was confident they could rely on the country to replenish their larder. At last, when the bitter truth was borne in on them, they were truly between the devil and the deep sea. With the Rocky Mountains, forming an impassable barrier on one side, and the prairie with its muskegs and lakes on the other, they, like us, just had to decide, whether or no they would push on, or face about and go back. Naturally, an outfit would push as long as ever there was the slightest chance, and often, even longer. Then, in final desperation, they would at last be driven into turning back, both men and horses by this time terribly emaciated and weak, through hardships and short commons. They would then meet an outward-bound outfit, who, by the unwritten law of the North-West, could do no less than grub stake them; that is, give them sufficient to eat for a few days at least. This act automatically lessened the outward bound outfit's chances of getting through, and so the bad work went on, outfit after outfit pushing away north, having to reduce their own stock by helping those who were starving on their way back, only to eventually land in the same predicament themselves. The cumulative effect almost beggars description.

It should be borne in mind that it was not a case of just a few men, but of thousands. The total number will never be known, but to my mind, it would be no exaggeration to say that at least ten thousand men lost their lives on the overland trail. Outfits, made up of experienced men, well provisioned, frequently with a sectional boat and every contrivance that years of experience in that country could suggest, came to grief; their whole expedition sapped and crippled, in efforts to save others.

I was invited to join up with an outfit of this description when first we arrived in Edmonton. Their supplies ran to a full ton, not including the sectional boat they had. These men were real old timers and I should have been one of their party, only for the fact that I was an utter greenhorn, and did not realise, until it was too late, that an invitation though given in seemingly quite a casual manner, was meant in all seriousness. By the time I did wake up, I had made arrangements with my own chum and the others, to forge our own trail.

As it turned out I should not have been a scrap better off anyhow, for, despite their experience, none of them were ever heard of again.

Yes, Edmonton was full of men just broke to the world, who had what they stood up in, and absolutely nothing else. So when Bill and I got back with all our worldly wealth comprised in the half cup of rice and three cents, it was not long before I hit the trail for happier hunting grounds.

We decided, in the circumstances, it was best for us each to play his own hand, so we parted, and within a week I found myself cow punching on the prairies.

There were three or four of us cowboys with some thousands of head of cattle to look after. Here again was a new experience. A happy life; a careless life. The stars for your blanket, the prairies for your bed, and your horse still your best friend. Cook what you have with you, when you can, and how you can. Plenty to eat, plenty to drink, nothing much to do so long as you keep your eyes open, and the cattle well under control. But heaven help you when one of those brief, but terrific thunderstorms comes down and stampedes your bunch.

Some of these are fairly big horned beasts, and, in their maddened stride, will rip up a horse like a piece of tissue paper. There is only one thing to do and that is to get to the leaders of the rush, and head them off. You work away from the wind, as the tendency of cattle is always to turn tail to wind, and so you throw the head round, forming a huge circle, until, finally, with luck, the head of the stampede catches up with the stern. At that moment, it is very necessary to be on the outer rim, for as one end catches up with the other, so they form literally a gigantic whirlpool, and the whole lot run up together in one solid mass. Not infrequently, a good bit of damage is done, but that cannot be helped. You will know all about the damage if you happen to be on the inside. Then there is only one way you will get out and that is by walking across the backs of the steers; but you can say "good-bye" to your horse.

This went on for a few weeks, till, sitting by the camp fire one night, smoking and thinking things out, I realised that what I had set myself out to do, namely, to make just enough money to grub stake myself and to then head off again into the mountains, was impossible, partly because I had determined this next time to try the west side, where there is less water, and more gold.

The ordinary life led by a cowboy doesn't tend to gather in the shekels, or perhaps it would be nearer the truth to say that it isn't conducive to keeping them. Every so often a bunch of steers has to be taken to the railway, or somewhere near thereto, and having disposed of them, the temptation to "blue" one's hard-earned wealth, in one great and glorious spree is usually too great to be withstood. Not necessarily a drinking spree, because, actually, there is little of that done in Canada.

For my part, I never spent five cents on drink until I had made the grub stake which would carry me out of the country.

But a cowboy who has been out on the prairie, seen no one, spoken to no one for weeks on end, must do all the crazy things that come into his mind when he gets into civilisation. He is like a big boy let loose.

The night I was considering all these things by the fire, there came into my mind a promise I had made before I had left England, that if things went against me I *would* come back. There was no question about my being up against it, and a promise is a promise. Furthermore, I could gather together more money, on my own job, at sea, than I ever should cow punching; so, just as quickly as I made up my mind to get out, I decided to go back.

It was with a horrible sinking feeling in the pit of my stomach that I sold, and said good-bye to my old pal Rufus. It hurt like hell, and does even yet. Still, it had to be done, so I got it over as quickly as possible and started off back to England in dead earnest.

I had become a hobo.

This term applies to anyone who is trying to beat the country. He is not a tramp, as is generally known at home. He is best described as "a traveller without means of paying his way," an accepted fact in the country, and it is a war of wits between the hobos and the various means of transport, which, in those days, were mainly in the hands of the C.P.R. Jumping trains, riding the blind baggage, or making out on the rods were three of the recognised methods, and the brakies, your natural enemies; who would think nothing of swinging a five pound lynch pin on the end of a line, if they thought somebody was "riding the rods." If you were, and unluckily got a crack on the head, you simply fell off, and the train passed on. If you were lucky and could get into a van you travelled in luxury. Another good plan was to ride the blind baggage, the platform at the back of the last car, but from which you are more easily expelled. The third and last method is riding on the rods (suspension rods) under the car. That is where I usually parked, for although the least comfortable, I always found it the safest, and the place where one was sure to make the longest journey undiscovered.

I still had with me my inseparable companion the banjo, also a small sack in which I kept bacon and bread, my blankets, and another companion, a piece of cheese. I asked, when I bought this cheese, for the strongest the chap could find. It certainly was powerful. Perhaps that was why I was so successful in making such long stretches without being thrown off!

Anyway, I noticed that everyone gave it an astonishingly wide berth. However, I eventually parted company with both my cheese, and my blankets, my bread and my bacon, through a mistaken sense of hospitality on the part of a man in charge of one of the water tanks.

These tanks are situated just so far apart, where the engine may draw up in the otherwise uninhabited country, and get water. I had dropped off to fill my billy can, and the tanker, when he saw me arrive, gave the usual salutation, "Hullo, Bo. Where are you going." My invariable reply was, "Liverpool."

As a rule a hobo is making his way from one town to another, and the vision of a man heading for Liverpool, England, seemed to strike everyone as particularly humorous. It tickled this chap to the extent that he would have me take, as he expressed it, "a drop of something with a kick." He was a decent fellow and meant well, but whilst we were busy with our salutations the train sloped off with my worldly possessions, and I was left the proud possessor of a banjo. He was so sorry that I believe he would have stopped the train at the next tank, and had it held—had I urged him—until I had time to catch it up. In any case he made an excuse to flag the next train along, and whilst he was telling a little story to the brakie, I made myself as comfortable as I could on the blind baggage, which landed me as close to Winnipeg as I wanted to go.

I spent three weeks in that Prairie City; an exhibition was on at the time, which for me proved fruitful, and enabled me to collect sufficient currency to make the last long leg to Montreal. I had not been many hours in Winnipeg when I heard of a man who had built a house and was trying to get it finished, by way of painting and so forth; but he was a notoriously bad payer and the men that were working for him had quit, as they could not get their money.

His name was Chamberlain, so I made my way over to where he lived and dug him out.

"Did he want a painter?"

"Yes, he wanted a painter. Was I a painter?"

"Yes, I was."

"Well," said he, "go right ahead and get it finished."

I did, though it was a pretty tall order. I found some paint brushes and so forth and sailed in. We neither of us discussed wages. As a matter of fact a painter's pay was three dollars a day, with which I credited myself.

After my experiences with jamb piles and muskegs, work with a paint brush, in either one hand or the other, was child's play, and, in any case, I had served in the hardest school in which one can learn painting, and that is a British sailing ship.

Chamberlain seemed tickled to death with the hours I worked and the ginger I put into the job; in fact, we became great friends, and he cordially invited me to work any number of hours I cared. I took him at his word. In the evening I usually walked into the town, and bought myself provisions to cook overnight, which served me for the next day. Good solid food, but no luxuries. One day old Chamberlain asked me where I lived. I told him "on the prairie."

"Hell, you don't mean to tell me you sleep out there every night, no wonder you get up early in the morning."

I told him I had been sleeping out there for very nearly twelve months. However, he eventually made me take a room in the house. I did, for one night, and felt very nearly suffocated, and I gave up again in favour of the open air.

The time finally came when the job was finished, and up till then no mention of pay had passed between us; although some of the former hands, in the goodness of their hearts, had walked all the way out to where this house was situated on the prairie, to tender the information that I should certainly never get any money. Well,

I might, or again I might not, but my impression was I should get what I had worked for. We left it at that. Later on, Chamberlain informed me he was getting a mortgage through on the house, and until that was through he could not pay me.

He happened to tell me that his solicitors were Andrews and Pitblado, and it also just happened that while working on the Exhibition grounds, I had made contact with Andrews, who was, at that time, Mayor of Winnipeg. It came about that he met me on the grounds where I was working and sent me over to bring a huge wooden form. The band of the Black Watch were playing out there at the time, and one can get an idea of the size of the form, when four forms accommodated the whole band. They were made of just rough hewn timber, I thought it a tall order, but as I was in the very pink of condition I actually managed to hoist it on my shoulder and proudly marched off with it across the grounds. By luck, I met Andrews, who asked me a bit fluently, what I thought I was doing. I told him I was carrying a form, and that, furthermore, he had sent me for it.

"Put the damn thing down. Do you think I sent you alone. Where's the other man?"

Well, I had not seen him, but nothing would suit Andrews but to leave the form there for others to collect whilst he took me away and put me on another job, which was all to do with ropes and tackles, and right into my hand. I may say I had casually told him when walking across the grounds, in reply to his enquiry, that I was a sailor, had been out on the gold rush, and was then a hobo, bound back to Liverpool to pick up my job again, and we became quite good friends.

This was the chap who was getting the mortgage through for Chamberlain, and to whom, by good luck,

I had to apply for my dollars, so, having got Chamberlain's signature to my time sheet, I trotted off down town to interview Andrews. I had enough money coming to me then—if I could collect it—to see me through to Montreal, no longer as a hobo, but as a real, self-respecting passenger—what a change! When I asked for Mr. Andrews the clerk accommodated his tone of voice to my appearance, which, beyond being clean, was hardly millionairish, and the few words we had quickly brought Andrews out of his office to see what was going on.

I must say his office was reached by a steep flight of stairs, which led directly into the street, and down which I was proposing to toboggan the clerk.

"Hello, my lad," said Andrews, "what's all the row about?"

I told him.

He whistled when he saw the account, and told me the mortgage was not through. At the same time he knew exactly where I stood, and, to make a long story short (good fellow that he was) he paid me in full on the spot.

I then journeyed down to the Manor Bar, where kindred spirits used to foregather, and, to their surprise, stood them all a good round of drinks. One of the chaps who had quit Chamberlain's place before I took on, and who had been cocksure I should not get my pay, asked me "where I had got the wad." I told him.

Said he, "How did you manage to collect it?"

"Well, of course," I said—trying a good leg pull—"you don't want to go round to these lawyer's places eating humble pie; you want to go in and threaten to break up the furniture, and take them to pieces. Throw things about a bit, and say, if they don't anti up, that you'll include them in a quick passage to the street.

Just let them know you are some sort of a chap. See then, how quickly they will come across with your money."

He gazed at me the whole time I was talking, and then, just walked out.

Half an hour or so later I had boarded the train at the Depot, and was sitting on the steps of the car yarning with a few of the fellows who had come to see me off, when another pal came on to the platform roaring with laughter, and said to me, "Say, what on earth did you tell Charlie?" When I told him the yarn, he said he had just come past Andrews and Pitblado's office in time to see Charlie thrown down the stairs into the street. We were still laughing over poor Charlie as the train drew out, and I started on the last lap for Liverpool.

Having made a good grub stake in Winnipeg, and being able to stick to one train for a change, it seemed a very short time before I was in Montreal, with its familiar ships and shipping. Here I was back in my own territory, and in touch with my old friend, the sea. My troubles, as far as the trail was concerned, were over. Crossing the ocean—or even going round the world—presented less of a problem than did a few hundred miles by land. Looking back over it all, I felt I had achieved my object to some extent. At any rate, I had been up through the North-West. I'd tried it out, I'd had a great time, and I'd got back—the next bit to Liverpool hardly counted. Admittedly I had gone broke; on the other hand I *had* got back, which was more than thousands and thousands of others had done. There were hundreds in Winnipeg alone—many of whom were there when I arrived on the way out, and were still there when I left on the way back—who, poor devils, had no idea how to make their way back home.

It was not long before I was on board ship, and in my own element again. I was not on board in the capacity of an officer. I took the first job that was going, and that was cattle-man—not very thrilling, with all the beasts tied up by their head stalls, and I could not help but compare them with similar animals out on free range. Here they were in their hundreds; there they had been in their thousands. Neither were the cattle-men quite the type one meets "punching" on the prairie; they were inclined to be a wee bit impulsive at the wrong time. For instance, when I came down a bit late for the first day's dinner, every scrap of food had been cleaned up, on the basis of "first come, first served." Perhaps I was more at home on this job than they had realised. However, believe me, it never happened again, and when a few of the niceties of shipboard life had been duly instilled, they proved quite good fellows—if a bit crude.

CHAPTER TWENTY-FIVE
BACK TO SEA

Two o'clock one bright spring morning found us "tied up" in the Hornby Dock, Liverpool, just a little over twelve months since I had left. As all my money had been exhausted in making my way to Montreal, I stepped off the ship with a pair of buckskin pants, serge shirt, huge sombrero hat, and the world before me again.

A few miles hard walking brought me to my old rooms, where I must hide myself until such time as I could have a suit of clothes made by my friendly old tailor.

What agony it was to encase oneself again in boiled shirt and stiff collar, but it had to be done; respectability once more, and then a ship. There was no time to lose as I hadn't a penny in the world, and I certainly was not going to apply at home for money.

Down to the docks I went for an interview with old Jack Rattery, the Marine Superintendent of the African Royal Mail. He was commonly known as "Three Fingered Jack" having had two of them bitten off by a negro down the West Coast. Bully Waters at one time had been his mate, and they were great pals; also two of a kidney. Furthermore, Rattery had told me, when I left the *Niagara*, that Bully Waters, despite the lurid passages at arms and wordy battles that had taken place between us, had, to my unbounded astonishment, given me a most glowing character. This being so, I knew I was sure of a ship as soon as Capt. Rattery could find me one. He wanted to know where I had been. I merely told him, "Where ships don't go. But I'm looking for a ship now, sir."

I had also seen a brand new ship in dock about to sail on her maiden voyage, and I asked him to appoint me to her. Good fellow, he gave me the job. Right glad I was to be back again on pay, with the hopes of wiping out some of the huge debts that had accumulated with my tailor and elsewhere. Sextant to buy, telescope to buy, glasses to buy, instruments of various kinds, books, in fact the whole complete outfit, including uniform and mufti, for I had sold everything before I had left. Still, what matters; I was back in the good old familiar surroundings, again serving my eccentric mistress. Good solid pieces of gold rolling in every voyage from over the pay desk, instead of digging them out of the earth—much more of it too—so why worry? Everyone would soon get paid and I'd quickly make enough to hit the lone trail again.

Being a new ship and the biggest on the run, we gave a banquet in every port, and we did not have to go looking for the makings of the banquet with a rifle. Any amount of game here, if it was in the frig. When we got down to Lagos, Opobo and Calabar, the guests were nearly all native chiefs, and we had to entertain them. These chaps are big noises in Africa, and come down in their war canoes, pulling twenty paddles aside. The canoes are wonderful pieces of craftsmanship, and take years to build. It was a touchy business getting the different tribal chiefs to the gangway, and on board, without any fighting. They are all pretty warlike and ready to jump at each other's throats on the slightest pretext. At the signal from the officer on the gangway, up they came dashing to the side ladder (and they have a speed of anything up to ten knots) and if another war canoe were slow in getting away, they would think nothing of ramming it, and if that happened, then the fat would be in the fire. It was only by virtue of the tact of the white officer on the gangway that many a full blown scrap was nipped in the bud.

Once on board, they were kept separate as much as possible by the whites, and eventually, marshalled down to the saloon. Some of these chaps had been educated in England, even at Oxford or Cambridge, but, curiously enough, as soon as they get back to their tribe, the veneer of civilisation almost invariably drops right away and they re-adopt both native habits and clothes. It is a bit of a shock to have one of these war canoes come alongside and a fellow in native rig stroll up the gangway, hold out his hand, and greet you in fluent English, with a full Oxford accent—we used this educated section to help the white men separate the more primitive-minded—and they needed separating!

On one occasion in Old Calabar, we were entertaining about fifty native chiefs. They had been a bit jumpy from the start, but, with a little tact, we had managed to keep peace. Everything went on happily, and we got them divided up and sitting round the long saloon table, but by the time they had imbibed a certain amount of "bubbly water" they were just about fit for anything. We had a Piper on board, who, as a rule, used to march up and down the promenade deck above, and pipe during dinner. The Captain had a brain storm in the middle of this dinner, that very nearly sent up the balloon. He passed an order for the Piper, who, without any warning, marched right up one side of the long table and down the other, with his deafening skirl. This set our guests fairly dancing in their chairs, eyes glaring, and hands itching for a spear or a knife, or any other professional instrument. It only needed one man to start in and the whole pack would have been on their hind legs, with anything near the shape of a knife they could grab off the table. For a minute or two it looked bad, and the skipper did look a bit glum. However, nobody moved. The white men studiously kept on talking, and so managed to keep the others in their seats. After a bit, the hotheads also cooled down and the dinner went along happily up to the ice cream stage.

Most of them had never seen ice-cream before, much less tasted it. The first chap to put a spoonful in his mouth just went up like a rocket.

Ice to them is just the same as heat; they think it burns. It was fortunate for us that there were only two or three of them who got the ice-cream down at the same time, but, believe me, they needed some pacifying. Only the fact that everybody else stuck fast to their seats, and seized these fellows by their wrists, whilst others went on eating their ice-cream, gradually brought them to their senses again. They are proud and touchy chaps, and really thought a game had been played on them.

That voyage ended my West Coast experience, and I have never been down there since, despite the saying, that, once a fellow has the coast in his veins, he can never leave it. It certainly has an extraordinary attraction of its own, that must be experienced to be realised. A fortnight out of Liverpool, and it's back to nature with a bump. Natives, pure-blooded negroes, perfect physical specimens, but as full of superstition as they can hold. Anything their childlike minds can't quite grasp, it's, "Oh, Massa, he be Ju-ju too much." Show them the simplest conjuring trick and they'll run a mile. I appeared to take a two shilling piece out of one chap's nose. He never let go of his nose for the rest of that day, in case another should come. Awful thieves, but perfectly trustworthy, whilst you watch them.

An officer, who had been mate of one of the Branch boats for years at Lagos, had a perfectly marvellous record for good steady work amongst his boys and he was hardly ever known to have a case or bale broached on his ship. One day I asked him how on earth he managed it, for certainly he paid far less attention than was customary to his loading from the liner, and discharging ashore. After much urging, in a burst of confidence and gin, he let me into his secret. He had a glass eye, also a spare one. If they were handling any cargo that held special attraction, he just went down below, extracted his eye, and placed it on a convenient bale and said, "Now, you Bushmen, I go for watch you all time."

Entering at Forcados, a 5,000 ton ship, big as she is, can navigate up the creeks for scores of miles. Mangrove swamps on either hand most of the way, no room to turn and little room to pass. In some places it is so narrow that her nose must be driven up into the jungle, whilst the tide is allowed to swing her stern, and so negotiate a sharp bend. Here and there clearings with native villages, and men who never saw a wheelbarrow, yet stand and stare at a modern steamship, a fortnight out from Liverpool. No Pilots; just local knowledge gained by Officers and Captain through years of experience. Here's a whitewashed tree where you take the right fork for Benin. There's a barrel on a stump, where you turn off for somewhere else. High pay, yes, and one earns it. Furthermore, I needed it. The life served me in another way, as, being Second Officer of a Royal Mail and passenger ship for a certain time, qualified me for a commission in the Royal Naval Reserve, also my Master's Ticket, which I had yet to get.

One way and another, I had had a good time, but had lost a lot of necessary sea time through periodically chasing some hare-brained idea. Still, in the end, I made it all up and even caught up with chaps of my own age. For one thing I had never lost a minute over my exams. by failing—and it's not uncommon to fail three or four times for one ticket. I know one chap who went up seven times for his Master's certificate. Then again, by taking the West Coast run, I got better promotion and my time counted more. Anyhow, I went up, when I got home, and, my luck still holding, passed for Master at twenty-three.

I had now the world at my feet, or so I thought anyway, and when I had had a sufficiently good time I marched off to find a ship, but, of course, only when funds were completely exhausted. I still had had a tremendous amount of leeway to make up and debts to pay, owing to my little jaunt out in the North-West, and I still had the North-West in the back of my mind, for as I have said before, I only came home with the intention of making sufficient money to outfit myself and go again. As a matter of fact, I became involved in a much more attractive scheme, which rather eclipsed the cold of Canada, and that was running sandalwood from New Guinea to China.

New Guinea is one of the few remaining unspoiled spots of the world, where there is a fortune waiting for those sufficiently enterprising to take up the export of sandalwood, sandalwood oil and so forth. Furthermore, New Guinea is the only place where the Bird of Paradise can be found, and though he is merely a glorified edition of old Jim Crow, he has a wonderful market. Then again, there is gold up the Fly River, and many other things to attract those unfortunately born with the love of the unorthodox; wanderlust, or whatever you like to call it. However, nothing more need be said about New Guinea, for it came to nothing, in fact, the idea was effectually scotched by my getting married. My wife made one stipulation, and that was that if I went on that expedition, she went too. It is no climate for a white woman, so there the matter ended.

CHAPTER TWENTY-SIX *SHANGHAIED*

HAVING got my Master's Certificate, I decided to try the Atlantic again, and I'm not likely to forget my first ship; she was a real poem. It had become, as usual, a financial necessity to find a ship, and one day, as I was walking along Castle Street, Liverpool, I noticed Greenshield, Cowie & Co's, plate. These were the owners of the old Knight Line, under whom I served in the four masted barque *Knight of St. Michael*. On the impulse of the moment, I slipped in and asked for the managing director, and was shown in the sanctum of sanctums. "Oh, yes," in his deep sonorous voice, he "remembered me quite well," and we talked over some of the old days. Yes, he would appoint me to one of their steamers, in fact "the very best of the Line, the *Knight Bachelor*, lying in London; join her right away." Very hearty and very blunt, he held out his hand to say good-bye. This was all very well but I wanted to know in what capacity. "Third Mate," said he. "Indeed," I replied, "but I am looking for a berth as at least Second Mate, or even Mate."

"Well, of course, Lightoller, you will be no time as Third Mate. In view of the fact that you served so long and so loyally in our sailing ships, we can never forget——" And so on and so forth.

To make a long story short, I allowed myself to be bamboozled into going out of that office with my sailing orders in my pocket. "Well," I thought, "it's a good ship, and the Western Ocean, and I will take good care that I am going to get my step up pretty soon." I still had malarial fever in my veins, and well I knew it on the train journey down and across London. I arrived at Tilbury Dock feeling like the complete West African dishcloth. All I wanted, was to get my head down, and forget I was alive. I had, in my sub-conscious mind, all the comforts that one associates with the Royal Mail. A nice airy cabin, a bunk with clean white sheets, a boy to attend you, and practically every wish anticipated. Doctor, stewards and all the rest of it. Arriving at Tilbury Dock I asked a porter wearily where the *Knight* boat was lying. He replied, "Oh, just near by, sir. Over the bridge," and suggested he should put my baggage on a truck and run it over. "Right," said I, my one anxiety being to get to my cabin, and try to forget this damnable fever. We trudged along, I simply following the porter, conscious of little but a terrific temperature. Suddenly the porter stopped. "Well," I said, "why have you stopped?" "Here is your ship, sir." I looked up. What a horror! About the dirtiest thing I'd ever clapped eyes on. Her rusty iron sides streaked with the horrible overflow from the cattle she had evidently been carrying. Smelling like nothing on earth. "But, this isn't the *Knight Bachelor*, surely?" I exclaimed. "Oh, no, sir, the *Knight Bachelor* sailed last week; this is the *Knight Companion*." Had I had the strength she would certainly have been no companion of mine. However, I was just about at the end of my tether, and thought, "Come, let's get on board, and between some blankets."

The deck was simply a jungle of old cattle pens, ashes, coal, dirt and filth of every description.

A man came up to me and asked me what I wanted. I said I wanted the Mate. In a very nasal voice he informed me he was the Mate. I really thought he was pulling my leg, and I told him abruptly, that I didn't feel like joking with him, "*Where was the Mate?*" This time he asserted, a little more forcibly, that he *was* the Mate. I apologised, and said I was the Third Mate. His reply was, "When are you going to turn to?"

"I am going to turn in," I said. "Can you tell me where I can find the steward who will show me to my cabin?"

"Well," says my bucco, of the collarless flannel shirt, "I guess, in this ship, we find our own cabins."

After climbing over a pile of coal and ashes I found mine. It really wanted scraping out—before it was washed!

I know I was a fool, but really malaria, when you do get it, simply takes the heart out of you, and all I wanted was to get my head in line with my heels, get under a pile of blankets, and forget the world. I managed to dig out some blankets, and when the Mate found out how thoroughly bad I was, he became pretty decent about it and did what he could.

The West Coast sufferer's remedy is simple, if drastic, and consists of a tin of quinine powder and a packet of cigarette papers. Put as much quinine in a cigarette paper as it will hold, seal it up and swallow it. After a few of these, a couple of brass bands will start up in your head; but you get used to that also, and as it does not last more than a couple of days, one is soon about again.

Curiously enough, I had one more violent attack after this, and one only. That happened when bound down the river on that voyage out. I had one final and terrific upheaval off the Nore Lightship, which I thought was going to be the end of all things; it was actually the end of old malaria.

I have often grinned over the way I got shanghaied into that wretched ship, although it was a glorious voyage. Out to the West Indies, and round the Gulf of Mexico, Barbados, Portobello, Vera Cruz, Tampico, Progresso, and all those old historical places with which the West Indies teems. One could easily write a book about each individual place, its inhabitants and their quaint and comical customs, though this applies more to some of the islands and the northern side of the Gulf. The inhabitants of the southern and western parts are mainly the Latin race in about its worst form. An Englishman appreciates a joke, but not when it's pointed with a knife, and no matter whether it's Mexican, Columbian, or Venezuelan, they are an untrustworthy lot, and forever digging buttonholes in their fellow men.

Whereas the West Indian negro is just a child of nature, full of fun and harmless devilment, stinks like a polecat, but sings divinely. They are in fact, born songsters. See them sitting in a row, with ragged hats, say on the New Orleans Levee, dangling their bare, and often dirty feet over the stringer piece, is a sight in itself. Up and down the line goes a word, a joke, and a deep throated laugh. Then, without the slightest premeditation, the whole line bursts into a quaint, chanting song, each part perfectly taken and harmonised. If you don't have creeps running up into your back hair, then you've no ear for music. And the water round the islands, clear as crystal; in fact there are mighty few places where you cannot see your anchor at five fathoms. All-coloured fish swimming about, great big rainbow hued conch shells, and, of course, our old friend, John Shark.

The natives here, like the West African natives, are born to the water, and will dive off the rail, after a threepenny bit has actually touched the water, and pick it up long before it reaches the bottom. One evening we thought we would have a try at bringing up some of these bright coloured conch shells ourselves. We had seen how the natives go down, and how when they got to the bottom they slipped their hands under the shells, detaching them from the rock, and brought them up stuck to their hands. This sport came near to be our undoing.

That evening, whilst we were leaning over the rail, smoking and yarning, someone spotted a huge conch shell a little way out from our quarter. Like a fool, one of the chaps was going to have that shell! So, clothed in a birthday suit, he jumped up on the rail and dived over the side, and down. After a struggle he got his hand between the fish and the rock. The fish then attached itself to his hand, and short of putting the shell in between his feet and pulling with all his might, it was impossible to get the thing off, for your fingers are sucked right into the shell itself. This, however, did not worry him. Up he came, but at an angle that took him still further away from the ship. Once again on the surface, he waved his capture above his head, still stuck to his fist, swimming slowly at the same time, towards the gangway. At this moment, we spotted a sinister black shape, still some distance away and below water. One of the chaps sang out, "Come on, you ass, buck up." He caught an anxious inflexion in the voice, and glanced round on the surface of the water, but there was nothing to be seen from water level, so he thought it was just his imagination, and continued to swim leisurely towards the ship. Two or three of us rushed down the gangway, whilst another fellow hailed him, and this time there was no mistake about the anxiety. He looked again, and there, sure enough, was that black fin, now cutting the water like a knife, and about a hundred yards away from him. He had not twenty feet to go, but, as he said later, the leaden feet one experiences in dreams, trying to run away from some overtaking horror, was mild compared with his feeling of pure unadulterated terror. Of course, try as he might, he could not get that infernal shell off his hand. He went through all the gyrations imaginable, trying to swim with it, trying to tow it, trying to pull it off, trying to do anything that would bring him to that gangway. By this time we were down the gangway and on the platform, waiting to make a grab. There was no boat in the water, and no time to lower one, so no help was available from that source. Did he bring his feet up when we grabbed him under the armpits? Did he not! We beat John Shark by a good ten yards. After that episode however, diving for shells became unpopular—much to the amusement of the natives.

A round of the islands, and we loaded up in New Orleans for home. Deep loaded with grain, and cattle on deck, she wallowed her weary way, far worse than the proverbial canal barge. All went comparatively well until crossing the Grand Banks of Newfoundland. Here, owing to the shallowness of the water, a wall sided sea gets up that is the terror of all small and moderate-sized ships. It is well known to all Western Ocean sailors, and with a small deep loaded ship, it behoves one to treat it with respect, and heave to in plenty of time.

One afternoon it blew up and there was every indication that we were in for a dirty night.

The *Knight Companion* was really an Eastern trader; so was the Captain. The ship was not built to face the Western Ocean, and the Skipper lacked Western Ocean experience. She was running heavily all that afternoon, and when I left the bridge, I half suggested that it was getting time to heave-to. The skipper jokingly, though half seriously said, "Oh, I thought you Western Ocean sailors were never afraid of bad weather." There was nothing more to say so I went below. Even then she was lurching and labouring far too heavily for anyone to remain long in his bunk, so I made myself up a bed on the floor of my cabin and jammed myself in as best I could. The pitch and heave to the following sea rapidly grew worse, one could feel her difficulty in rising and getting away from the seas racing after her, and threatening to overwhelm her. An hour or so later I felt that horrible and unmistakable feeling of a ship pooping. A sea had broken over her stern, and she shuddered horribly as it tore its way along the decks, crushing and smashing everything in its wake.

There was no object in dashing up on deck and chance getting washed overboard; if the ship were going down one might as well stay where one was. A few minutes later I felt her broach-to, and over she went, almost on her beam ends, being pounded all the time by the huge seas breaking on her. After a few long drawn minutes she eventually came to, head on to wind and righted.

Of course, by this time my cabin, along with everybody's, was all afloat. Water everywhere, but evidently some of the fires in the stokehold were still alight, and the ship was able to keep head to wind. I went on deck. What a ghastly wreck! The sea had simply crushed down flat the whole of the cattle pens fore and aft, and cattle in all shapes and forms were lying dying, maimed, bruised and broken, all over the ship. Numbers had, of course, mercifully been washed overboard. Unfortunately, steam had been left on deck, and was running through many of the pipes, which only added to the horror. There was nothing for it but to release what we could, and simply let them wash overboard.

Seas breaking over us all the time, but the main aim and object was to save the ship.

We remained hove-to for the best part of forty-eight hours before the gale eased down and we were able to keep her away again for our home port. So much for the Western Ocean in general and the Grand Banks in particular. When we did get home I wasted no time in getting ashore, and finding something a little more orderly and seaworthy.

After another year or so of knocking around, a good part of the time spent ashore, mostly doing things of not much interest to anyone but myself, I discovered one day that I had arrived at the mature age of twenty-five, and it struck me that it was just about time that I quit this roving and settled down to something really permanent. I fully realised that I might quite easily have been much ahead of where I was; still, I never regretted the time I had lost. I had had good times and I had enjoyed them. Experience is always a good companion, if you look at it that way. Granted there had been a considerable element of luck that had always enabled me to catch up; in fact, in the end, when I joined the White Star Line, I was still ahead of the average age.

CHAPTER TWENTY-SEVEN — *WHITE STAR LINE*

So, in the year of Our Lord 1900, armed with a letter of introduction and full of good resolutions, I made my appearance at 30 James Street, Liverpool, the headquarters of the wonderful White Star Line. It was customary in those days to have to wait anything up to six months before getting an appointment, so, feeling very virtuous at having done the great deed, I slipped away for a few months' holiday. Within a week, to my utter disgust, I had orders to report; and on arriving in Liverpool, found I was appointed to the R.M.S. *Medic*, the first of the five huge White Star Liners that were to open the new Australian service. I suppose I ought to have felt flattered at being picked out from among the many, but it was rather a staggerer, since all my outfit happened to be roaming somewhere round the railways, more or less lost, and certainly unobtainable.

When the Marine Superintendent told me the ship was sailing within a couple of days, I blurted out, "Good Lord, I've no clothes." His reply was short, and to the point. "Get some." I did, and rambled off to Australia with slightly less than half an outfit. But it was the White Star Line, the summit, at that time, of my ambition.

What a change after that precious old cattle truck. Here everything spotless and clean; everything just-so, discipline strict, but in no way irksome. Navigation such as I had never known it.

I soon fell into things and became frightfully keen at my job. Crowds of passengers, and plenty going on. I lasted a whole voyage, and then I sent in my resignation in preference to being fired! Undoubtedly my own fault for again doing those things usually left undone by the discreet and wisely minded.

It came about this way. We were lying in Sydney, in Neutral Bay, and for one reason and another our sailing had been delayed. She was a show ship, the biggest that had ever been out there, and the people in Australia gave us the time of our lives. Everything and everywhere it was *Medic*.

I was always extremely fond of small boat sailing, and it was partly this amusement that got me into the scrape. I, as fourth officer (since she did not carry a fifth), with four midshipmen, had rigged up one of the ship's boats. We fitted her with a false keel, and used to sail her all over the harbour, that most wonderful of harbours in the wide world, and the boat was no slouch either.

One day we had been across to Rosecutter's Bay, and, as an excuse for the jaunt, had taken sandbags, to fill up with sand and bring back for the purpose of holystoning the decks. Now, standing in the middle of the harbour is a rock, on which is built a fort, known as Fort Dennison, or more commonly Pinchgut, owing to the starvation diet on which the convicts were kept whilst confined in the fort. Mounted on this fort is a huge gun, that covers the whole of the harbour.

We were coming off with a light breeze, clad in our white ducks, thoroughly enjoying life, and went to pass windward of the fort. The boat did not seem inclined to lie up to it, and as it was of no consequence whatever, we ran close under the lee. One of the boys, Watson by name, lying on his back along one of the thwarts, and looking up as we passed close under the fort, noticed the projecting muzzle of this huge gun. "What a lark," he blurted out, "to fire that gun some night. Wouldn't it shake 'em up?" I looked up, and as they say in Yankeeland, fell for it. It was a proposition that appealed. So, with each one sworn to secrecy, we set about what proved to be a task that took over six weeks to accomplish, but it was worth it.

First, there was the powder to get, and, to avoid suspicion, it had to be obtained in very small quantities. There was fuse to get also, but before we committed ourselves very deeply, bearing in mind our very limited exchequer, it behoved us to go off some night and reconnoitre, and find out what sort of a gun it was, and if it *could* be fired. For this purpose we commandeered a scow from Cavill's Baths that lie off the Domain.

Sydney Harbour is reeking with sharks, as in fact is the whole of the water round Australia; any baths therefore, must have a shark-proof netting, and it is customary to have floating pontoons, on which are built the dressing rooms, and from which the shark-proof netting is suspended. These iron tanks rapidly become fouled in the warm water, and it was for the purposes of cleaning these tanks that this one man scow was used. It was capable of carrying one man, and one drum of tar, with a fair amount of safety.

Two of the boys were wise, and at this juncture backed out of the escapade, so the remaining two and myself boarded our noble scow one night, and proceeded to paddle out into the middle of Sydney Harbour. Our good Guardian Angel must have been pretty wide awake. Although it was dead calm and the surface like glass, we could not paddle quickly because the water came over the bows. As to what would have happened if the slightest breeze had sprung up, doesn't need a very vivid imagination. However, I cannot say it bothered us; we wanted to get there and we got there, climbing up the lightning conductor and into the turret-like top of the fort.

The interior was a huge circular well, round which this massive gun carriage was supposed to revolve. The gun was an old muzzle loader, and I should think the whole outfit weighed somewhere in the region of twenty tons.

I was walking round the parapet on the inside with cat-like tread, looking to see what I could find, when I suddenly realised there was a face staring at me out of the darkness, within about two feet of mine. Instinctively I drew back my arm, in a way wondering who would get in the first knock, when I realised that my opponent was my own reflection in the glass of the door, which led to the lower regions of the fort.

We found the bore and vent all clear, with ramrod, sponge, and extractor all complete. As the latter two could only be required in the event of a second shot, they did not interest us. If we could ram home and bring off the "One Gun Salute" as it was eventually called, we were going to rest on our laurels. Having completed our examination we returned down the lightning conductor, into the scow, and back to Cavill's Baths. That occupied one whole night, from just before midnight until five o'clock in the morning, and not a soul a penny the wiser.

We slowly collected powder, fuse, and masses of white cotton waste, which we marled down, with the object of ramming home in the form of three large wads, and so completing the charge. There were fourteen pounds of blasting powder alone, apart from a similar amount of fine grain, the former, of course, went in the rear of the charge as it burns slower.

What really topped off the crazy joke, and gave it a real artistic finish, was the idea of hoisting the Boer colours on the flag staff of the Fort.

England was then in the throes of the Boer War, with Australia more loyal, more patriotic, more fervently keen for Empire rights, than was even displayed at home. It is notorious that the Australians are always more British than the English themselves, loyal to the heart's core, and every thought for the homeland. The scene on the quaysides, and in the towns when a contingent was leaving for South Africa, simply staggered belief. The people were patriotic mad, and had there been the ships and the necessity, every man jack in Australia would have volunteered.

It was under these conditions that we conceived the glorious idea of hoisting the Boer Flag and flaunting a real roaring red rag to the Australian bull. It had, of course, to be made, and must not be made out of bunting, otherwise it would at once be traced to some ship in the harbour. Actually it was made out of linen pinched from the surgery, and painted with the Boer colours. All this had to be done behind locked doors, and after many days we were ready at last to put our scheme to the test.

We had located a boat which we could commandeer, and at eleven o'clock one night, with a nice fine drizzle falling, sufficient to keep most people in doors, we loaded up. I had the honour of carrying the fifty feet of fuse round my waist, and the bag of powder slung round my shoulder and under my armpits, covered by my coat. Three huge wads of waste and the coil of signal halyards, for hauling the ammunition up, were distributed equally between us.

With this, the three of us marched up George Street, Sydney, perfectly confident that every policeman we came to was going to arrest us on suspicion and trembling in our shoes in consequence; not so much I'll say, in fear of ourselves, but that our plot might fail.

It did not.

We got our boat; then out to the fort, and up the lightning conductor. Everything worked nicely to plan. Having hauled up the powder, I laid on my back, and with my heels on the inside edge of the Fort, I was just able to reach the muzzle of the gun, jam in the flannel bag containing the powder, and ram it well home. Next followed the two wads of waste, and they also were rammed well home. Then, finally, the third wad, which had first been soaked in water.

Our only disappointment so far had been that we were unable to train the gun until it bore on a Russian man-o'-war then lying in the harbour. If this had been possible, we intended to insert one of the sandstone balls from off the top of Government Garden Gates, which would have burst on impact with her decks, and left little or no trace, but added considerably to the fun. This did not come off, however, as the gun couldn't be trained.

Having rammed the charge home, until the thud of the rammer was loud enough to bring out the sentry, we quit. The plan was for the other two boys to hoist the flag, let go the piece of signal halyard, that we had used to haul up the ammunition, get down to the boat, turn her stern on the rocks, haul the signal halyards into the boat, lay on their oars, and stand by.

I had allowed three minutes for this operation.

In the meantime the fifty feet of fuse had to be coiled round the breach of the gun; the pricker then driven down the vent to pierce the flannel bag of powder, a small box of fine grain powder poured down the touch-hole, the business end of the fuse stuck down the vent, and then to stand by with a match. All this I finally finished, and there was still one minute to wait; it seemed like an hour.

At last the great moment arrived. Striking the match, I lit the frayed out end of the fuse, and, as it spluttered and hissed, blew out the match, and put it into my mouth. The flag was now gaily fluttering in the breeze, as I dashed for the lightning conductor, to find, in the first place, that Watson had forgotten to let go one piece of signal halyard. This I cast off; then I more fell than climbed down the side of the fort, on to the rocks below, only to discover that a plank in the boat had been stove in on the rocks, by the wash from a passing tug, and she was half full of water.

There was no choice; the fuse was burning, so we had to go. In we jumped and pulled like mad. The others were both Conway boys, and they could pull. I had to strip off my shirt and jam it into the hole, and hold a foot on to it to keep the boat afloat at all.

It was impossible, in the circumstances, to return her. We had to land, just at the nearest point, draw her up where she would be safe, and scoot for our lives.

We went through the Domain, over the fourteen feet spiked gates of Government Gardens, and across Government Gardens—where Watson came to grief by putting his toe in one of the hoops round a rose bed, turning a complete somersault, landing on his back in the middle of the bed. We picked him up, and some of the more prominent thorns out, and continued the race. As yet we had not stopped even to put on our shoes.

We went over the gates on the far side of the gardens, and on to Circular quay. There we pulled up to take breath. They, of course, wanted to know, "was everything all right?" "Had the fuse been lit?" "Would the gun go off?" and so on. I said I'd done everything, but the only thing I had a doubt about was that, in my excitement in driving the pricker down the vent hole, I could not say for certain if it had pierced the flannel bag. If this had not been done, I was afraid the main charge would not ignite, and, of course, the gun would not go off. This was going to be a mighty grievous disappointment; still, we consoled ourselves whilst putting on our boots, with the thought that, at any rate, they would find the Boer colours flying.

At this instant, the whole sky lit up with a flash like lightning. Each of us stopped in his tracks, and held his breath. Was it, or was it not the gun? Surely not, with a huge flash like that. More likely lightning.

We waited and waited.

Then it came, and no mistake indeed. There was a crash like thunder, we could feel the concussion even where we stood.

We danced and shouted; threw down our caps and danced on them, and even shook hands, and, in short, behaved like lunatics. *We'd done the trick.*

We soon realised that it behoved us not to act like imbeciles, or we should attract attention; so, very sedately and circumspectly, we made our way back on board. The Quartermaster had been disposed of when coming ashore, by sending him on a wild goose chase to make some coffee, and whilst he was away from the gangway we slipped ashore unseen. Coming back, our luck was still in, and we each got to our cabins without anyone being the wiser.

How we chuckled during the remainder of our stay in Sydney. The noise, the uproar, the jeers and recriminations! Imagine the feelings of the inhabitants when they found the colours of Britain's hated enemy, fluttering in the breeze, and on the flagstaff of the harbour's main fortification. Oh! it was great. The military authorities tried to throw the responsibility on the naval authorities, who retaliated by insisting that the Fort was a military garrison, and not their responsibility at all.

Somehow they managed to keep the papers in the dark for a couple of days, with the result that when the papers *did* get hold of it, they pulled the official leg, until the authorities were jumping mad, and would have cheerfully hung, drawn and quartered the culprits had they caught them, but luckily for our hides, they never did.

CHAPTER TWENTY-EIGHT *ALMOST A PENALTY*

It was not until I got home that the full measure of my iniquity was brought home to me. It had leaked out on board, and though I hate to say it, one of my own shipmates was mean enough to give me away to the Powers at 30 James Street, Liverpool. They, on their part, had no choice but to sit up and take notice, for it was reported under the guise of "endangering the Midshipmen's lives." That, and one or two other things that had been done, which probably would have been best left undone, although they were quite good sport in the doing, finally caused me to realise the immediate necessity of writing my resignation, before I was asked for it; and so nearly ended my brief career in the White Star Line. Nearly, but not quite so.

The Marine Superintendent, dear old Daddy Hewitt —now long since passed beyond—put me on the carpet, and gave me the darndest dressing down I ever had in my life; but before making his final decision, he insisted on my giving him full and complete details. Thinking that as I had the order of the boot anyway, it was of little consequence how I told it, or how he received it, I simply told it in my own words, neither hiding nor elaborating anything. I suppose I enthused a bit towards the end, for I noticed that he kept putting his hand up and rubbing his old grey beard—not that I paid much attention—until, just as I had finished, he went off into a roar of laughter. My dejected spirits immediately shot up, and I thought, "Come, it isn't so bad if he can laugh," and in the end it wasn't. He picked up my resignation which was lying in front of him, tore it in half, and growled out, "Get out of here, and back on board your ship."

I was taken out of the Australian Line as it was not thought advisable for me to go back until things had simmered down a bit. As a matter of fact, in effect, I got slight promotion, through being transferred to the Atlantic, but before finishing with Australia I must just give this example of the wonderful Australian hospitality we experienced whilst in Sydney.

These boys and I had been across the harbour to Rosecutter's Bay, as usual for sand, and had decided to have a ramble along the cliffside, catching lizards, crabs and so forth, when I suddenly realised that I had left my good watch in the boat, and with one of the boys, who volunteered to come with me, went off back. The other two went on; Watson, of course, one of them. Roach and I sat there on the gunwhale of the boat dangling our feet in the water, for half an hour or so, until we suddenly heard hails and yells from Watson and Freke who suddenly appeared bounding down the cliff with two men in pursuit. Roach and I shoved the boat off, turned her round stern on, hoisted the mainsail, and stood waiting, up to our knees in water. When the two men saw this manœuvre, and that evidently these boys were from the boat, they stopped. Watson and Freke tore across the beach and into the water. We all tumbled on board and sheeted home.

They were in convulsions of laughter, and could hardly explain, when I asked them with some annoyance, what on earth they had been up to. If there was any possible mischief to be got into, trust Watson to be in it. His story was that they were returning to the boat along the top of a cliff, when they came to a fence that reached right to the edge. In the fence was a gate. The only alternative to returning the way they had come, was to open the gate and walk into what proved to be a garden. They walked in, and the path led them up to a house. Around the house was the invariable wide, sun screened veranda. On this veranda was a tea table, tea already made and the table all set out with cakes, fruit, and all the etceteras that appeal to the heart of a hungry boy. With inconceivable cheek, Watson planted himself in a chair and invited Freke to a cup of tea. Freke, although he should have known better, sat down, and they both sailed in to a downright good tuck in. In the middle of it, Watson, who was facing the hall of the house, noticed in the shadows, a lady and two gentlemen, calmly standing watching the whole proceeding. "Cave," yelled Watson, and made his exit. The two gentlemen, who proved to be father and son, came running out and called to them to stop. As Watson emphatically said, "We were not doing any stopping."

"Well," I said, "of course, you are for it this time."

Although they had only duck pants and soft shirts on, their badge cap must have given them away. Anyway, they were the only midshipmen in Sydney at that time, and I think everyone on board the *Medic* was far too well-known for them not to have been spotted. I decided there was only one thing to do, and that was to get back as soon as we could next day and make full apologies, for although it might only be a joke, played on the spur of the moment, if it got into cold print it would look beastly. So next day back to the beach we went, and, in a weak moment, I gave way to their entreaties that I should go up and make peace for them.

I went up, and the lady of the house came to the door. I commenced "I've come to apologise for the outrageous behaviour of those two young midshipmen yesterday." I got no further. Here you have the true Australian.

"Oh, don't say a word about it," she said. "I *thought* those two boys were off the *Medic*. We thoroughly enjoyed the joke. We called them to come back. We wanted them to join us—but they wouldn't."

"No," I said, "they told me you had called them, but, as they put it, 'they were not stopping.' You see they are not used to your Australian ways. In England such a thing would not be looked upon in the light of a joke, by any means."

Nothing would satisfy her but that I should bring the boys up to the house, and she would give them tea, right there and then. I could have hugged her.

I went back to the boys, pulling a long face, and said that nothing but their personal attendance and an abject apology would meet the case. "Come on, now," I said, "and take your medicine." They came, a most dejected looking pair. And their blank amazement was really well worth seeing, when Mrs. Penrose, the dear old motherly soul, almost threw her arms round them. She gave them all they could eat, and far more than was good for them. From that hour, her place was open house to every officer and midshipman on board—particularly the midshipmen. Parties and picnics, afloat and ashore, during the remainder of the time we were in Sydney, and very loth they were to leave it.

Poor old Watson!

When in Cape Town, we both tried to join the S.A. Light Horse. We couldn't get a scrap of help, and unless we left the ship, they would not look at us. We tried all we knew how, to get the Powers to use their

ALMOST A PENALTY

influence with the White Star Line, to sign us off, but there was nothing doing, and as I couldn't afford to burn my boats, we went home. Having got home, the glamour of war, to me, had faded to a certain extent, and in any case, I realised I had got to stick at sea, and stick to the company, if I was going to do any good at all. Watson was younger and went back —and he stayed there. Shot in action on the Tugela River.

CHAPTER TWENTY-NINE — *GREYHOUNDS OF THE ATLANTIC*

WITH the exception of one other voyage to Australia, which, as a matter of fact, although promotion at the time, was actually a punishment voyage, for a certain scrape I got into, the whole of my twenty years with the White Star Line, was spent on the Atlantic service; fifteen in the mail boats, and if ever there was a kill or cure, it was a Western Ocean mail boat in winter time.

In those days, although the ships were much smaller, everything was devoted to making a passage, with the result that the ship was driven smashing through everything and anything in the way of weather, pretty well regardless of damage done. Those ships were stronger in proportion than the mammoths of to-day.

I have seen a big modern liner push a plate in, where the old time ship would have just bumped and bounced off, without a scrap of damage. Three times in the old *Majestic* I have seen the look-out cage, situated half way up the fore-lowermast, and built of steel, flattened in against the mast, but little or no damage on deck.

The officers' quarters were situated on the fore deck, and formed a kind of breakwater to the saloon. Immense nets were spread from the fore part of our quarters to the after part of the fo'c'sle to break up the seas as they came thundering on board. The ports, with their inch-thick glass, were protected in bad weather with thick oak shutters, with small two inch bull's-eyes let into them. Notwithstanding these precautions, one afternoon, for instance, we shipped a sea, or, to be more correct, we drove into and under a sea, that dropped on top of us; and the first thing it touched was the nets. These it tore to pieces, and struck the fore part of our place with such force that although built of steel, and of immense strength, the fore part was completely bent in. The glass bull's-eye was driven through the inner port, and a piece of this glass actually took a cup out of the hand of an officer sitting at the table having afternoon tea, leaving the handle in his hand. Any meal in those circumstances, was a series of gymnastics, and although not amusing at the time, very often became the subject of an interesting yarn when swapping lies with kindred spirits, later on.

On one occasion a huge roast of beef was planted on the Second Officer's pillow. He was on the bridge at the time, and although immensely fond of a practical joke at other people's expense, could never bear to have one played on himself; but this one was on him all right. The roast of beef was on one end of the mess room table which ran athwartships, and it was the custom, in this ship only, for the First Officer to carve. The boat gave one of her terrific lurches, which, when accompanied by the propellor coming out of the water, engenders a sensation immeasurably worse than an express lift dropping from the upper floors of a skyscraper.

The First must have thought the Chief was going to check the beef. One did not, neither did the other, with the result that it came careering across the table, and having got a good start, each officer cheered it on its way. At the far end of the table the dish was brought up with a jerk by striking the fiddle, or wooden stretcher that is placed there to keep the cutlery and plates within bounds. The edge of the dish had just sufficient lip to give the roast an upward trend, and, although there were two bunks, one above the other, and over ten feet of space, the roast described a graceful parabola through the air, across the rest of the messroom, through Barber's cabin, and came to rest on his pillow. The mess room steward at once set out to retrieve it, but we unanimously agreed that it was in far too good a place to be disturbed.

Barber had a habit of coming off the bridge and asking the steward what the others had had for their meal, as, of course, in these ships, there is a pretty long menu. We had coached the steward, before we had retired to our cabins and when Barber had made his usual enquiry, "Well, Davies, what have you got," followed by, "What have the others had? Oh, all right, I'll have the roast beef too," Davies replied, "The roast beef is in your bunk, sir." At first, Barber didn't know what to make of it, then, when he did realise this, as the song goes, "The air went blue for miles all round," and, to this day, he firmly believes that it was put there. When you take into consideration that the edge of the bunk was five feet from the deck, and ten feet from the edge of the table, it certainly did seem pretty near an impossibility, but at the same time, it will give a fairly clear idea of the contortions of a Western Ocean mail boat in an Atlantic gale.

These ships are not only the cream of the service, but the cream of the Mercantile Marine, and it is considered a feather in one's cap to be appointed to one. Therefore, despite the rigorous conditions, and the powers of endurance one has to exhibit, there is never a word of complaint. Time and again I have seen the ship driven into a huge green wall of water, crowned with that wicked, curling breaker, which it seemed utterly impossible for anything to withstand. An immediate dash is made for an iron stanchion, and, gripping this with might and main, one awaits the crash.

Not infrequently the steel fronted bridge, stanchions and rail, are driven back, and nearly flattened to the deck,— to the discomfort of the O.O.W.

It certainly was not a paying game, though the Mail Boat companies were slow to discover it. As ships grew bigger and faster, and did more damage in consequence, Captains were warned to be more circumspect, and, when the occasion demanded, to slow down.

The bigger the ship, the longer she could be driven before she would take any weighty water on board, but when she did, then it was proportionately heavier. But the increased strength of the liner by no means kept pace with the increased volume of water she could, and would, ship.

Then again, there is the increased speed of these vessels, and, of course, the seas have attained an increased speed by the time one does get its head up and come aboard, the cumulative effect is sometimes astonishing, and not infrequently, disastrous. In a word, we cannot drive the ships to-day like we used to, even if we would; just because their strength has not, and in point of fact, could not, increase with their size. The temptation to drive is there, but if she is not eased down something will happen, as happened to one of our biggest and best ships, the *Olympic*.

She had a steel hatch on the forecastle, weighing about three tons. This was built with a turtle back, and comparatively close down to the deck, so as to give a sea, when it did come, the least chance to get a grip. It was secured all round inside and underneath by one and an eighth inch bolts, fifteen inches apart, each bolt individually screwed hard down before leaving port. Would you think it possible to lift it? Yet she had such a hatch ripped off like a piece of paper and flung down the fore well deck.

Wicked though a Western Ocean gale can be, fog still remains a sailor's worst enemy, and this applies more so when he is in the region of ice than anywhere. For this reason the steamship lanes, as they are called, on the North Atlantic route, are altered to clear the Grand Banks altogether when ice is around.

Apart from the ice and fog, an added anxiety when crossing these banks is the cod fishermen, who put out from Newfoundland, and many other ports in the United States. One whole fleet comes over from France, mainly Fécamp.

A blanket of fog will suddenly shut down, with not only these vessels scattered about, but also their dories, small light skiffs, of which a large schooner will carry perhaps fifteen to twenty. The dories have no means whatever of indicating their presence to an oncoming ship; in fact, the schooners are not really very much better off, particularly when one takes into consideration the unreliability of sound in fog.

The Atlantic Mail Boats have been unfairly blamed for the loss of a great number of these schooners, whereas, knowing, as we do, the difficulties under which the fishing is carried out, every possible precaution and care is taken to avoid a collision. Two look-out men are always on their stations. In fog, these are always doubled, as also is the look-out on the bridge. The ship is slowed down, and an automatic steam whistle blows every minute. It has never been my misfortune to run one of these poor devils down, although, heaven knows, I have been close enough to them. A slight loom ahead, helm hard over, and gliding by, within biscuit throw, goes a big topsail schooner. A quiet exchange of glances on the bridge, a sort of general sigh at the escape, and everyone again freezes into immobility, and intense concentration—watching and listening.

The risks the individual fishermen take are not only confined to laying across the steamship lanes. They'll face almost any weather, and almost always freezing at that. I have seen dories out and fishing in weather one would have thought it impossible for a small open boat to live in. Up round the Virgin Rocks, where the water breaks in a heavy sea, it is a common custom in an increasing gale for these small boats to hang on and hang on, each man daring the other. This is one of the best fishing grounds, and the boats lie-to at anchor. The sea steadily rises, banks up, and eventually breaks. Many is the dory that has been lost here through sheer daredevil hanging on. See a couple of them riding at the sea when it has become an absolute wall. With a careful manipulation of the warp, they run their boat up the precipitous side of the sea, give a sharp snub on the rope, and she is over the top just as the crest is about to break. One by one the boats will slip and run, as the seas get too big for them and threaten to break. But there are always one or two foolhardy ones that will strive for the honour of being the last to leave, and not infrequently they are the last—the long, long last. A slight misjudgment of the curl of the crest, maybe the anchor drags just as he goes to snub her over the top, or perhaps the rope itself breaks. Then the flimsy dory is picked up on that wall of water, flung in the air, and finally crushed to matchwood—another victim of the Virgins.

I got my severest mail boat training during the seven hard, though happy years I spent in the Queen of the Seas, as the *Oceanic* was then called. A wonderful ship, built in a class of her own, and by herself.

The usual custom is to build twin ships, as with the *Britannic* and *Germanic*, *Teutonic* and *Majestic*. Then, in lone and stately majesty came the *Oceanic*. She was an experiment, and a wonderfully successful one; built by Harland and Wolff, regardless of cost, elaborate to a degree, money lavished where it was necessary, but never gaudily as is so common nowadays. Her smoke room doors were a masterpiece in themselves, and cost £500. There was eighteen carat gold plating on the electric light fittings throughout the saloon and staircase, and paintings by well-known artists, worth a cool thousand apiece. Hand carvings of delicate work, and the joy of souvenir hunters. Every deck plank was picked wood. Last, but by no means least, her Captain, John G. Cameron. A martinet to his fingertips, who set a standard, that I for one, found it difficult to live up to. He was deep voiced and bluff, but a splendid seaman, and proud of his ship. With his blue eyes and ginger beard he was a broad shouldered edition of Captain Kettle. Head erect and shoulders back, he would walk out on the bridge, and fire off a volley of questions, and woe betide the unfortunate officer that hadn't an answer ready. Not to be able to answer each, and every one, as quickly as they were shot at you, in his deep staccato tones, was to invite the brief but pungent query, "Then what the hell are you here for?" To give any back chat or even look what you felt would not only put a term to your services in that ship, but probably ruin your prospects in the Line. Yet to be appointed to her was the most signal compliment. Of course, we all knew the questions he was most likely to ask, and had answers ready. They usually ran: "What are the revolutions?" "What's on the log at eight bells?" "How's the barometer?" "Where's the wind?" "What time does the moon rise?" This latter was not an easy one to answer correctly, and meant a lot of figuring out. As a rule a broad guess was near enough, for John G. didn't always bear your replies in mind. One officer, six feet three inches, and misnamed "Little," well liked throughout the Line, and not least by John G., was saluted one evening with the usual rattle of questions, the last one being, "What time does the moon rise?" to which Little replied, "Eleven-fifteen, sir." It then being seven-thirty o'clock and Cameron in full mess kit on his way down to dinner. With that Cameron turned smartly round and left the bridge, but as he was going down the ladder to the promenade deck, behold a cloud rolled away, leaving a full moon high up in the sky. Cameron saw it and, for a wonder, remembered what Little had said, so when he returned to the bridge after dinner, with his cigar a-cock-bill, his first question was in a particular "Now I've got you, my lad" tone:

"You told me the moon rose at eleven-fifteen, sir?"

Little, not to be caught out, replied:

"I'm awfully sorry, sir, I got hold of last year's calendar."

"You did, did you? Bring it here and let me see it," said Cameron, with a suspicious squint out of the corner of his eye. Little immediately replied, in a tone of deep respect:

"I threw it overboard, sir, so that no one else should make the same mistake."

Cameron looked straight at him and then turned on his heel with an irrepressible chuckle, and the slow, but pungent remark, "You damned liar."

He never minced matters in his remarks to his officers, although heaven help the man who took them literally.

The *Oceanic's* bridge was covered with expensive white rubber, laid in narrow strips, representing planks. This had to be scrubbed every morning with bath brick, until it was snow white. Incidentally if it was not scrubbed and got salt water on it, it became so abominably slippery that we had to lay down coir matting to walk on. She had a bow fronted wheel house, and covered in bridge amidships. After a shower I used to amuse myself, when she had got a slight roll on, by trying to slide from one side of the bridge to the other, without touching anything. It was rather difficult to negotiate the forward bulge of the wheel house, steering between this and the wheel on the bridge. With much practice I became so proficient that four out of five times I would make the passage without touching. One morning, after several ineffectual attempts, I at last came across in one beautiful sweep, shooting both wheel house and wheel, when, to my horror, on the opposite side, out stepped John G. Cameron.

"And what the hell do you think *you're* doing, sir?"

I replied, "I'm awfully sorry, sir. I slipped."

"Slipped, did you? I wish you had broken your damned neck, sir, as you nearly broke mine."

And with that the incident was closed.

No passengers were allowed on the boat deck, so all these little episodes were kept a jealous secret. No doubt we were looked upon as models of rectitude and correct behaviour—or at least what they could see of us above the dodger. On the bridge, with rare exceptions, no doubt we were, but it was a different tale when we got below—that is, to our own quarters.

Then the fun started, particularly at four o'clock in the afternoon, when my watch ended and afternoon tea was served. It was usual for almost everyone off watch to have a caulk after lunch—sort of fortification for the night watches—when there's NO fooling. Unless a chap was off colour, and pinned a notice on his cabin begging that he might not be disturbed, he had to come out of his own free will or be brought out, usually by inserting a lighted blue light (which gives off a terrific amount of pungent smoke) in a copper fire nozzle, and applying the business end of the nozzle to the ventilator at the bottom of his door. On one such occasion the deck steward had to make a hurried visit, so that he could assure some passengers that the ship was not really on fire.

From Second Officer of the *Oceanic* to First of the *Majestic*, then temporary Chief of the *Majestic* and back again to First of the *Oceanic*, such were the moves covering the next couple of years.

CHAPTER THIRTY — *LOSS OF THE "TITANIC"*

FROM the *Oceanic* as First, I was appointed to the *Titanic*, of tragic memory, as First, and three very contented chaps took the midnight boat for Belfast, where she was completing. Murdoch, Chief, your humble, First, and Davy Blair, Second; Captain E. J. Smith, Commodore of the Line came over a little later on. Captain Smith, or "E.J." as he was familiarly and affectionately known, was quite a character in the shipping world. Tall, full whiskered, and broad. At first sight you would think to yourself "Here's a typical Western Ocean Captain." "Bluff, hearty, and I'll bet he's got a voice like a foghorn." As a matter of fact, he had a pleasant, quiet voice and invariable smile. A voice he rarely raised above a conversational tone—not to say he couldn't; in fact, I have often heard him bark an order that made a man come to himself with a bump. He was a great favourite, and a man any officer would give his ears to sail under. I had been with him many years, off and on, in the mail boats, *Majestic*, mainly, and it was an education to see him con his own ship up through the intricate channels entering New York at full speed. One particularly bad corner, known as the South-West Spit, used to make us fairly flush with pride as he swung her round, judging his distances to a nicety; she heeling over to the helm with only a matter of feet to spare between each end of the ship and the banks.

For some time previous to being appointed to the *Titanic* "E.J." had been in command of the *Olympic*

—since she was launched in fact. Murdoch also came from the *Olympic*, whilst Blair and I were from the *Oceanic*.

It is difficult to convey any idea of the size of a ship like the *Titanic*, when you could actually walk miles along decks and passages, covering different ground all the time. I was thoroughly familiar with pretty well every type of ship afloat, from a battleship and a barge, but it took me fourteen days before I could with confidence find my way from one part of that ship to another by the shortest route. As an instance of size, there was a huge gangway door through which you could drive a horse and cart on the starboard side aft. Three other officers, joining later, tried for a whole day to find it. No doubt with the help of a plan it would have been fairly simple, but a sailor does not walk round with a plan in his pocket, he must carry his ship in his head, and in an emergency such as fire must be able to get where he wants by sheer instinct—certainly without a chance of getting lost on the way.

Touching on fire, the modern ship's equipment is such that it is almost impossible, with fair play, for a fire to get a serious hold. I say this, despite the fact that quite recently no less than three modern liners have been burned out. Generally speaking, the fire-fighting equipment is based on something like these lines.

Close adjacent to the bridge is the Master Fire Station, where a Fireman in full regalia is on duty night and day, and must never be more than six feet away from the door of his station. In his little cubby hole, he is surrounded with instruments which keep him in close touch with secondary Fire Stations situated in commanding positions throughout the ship. In front of him, in the Master Station, on the bulk-head, is a glass fronted air tight case, into which are leading numbers of little tubes, coming direct from the Secondary Fire Stations. By suction a current of air is drawn through these tubes and into the case. As the air comes through the tube it impinges on a filament resembling tinfoil, causing this to vibrate, and therefore proves that a current of air is actually passing through. If the other end of the tube should be blocked, or stuffed up by some unconscious humorist, this filament at once becomes stationary.

Now, if anyone were to stand close to the other end of the tube, say smoking a cigarette, the smoke would be drawn into the tube, passed up to the Fire Station, and strike this filament. The smoke would then become exaggerated until it resembled a ball of wool, and would immediately catch the notice of the man on duty. If he wishes, he can ascertain for his own satisfaction whether it is just tobacco smoke, or something more dangerous. Probably if he finds it is merely tobacco smoke he will conclude that someone is standing nearby the tube smoking, and may wait a reasonable time for it to disappear. If he is not satisfied he will telephone down, calling that Station; and, the man on duty replying, he will ask, more or less politely, if anyone is smoking near that Detector? Probably the man on the Secondary Station will find that it is just tobacco smoke and report it. If, on the other hand, it were, for instance, the result of some careless fool throwing a cigarette down on the carpet, and setting it alight, very few moments would elapse before it was known on the bridge, and communication made to the necessary points.

Hoses are always ready, rigged in readiness and attached to hydrants, so that even in the case of a really serious fire suddenly breaking out, it would be known at headquarters within a very few seconds, "fire stations" signalled, and a Fire Party with hoses, buckets and blankets would be on the spot within three minutes.

In these circumstances it is extremely difficult to arrive at any satisfactory conclusion as to how, with fair play, a fire could break out on a modern ship like say the *Atlantique* without being instantly detected. Admitted there were no passengers on board, yet the ordinary fire precautions would still be in operation. With the *Europa* it was different; she was still in the builders' hands, but judging by what one knows of builders, the fire precautions are just as stringent whilst the ship is being built as they are when she goes to sea; in British shipyards, anyhow, and I don't suppose the Germans are a whit behind us.

But to return to the *Titanic*. Putting a new ship in commission is, at the best of times, a pretty strenuous job. With the *Titanic* it was night and day work, organizing here, receiving stores there, arranging duties, trying and testing out the different contrivances; makers of the hundred and one instruments with their chits to be signed certifying that this, that and the other was in perfect working order. All the navigation instruments fell to my lot, as also did firearms and ammunition.

These latter are looked on mostly as ornaments in the modern ship.

Revolvers, rifles and bayonets, in the Merchant Service, are rather superfluous. A man governs by accepted discipline, tact, his own personality and good common sense. We have no King's Regulations to back us up; neither do we need them; nor yet do we require firearms, except on the rarest occasions. Curiously enough, the *Titanic* was to prove the only occasion at sea that I have ever seen firearms handed out, and even then it was not Britishers they were used to influence.

After running our trials we finally took over from the builders and proceeded round to Southampton. It was clear to everybody on board that we had a ship that was going to create the greatest stir British shipping circles had ever known. For one thing, she was the first ship to be fitted with a third screw, driven by a low-powered turbine. For manœuvring, the two wing screws alone were used, but once clear of the land, steam from low pressure cylinders was turned into this turbine, and undoubtedly it gave her a wonderful turn of speed.

Unfortunately, whilst in Southampton, we had a re-shuffle amongst the Senior Officers. Owing to the *Olympic* being laid up, the ruling lights of the White Star Line thought it would be a good plan to send the Chief Officer of the *Olympic*, just for the one voyage, as Chief Officer of the *Titanic*, to help, with his experience of her sister ship. This doubtful policy, threw both Murdoch and me out of our stride; and, apart from the disappointment of having to step back in our rank, caused quite a little confusion. Murdoch, from Chief, took over my duties as First, I stepped back on Blair's toes, as Second, and picked up the many threads of his job, whilst he—luckily for him as it turned out—was left behind. The other officers remained the same. However, a couple of days in Southampton saw each of us settled in our new positions and familiar with our duties. Board of Trade surveys were carried out to everyone's satisfaction. Life boats and all Life-saving equipment tested, exercised and passed. "Fireworks" (distress rockets, distress signals, blue lights, etc.) examined, tried and approved. All these, and a hundred and one other details pertaining to a crack

Atlantic Liner preparing for sea were gone through. Being a new ship, and the biggest in the world, even more scrupulous care was exercised than is usual, or applies to a ship on her settled run. The Board of Trade Surveyor, Captain Clark, certainly lived up to his reputation of being the best cursed B.O.T. representative in the South of England at that time. Many small details, that another surveyor would have taken in his stride accepting the statement of the officer concerned, was not good enough for Clark. He must see everything, and himself check every item that concerned the survey. He would not accept anyone's word as sufficient—and got heartily cursed in consequence. He did his job, and I'll certainly say he did it thoroughly.

At last sailing day arrived, and from end to end the ship, which for days had been like a nest of bees, now resembled a hive about to swarm.

As "zero" hour drew near, so order could be seen arriving out of chaos. On the stroke of the hour, the gangway was lowered, the whistle blew, ropes were let go, and the tugs took the strain.

She was away.

CHAPTER
THIRTY-ONE *LEAVING SOUTHAMPTON*

BEFORE she cleared the dock we had a striking example of the power that lay in those engines and propellers.

The *Oceanic* and *St. Paul* were lying moored to the wharf alongside each other. They happened to be in a position where the *Titanic* had to make a slight turn, which necessitated coming astern on her port engine. The terrific suction set up in that shallow water, simply dragged both these great liners away from the wharf. The *St. Paul* broke adrift altogether, and the *Oceanic* was dragged off until a sixty foot gangway dropped from the wharf into the water. It looked as if nothing could save the *St. Paul* crashing into the *Titanic's* stern, in fact, it was only Captain Smith's experience and resource that saved her. The *Titanic*, of course, dwarfed these two ships, and made them look like cross-channel boats, and the wash from her screws had a corresponding influence. Just as a collision seemed inevitable, Captain Smith gave the *Titanic* a touch ahead on her port engine, which simply washed the *St. Paul* away, and kept her clear until a couple of tugs, to our unbounded relief, got hold, and took her back alongside the wharf.

To the casual observer the whole incident would have been just a thrill—perhaps not much more even though there had been a collision. For us it would have been something much deeper. It is difficult to describe just exactly where that unity of feeling lies, between a ship and her crew, but it is surely there,

LEAVING SOUTHAMPTON

in every ship that sails salt water. It is not always a feeling of affection either. A man can hate a ship worse than he can a human being, although he sails on her. Likewise a ship can hate her men, then she frequently becomes known as a "killer," and in the days of sail would regularly kill a man voyage after voyage.

The greatest care had to be taken whilst threading our way down the then comparatively shallow channel of Southampton Water and eventually out to Spithead. There was a general feeling of relief when at last we got her into her proper element, deep water.

We then went across to Cherbourg—a short run which barely warmed her up. Then a longer leg to Queenstown, and finally, the following day, we opened her up on the long run to New York.

Each day, as the voyage went on, everybody's admiration of the ship increased; for the way she behaved, for the total absence of vibration, for her steadiness even with the ever-increasing speed, as she warmed up to her work.

As day followed day, officers and men settled down into the collar, and duty linked up with duty until the watches went by without pause or hitch. We were not out to make a record passage; in fact the White Star Line invariably run their ships at reduced speed for the first few voyages. It tells in the long run, for the engines of a ship are very little different from the engines of a good car, they must be run in. Take the case of the *Oceanic*. She steadily increased her speed from $19\frac{1}{2}$ knots in her early days to $21\frac{1}{2}$ when she was twelve years old. It has often been said that had not the *Titanic* been trying to make a passage, the catastrophe would never have occurred.

Nothing of the kind.

She was certainly making good speed that night of

April 12th, but not her best—nothing compared with what she would have been capable, in say a couple of years' time. The disaster was just due to a combination of circumstances that never occurred before and can never occur again. That may sound like a sweeping statement, yet it is a fact.

All during that fatal day the sea had been like glass—an unusual occurrence for that time of the year—not that that caused any great worry. Again, there had been an extremely mild winter in the Arctic, owing to which, ice from the ice cap and glaciers had broken away in phenomenal quantities, and official reports say that never before or since has there been known to be such quantities of icebergs, growlers, field ice and float ice, stretching down with the Labrador current. In my fifteen years' experience on the Atlantic I had certainly never seen anything like it—not even in the South Atlantic, when in the old days of sailing ships, we used to sometimes go down to 65° south.

These were just some contributory causes, that combined, and brought into existence, conditions of which the officers of the ship were to a great extent ignorant.

Wireless reports were coming in through the day from various ships, of ice being sighted in different positions. Nor was that anything unusual at this time of the year, and none of the reports indicated the extent of the ice seen. A report would read "Iceberg (or icebergs) sighted in such and such a latitude and longitude." Later on in the day we did get reports of ice sighted in larger quantities, and also two reports of field ice, but they were in positions that did not affect us. The one vital report that came through but which never reached the bridge, was received at 9-40 p.m. from the *Mesaba* stating "Ice report in Latitude 42N to 41–25N. Long. 49 to Long. 50–30W. Saw much heavy pack ice, and great number large icebergs. Also field ice. Weather good, clear." The position this ship gave was right ahead of us and not many miles distant. The wireless operator was not to know how close we were to this position, and therefore the extreme urgency of the message. That he received the message is known, and it was read by the other operator in his bunk. The operator who received it was busy at the time, working wireless messages to and from Cape Race, also with his accounts, and he put the message under a paper weight at his elbow, just until he squared up what he was doing, and he would then have brought it to the bridge. *That delay proved fatal and was the main contributory cause to the loss of that magnificent ship and hundreds of lives.*

For the last hour of my watch on that never-to-be-forgotten night, I had taken up a stationary position on the bridge, where I had an unobstructed view right ahead, and perhaps a couple of points on either bow. That did not signify that I was *expecting* to see ice, but that there was the *possibility* of seeing ice, as there always is when crossing The Banks; ice *may* be sighted. In point of fact, under normal conditions, we should have proved to be well south of the usual ice limit; only in this case the ice limit had moved very many miles south, due solely to the immense amount of ice released in the Arctic.

In ordinary circumstances the cold current carrying the icebergs south, strikes the warm current flowing to the north-east and under-runs it—that is to say the cold current goes under the warm current, on the same principle that warm water always rises. The effect of this is to melt the iceberg around the water line. It soon "calves" or breaks up into smaller pieces, which again break up, continuing to float in the warm surface current for a short time, until completely melted. And so the work of disintegration goes on in an ever-increasing ratio, thereby forming the "ice limit."

It is often said you can tell when you are approaching ice, by the drop in the temperature. The answer to that is, open a refrigerator door when the outside temperature is down, and see how close you have to get before you detect a difference. No, you would have to be uncomfortably close to "smell" ice that way.

Ten p.m. came and with it the change of the officers' Watches. On the bridge, after checking over such things as position, speed and so forth, the officers coming on deck usually have a few minutes' chat with their opposite number, before officially taking over. The Senior Officer, coming on Watch, hunts up his man in the pitch darkness, and just yarns for a few minutes, whilst getting his eyesight after being in the light; when he can see all right he lets the other chap know, and officially "takes over." Murdoch and I were old shipmates, and for a few minutes—as was our custom— we stood there looking ahead, and yarning over times and incidents past and present. We both remarked on the ship's steadiness, absence of vibration, and how comfortably she was slipping along. Then we passed on to more serious subjects, such as the chances of sighting ice, reports of ice that had been sighted, and the positions. We also commented on the lack of definition between the horizon and the sky—which would make an iceberg all the more difficult to see— particularly if it had a black side, and that should be, by bad luck, turned our way.

The side of an iceberg that has calved or broken away from its parent glacier will usually be black, where the fresh ice is showing, and is consequently more difficult to see at night. After considerable exposure, this side turns white like the rest.

We were then making an easy 22 knots. It was pitch dark and dead cold. Not a cloud in the sky, and the sea like glass. The very smoothness of the sea was, again, another unfortunate circumstance that went to complete the chain.

If there had been either wind or swell, the outline of the berg would have been rendered visible, through the water breaking at the base.

Captain E.J. was one of the ablest Skippers on the Atlantic, and accusations of recklessness, carelessness, not taking due precautions, or driving his ship at too high a speed, were absolutely, and utterly unfounded; but the armchair complaint is a very common disease, and generally accepted as one of the necessary evils from which the sea-farer is condemned to suffer. A dark night, a blinding squall, and a man who has been on the mental rack for perhaps the last forty-eight hours, is called on to make an instantaneous decision embodying the safety of his crew and his ship. If he chooses the right course, as nine times out of ten he does, all well and good, but if on the tenth time his judgment is, momentarily, in error, then he may be certain he is coming under the thumb of the armchair judge, who, a thousand to one, has never been called on to make a life and death decision in a sudden emergency.

Captain Smith, with every other senior officer (apart from myself), went down, and was lost with the ship, and so escaped that never to be forgotten ordeal carried out in Washington; repeated again in England and finally concluded in the Law Courts.

Murdoch, the First Officer, took over from me in the ordinary way. I passed on the "items of interest," as we called them, course, speed, weather conditions, ice reports, wished him joy of his Watch, and went below. But first of all I had to do the rounds, and in a ship of that size it meant a mile or more of deck, not including a few hundred feet of ladders, staircases, etc.

Being a new ship it was all the more necessary to see that everyone was on the top line. I had been right fore and aft several decks, along a passage known as Park Lane, leading through the bowels of the ship on one side, and bringing me out by a short cut to the after deck. Here I had to look round to see that the Quartermaster and others were on their stations, and then back to my warm cabin.

The temperature on deck felt somewhere around the zero of Canada, although, actually, it wasn't much below freezing, and I quickly rolled into my blankets. There I lay, turning over my past sins and future punishments, waiting until I could thaw, and get to sleep.

CHAPTER THIRTY-TWO

COLLISION WITH AN ICEBERG

I was just about ready for the land of nod, when I felt a sudden vibrating jar run through the ship. Up to this moment she had been steaming with such a pronounced lack of vibration that this sudden break in the steady running was all the more noticeable. Not that it was by any means a violent concussion, but just a distinct and unpleasant break in the monotony of her motion.

I instantly leapt out of my bunk and ran out on deck, in my pyjamas; peered over the port side, but could see nothing there; ran across to the starboard side, but neither was there anything there, and as the cold was cutting like a knife, I hopped back into my bunk.

In any case, to go dashing up to the Bridge in night rig, or even properly clothed, when not on duty, was bound to ensure anything but a hearty welcome. Another thing, to be elsewhere than where you are expected to be found, in a ship like that, would result in the man who is sent to call you, being utterly unable to find you. So I just waited.

The time we struck was 2-20 a.m. April 12th, of tragic memory, and it was about ten minutes later that the Fourth Officer, Boxall, opened my door and, seeing me awake, quietly said, "We've hit an iceberg."

I replied, "I know you've hit something." He then said: "The water is up to F Deck in the Mail Room."

That was quite sufficient. Not another word passed. He went out, closing the door, whilst I slipped into some clothes as quickly as possible, and went out on deck.

The decks in a modern liner are lettered from the boat deck downwards A,B,C,D,E, and so on. The fact of the water having reached "F" deck showed me that she had been badly holed, but, at the time, although I knew it was serious, I had not a thought that it was likely to prove fatal; that knowledge was to come much later.

Up to this time we had had no chance for boat drill, beyond just lowering some of the boats in Southampton. In any case, officers and men in the Mercantile Marine are always impressed with the vital importance of using their own heads, thinking for themselves and acting on their own initiative in an emergency.

Discipline in a Merchant Ship calls for the highest display of individual intelligence and application. Each man must think for himself. Whereas, in the Navy, the Bluejacket must do as he is told, nothing more, and nothing less. All perfect in its own way where a man is required to act with machine-like precision, but that won't work in the Merchant Service. If a man does no more than he is told, and makes that an excuse for leaving something undone, unseen or unattended to, he is quickly asked, "What the hell are your brains for?"

The result is that a crew come aboard a strange ship, and everything seems like the pieces of a jigsaw puzzle. But, there is just this difference between the two Services. Whereas each man in the Senior Service must be fell in, and detailed to his own particular job, to which he has probably been trained for years, but by which method each piece of the jigsaw must await the touch of the Master hand; in the Merchant Service the whole of the pieces shake themselves together without being "fell in" and "told off." Thus, in an amazingly short

COLLISION WITH AN ICEBERG

space of time they have all shaken down and become a homogeneous workable unit. If there should be a piece that won't seem to fit, then all I can say is heaven help him!

You may be sure that the crew of the *Titanic* had been put through a fine sieve, and particular care taken that there were no misfits. The result was that when the call came—not the call of bugles, but the call on every man to exhibit the highest individual effort, intelligence and courage, the response was absolutely universal—not a man failed.

The survivors of that night may thank God that our men did not wait for bugles and pipes. Nevertheless, they put up as fine a show as has ever been done in any sea tragedy in history. The final and conclusive proof lay in the fact that every single boat in the ship was cleared, swung out and safely lowered into the water and got away, without a hitch of any kind.

The ship had been running under a big head of steam, therefore the instant the engines were stopped the steam started roaring off at all eight exhausts, kicking up a row that would have dwarfed the row of a thousand railway engines thundering through a culvert.

All the seamen came tumbling up on the boat deck in response to the order "All hands on deck" just following the instinct that told them that it was here they would be required. It was an utter impossibility to convey an order by word of mouth; speech was useless, but a tap on the shoulder and an indication with the hand, dark though it was, was quite sufficient to set the men about the different jobs, clearing away the boat covers, hauling tight the falls and coiling them down on deck, clear and ready for lowering.

The passengers by this time were beginning to flock up on the boat deck, with anxious faces, the appalling din only adding to their anxiety in a situation already terrifying enough in all conscience. In fact it was a marvel how they ever managed to keep their heads at all. All one could do was to give them a cheery smile of encouragement, and hope that the infernal roar would soon stop. My boats were all along the port side, and by the time I had got my Watch well employed, stripping the covers and coiling down, it became obvious to me that the ship was settling. So far she had remained perfectly upright, which was apt to give a false sense of security. Soon the Bosun's Mate came to me and indicated with a wave of his hand that the job I had set him of clearing away was pretty well completed. I nodded, and indicated by a motion of my hand for him to swing out.

The *Titanic* was fitted with a well-known pattern of davit called the "Wellin." In operation it was merely a matter of shipping and manning the handles of the davits and the boats were quickly swung out. By this time it was clear that the ship was seriously damaged and making a lot of water. She struck the berg well forward of the foremast, and evidently there had been a slight shelf protruding below the water. This pierced her bow as she threw her whole weight on the ice, some actually falling on her fore deck. The impact flung her bow off, but only by the whip or spring of the ship. Again she struck, this time a little further aft. Each blow stove in a plate, below the water line, as the ship had not the inherent strength to resist.

Had it been, for instance, the old *Majestic* or even the *Oceanic* the chances are that either of them would have been strong enough to take the blow and be bodily thrown off without serious damage. For instance, coming alongside with the old *Majestic*, it was no uncommon thing for her to hit a knuckle of the wharf

COLLISION WITH AN ICEBERG

a good healthy bump, but beyond, perhaps, scraping off the paint, no damage was ever done. The same, to a lesser extent with the *Oceanic*.

Then ships grew in size, out of all proportion to their strength, till one would see a modern liner brought with all the skill and care possible, fall slowly, and ever so gently on a knuckle, to bend and dent a plate like a piece of tin.

That is exactly what happened to the *Titanic*. She just bump, bump, bumped along the berg, holing herself each time, till she was making water in no less than six compartments, though, unfortunately, we were not to know this until much later. Andrews, the designer, and nephew of the late Lord Pirrie was making the trip with us and it was he, familiar with every nook and corner in her, who made a quick tour of inspection with the Carpenter and reported her condition to Captain Smith.

Actually, the *Titanic* was so constructed and divided into watertight compartments that she would float, with any two compartments full of water; and the margin of safety made it fairly certain that she would still have floated, with even three of the four forward compartments full up. Although the water would have been above the forward watertight bulkheads, it would still have been kept out of the rest of the ship, despite the fact that the forward part of her would have been completely submerged. The whole ship would have assumed a fairly acute and mighty uncomfortable angle, yet, even so, she would, in all probability have floated —at least for some considerable time, perhaps all day. Certainly for sufficient time for everyone to be rescued; and, just possibly, until she could have been beached. But she could not remain afloat when she was holed in the forward stokehold as well. That made the fifth compartment counting from forward, that was smashed in by the iceberg, and this finally sealed her fate.

By the time all the boats were swung out she was well down forward, and the water was practically level with the main deck. Even so I still had no thought that she was actually going to founder. There had been no chance or time to make enquiries, but I figured up in my own mind that she had probably struck the berg a glancing blow with the bluff of her bow and opened up one or perhaps two of the forward compartments, which were filling and putting her down by the head; also that she would go so far, until she balanced her buoyancy, and there she would remain. Bulkheads were all new and sound and should be able to carry the pressure, and there was no reason to suppose they would not be equal to their task. All watertight doors had been closed automatically from the bridge, at the time of the collision—all except one place where there was no door, but which in any case would not have made any ultimate difference.

Although I was fairly confident in my own mind that she would not sink, one has no right to risk an error of judgment that may entail loss of life, particularly when it is the case of the passengers you are carrying. They are your trust, and must at all times be your first consideration, to the total elimination of all personal feelings, or personal impressions. It was fortunate we played for safety, for, as it turned out, she was holed in no less than six compartments along the starboard side, and *nothing* could have saved her.

Having got the boats swung out, I made for the Captain, and happened to meet him near by on the boat deck. Drawing him into a corner, and, cupping both my hands over my mouth and his ear, I yelled at the top of my voice, "Hadn't we better get the women and children into the boats, sir?" He heard me, and nodded reply. One of my reasons for suggesting getting the boats afloat was, that I could see a steamer's steaming lights a couple of miles away on our port bow. If I could get the women and children into the boats, they would be perfectly safe in that smooth sea until this ship picked them up; if the necessity arose. My idea was that I would lower the boats with a few people in each and when safely in the water fill them up from the gangway doors on the lower decks, and transfer them to the other ship.

Although boats and falls were all brand new, it is a risky business at the best of times to attempt to lower a boat between seventy and eighty feet at night time, filled with people who are not "boatwise." It is, unfortunately, the rule rather than the exception for some mishap to occur in lowering boats loaded with people who, through no fault of their own, lack this boat sense. In addition, the strain is almost too much to expect of boats and falls under ordinary conditions.

However, having got Captain Smith's sanction, I indicated to the Bosun's Mate, and we lowered down the first boat level with the boat deck, and, just at this time, thank heaven, the frightful din of escaping steam suddenly stopped, and there was a death-like silence a thousand times more exaggerated, fore and aft the ship. It was almost startling to hear one's own voice again after the appalling din of the last half hour or so.

I got just on forty people into No. 4 boat, and gave the order to "lower away," and for the boat to "go to the gangway door" with the idea of filling each boat as it became afloat, to its full capacity. At the same time I told the Bosun's Mate to take six hands and open the port lower-deck gangway door, which was abreast of No. 2 hatch. He took his men and proceeded to carry out the order, but neither he or the men were ever seen again. One can only suppose that they gave their lives endeavouring to carry out this order, probably they were trapped in the alley-way by a rush of water, for by this time the fo'csle head was within about ten feet of the water. Yet I *still* had hope that we should save her.

Passing along to No. 6 boat to load and lower, I could hear the band playing cheery sort of music. I don't like jazz music as a rule, but I was glad to hear it that night. I think it helped us all.

Wireless signals for help had been broadcast over the ocean ever since the first impact, and ships were coming to our aid. It was excusable that in some cases the Officer of the Watch on some ships could hardly credit his senses, or believe the wireless operator when told that the *Titanic*—that wonder of all mercantile wonders—was *sinking in mid-Atlantic,* and sending out calls for assistance.

The wireless operator of the *Virginian* told me that when he reported the fact to his Officer of the Watch, he was literally chucked off the bridge, for trying to play what the O.O.W. thought was an attempt at a practical joke; it was only as he was being pushed past the chart-room door, preparatory to being shot down the bridge ladder, that he landed out with his foot, and gave a terrific kick on the panel of the door. The wireless operator knew that the Captain was asleep in the chart-room, and that this crash would bring him out with a jump. The Officer of the Watch also realised when the report was officially made to the Captain, that it was no joke, and that the *Titanic* was truly in a bad way. They at once altered course and made all speed towards us.

On the *Titanic*, passengers naturally kept coming up and asking, did I consider the situation serious. In all cases I tried to cheer them up, by telling them "No," but that it was a matter of precaution to get the boats in the water, ready for any emergency. That in any case they were perfectly safe, as there was a ship not more than a few miles away, and I pointed out the lights on the port bow which they could see as well as I could.

At this time we were firing rocket distress signals, which explode with a loud report a couple of hundred feet in the air. Every minute or two one of these went up, bursting overhead with a cascade of stars.

"Why were we firing these signals, if there was no danger?" was the question, to which I replied that we were trying to call the attention of the ship nearby, as we could not get her with wireless. *That ship was the "Californian."* Here again we were to see exemplified, what has become almost proverbial at sea, that in cases of disaster, one ship, the first on the scene, will be in a position to rescue, and yet, through some circumstance or combination of circumstances, fails to make that rescue.

The distress signals we fired were seen by the Officer of the Watch on board the *Californian*, also by several members of her crew. Even the flashes from our Morse lamp were seen but finally judged to be "Just the masthead light flickering." Though at one time the thought evidently did arise that we were trying to call them.

To let pass the possibility of a ship calling by Morse, in the existing circumstances then surrounding her, was bad enough; but to mistake distress signals was inexcusable, and to ignore them, criminal. In point of fact the O.O.W. alone saw, and counted, five distress signals (or, as he reported them to Captain Lord, "five white rockets"). Evidently the Captain's curiosity was more than a little aroused for him to ask, "Are they company's signals?" To which the O.O.W. replied that he did not know, but they "Appear to me to be white rockets." Captain Lord merely told him to "go on Morsing," and if he received any further information to send it down to him.

It is an unqualified fact that every single one of our distress signals—unmistakable and urgent calls for help, were clearly seen by the *Californian*. These signals are never made, except in cases of dire necessity. The O.O.W. of the *Californian* fully appreciated this fact as was evidenced by his remark to the Apprentice on watch with him, "A ship is not going to fire rockets at sea for nothing."

Shortly after counting eight "rockets" he again sent down word to the Captain, with the added rider to the Apprentice, "be sure and wake him and tell him that altogether we have seen eight of these white lights, like rockets, in the direction of this other steamer."

Precisely at 2.40 a.m. this Officer of the Watch again called Captain Lord, this time by voice pipe, and told him that the ship from which he had seen the rockets, had disappeared.

He spoke truly. *A great sea tragedy had been consummated before his very eyes.*

CHAPTER THIRTY-THREE WOMEN AND CHILDREN —ONLY

THE quiet orderliness amongst the passengers, and the discipline amongst the crew, is a thing never to be forgotten. Many of the former came quietly with offers of help. The Bosun's Mate and six of the Watch having been lost to me, the work had become very heavy, and still heavier as I detailed two of the remaining Watch to go away with each boat as it was lowered. The practice was, to lower each boat until the gunwale was level with the boat deck, then, standing with one foot on the deck and one in the boat, the women just held out their right hand, the wrist of which I grabbed with my right hand, hooking my left arm underneath their arm, and so practically lifted them over the gap between the boat's gunwale and the ship's side, into the boat.

Between one boat being lowered away and the next boat being prepared, I usually nipped along to have a look down the very long emergency staircase leading direct from the boat deck down to "C" deck. Actually, built as a short cut for the crew, it served my purpose now to gauge the speed with which the water was rising, and how high it had got. By now the fore deck was below the surface. That cold, green water, crawling its ghostly way up that staircase, was a sight that stamped itself indelibly on my memory. Step by step, it made its way up, covering the electric lights, one after the other, which, for a time, shone under the surface with a horribly weird effect.

Still, it served a very good purpose, and enabled me to form an accurate judgment as to how far she had gone, and how quickly she was going down. Dynamos were still running, and deck lights on, which, though dim, helped considerably with the work; more than could be said of one very good lady who achieved fame by waving an electric light and successfully blinding us as we worked on the boats. It puzzled me until I found she had it installed in the head of her walking stick! I am afraid she was rather disappointed on finding out that her precious light was not a bit appreciated. Arriving in safety on board the *Carpathia*, she tried to make out that someone had stolen her wretched stick, whereas it had been merely taken from her, in response to my request that someone would throw the damn thing overboard.

It had now become apparent that the ship was doomed, and in consequence I began to load the boats to the utmost capacity that I dared. My scheme for filling up at the lower deck doors had gone by the board —they were under water.

Many were the instances of calm courage.

One young couple walked steadily up and down the boat deck throughout pretty well the whole of the proceedings. Once or twice the young chap asked if he could help. He was a tall, clean-bred Britisher, on his honeymoon I should say. The girl—she was little more—never made the slightest attempt to come towards the boats, much less to be taken on board, although I looked towards her several times with a sort of silent invitation, but no, she was not going to be parted from her man.

The order implicitly obeyed was, "Women and children only." The very highest tribute that it was possible for a human being to pay would hardly do justice to or give the praise due to the sheer calm courage shown by men, women and children amongst the passengers on that ship, individually and collectively. It made me unutterably proud of the English speaking race. The conditions were all strange; the ship was sinking and the boats were leaving, yet, neither man nor woman attempted to get into a boat without being ordered.

In the case of a Major Peuchen, a Canadian by birth, who went away in one of the boats, unwarrantable blame was attached, at a later date.

I was reduced to sending one seaman away in a boat, and on an occasion, after ordering away a sailor to take charge, I turned round to find there was only one left to attend the boat falls, for lowering away.

"Someone for that after fall," I called, and the next thing a man who had sailed with me for many years, Hemming by name, replied, "Aye, aye, sir! all ready." Unknown to me he had stepped out of the boat, back on board, to carry out what he considered the more important duty. Bravery and self-sacrifice such as this was of common occurrence throughout the night.

The boat was half way down when someone hailed me, saying, "We've no seamen in the boat," and at that moment I had no one available. I called to the people standing around, "Any seaman there?" No reply, and it was then that Major Peuchen, when he saw that there were none of the ship's crew available, said, "I'm not a seaman, but I'm a yachtsman, if I can be of any use to you."

The boat's falls, or ropes, by which the boat is lowered, hang up and down from the davit head, about nine or ten feet away from the ship's side. I said to him, "If you're seaman enough to get out on those falls, and get down into the boat you may go ahead." He did, and has been very unfairly criticised for carrying out what was a direct order.

It was about this time that the Chief Officer came over from the starboard side and asked, did I know where the firearms were?

As I pointed out before, it was the *First* Officer's responsibility to receive firearms, navigation instruments, and so forth. I have also said firearms on merchant ships are looked on as ornamental more than useful, and as First Officer I had simply hove the lot, revolvers and ammunition into a locker, in my original cabin, a locker that was of little use owing to its inaccessibility.

Then, later on, had come the "general post," whereby Murdoch, who was now First Officer, knew nothing about the firearms, and couldn't find them, when they were wanted—I say wanted, rather than needed, because I still don't believe that they were actually needed.

I told the Chief Officer, "Yes, I know where they are. Come along and I'll get them for you," and into the First Officer's cabin we went—the Chief, Murdoch, the Captain and myself—where I hauled them out, still in all their pristine newness and grease.

I was going out when the Chief shoved one of the revolvers into my hands, with a handful of ammunition, and said, "Here you are, you may need it." On the impulse, I just slipped it into my pocket, along with the cartridges, and returned to the boats. The whole incident had not taken three minutes, though it seemed barely worth that precious time.

As I returned along the deck, I passed Mr. and Mrs. Strauss leaning up against the deck house, chatting quite cheerily. I stopped and asked Mrs. Strauss, "Can I take you along to the boats?" She replied, "I think I'll stay here for the present." Mr. Strauss, calling her by her Christian name said, smilingly,

WOMEN AND CHILDREN—ONLY

"Why don't you go along with him, dear?" She just smiled, and said, "No, not yet." I left them, and they went down together. To another couple, evidently from the Western States, that I found sitting on a fan casing I asked the girl, "Won't you let me put you in one of the boats?" She replied with a very frank smile, "Not on your life. We started together, and if need be, we'll finish together." It was typical of the spirit throughout.

Boat after boat was safely lowered into the water, with its human freight of women and children, each with an ever-increasing cargo as it became more and more evident that the *Titanic* was doomed, and that the ship to which we had looked for immediate help, was also a false hope. Time and again I had used her lights as a means to buoy up the hopes of the many that I now knew only too well, were soon to find themselves struggling in that icy water.

Why *couldn't* she hear our wireless calls? Why *couldn't* her Officer of the Watch or some one of her crew, see our distress signals with their showers of stars, visible for miles and miles around?—a signal that is never used except when a ship is in dire need of assistance. What wouldn't I have given for a six inch gun and a couple of shells to wake them up. I had assured and reassured the passengers throughout these anxious hours, "She cannot help but see these signals, and must soon steam over and pick everyone up." And what an absolutely unique opportunity Captain Lord, of the *Californian*, had that night of rendering aid and saving close on 1,500 lives. Nothing could have been easier than to have laid his ship actually alongside the *Titanic* and taken every soul on board. Yet, not a thing was done, not even was their wireless operator aroused to see if there *were* any distress calls.

There are no police, fire brigades or lifeboats out at sea, therefore it becomes nothing less than a fetish—the tenet above all tenets in the religion among sailors, that absolutely no effort shall be spared in an endeavour to save life at sea. A man must even be prepared to hazard his ship and his life.

Just before launching the last two lifeboats, I had made my final hurried visit to the stairway. It was then conclusively evident that not only *was* she going, but that she was going *very soon*, and if we were to avoid the unutterable disgrace of going down with lifeboats still hanging to the davits, there was not one single moment to lose.

Hurrying back to the two remaining lifeboats still hanging in their davits, I met the Purser, Assistant Purser, and the Senior and Junior Surgeons—the latter a noted wag—even in the face of tragedy, couldn't resist his last mild joke, "Hello, Lights, are you warm?" The idea of anyone being warm in that temperature was a joke in itself, and I suppose it struck him as odd to meet me wearing a sweater, no coat or overcoat. I had long since discarded my great coat, even in pants and sweater over pyjamas alone I was in a bath of perspiration. There was only time to pass a few words, then they all shook hands and said "Good-bye." Frankly, I didn't feel at all like "Good-bye," although I knew we shouldn't have the ship under us much longer. The thing was to get these boats away at all costs. Eventually, and to my great relief, they were all loaded and safely lowered into the water.

The last lifeboat having got away, there remained No. 2 boat, which was actually a small sea boat used for emergency purposes (in fact often termed "The Emergency Boat"), hanging in the davits.

About this time I met all the engineers, as they came

trooping up from below. Most of them I knew individually, and had been shipmates with them on different ships of the Line. They had all loyally stuck to their guns, long after they could be of any material assistance. Much earlier on the engine-room telegraphs had been "Rung off—"the last ring made on board ships at sea, and which conveys to the engine-room staff the final information that their services below can be of no further use, that the case (from whatever cause) is hopeless. At the same time it releases engineers and stokers from duty, leaving them free to make the best of their way to the boats. Of course, in theory, each has his appointed place in a given boat.

Since the *Titanic* disaster, each undoubtedly has. But before that tragedy brought home to the world the utter fallacy of the "unsinkable ship" I'm afraid that many "appointed places"—as far as life-saving equipment was concerned—were just so much theory, concocted ashore with a keen eye to dividends.

Certainly there was no sailor who ever sailed salt water but who smiled—and still smiles—at the idea of the "unsinkable ship."

There was little opportunity to say more than a word or two to the engineers. Up to that time they had known little of what was going on, and it was surely a bleak and hopeless spectacle that met their eyes. Empty falls hanging loosely from every davit head, and not a solitary hope for any one of them.

In point of fact, they were lost to a man, *not one single survivor* out of the whole thirty-five.

CHAPTER THIRTY-FOUR *SHE FOUNDERS*

ARRIVING alongside the emergency boat, someone spoke out of the darkness, and said, "There are men in that boat." I jumped in, and regret to say that there actually were—but they weren't British, nor of the English speaking race. I won't even attribute any nationality to them, beyond saying that they come under the broad category known to sailors as "Dagoes." They hopped out mighty quickly, and I encouraged them verbally, also by vigorously flourishing my revolver. They certainly thought they were between the devil and the deep sea in more senses than one, and I had the satisfaction of seeing them tumbling head over heels on to the deck, preferring the uncertain safety of the deck, to the cold lead which I suppose they fully imagined would follow their disobedience—so much for imagination—the revolver was not even loaded!

"Any more women and children?" was the cry, and we had the greatest difficulty in finding sufficient to fill even this small boat—of those who were willing to go and leave others behind. Eventually, she was filled, and we lowered her away.

There now only remained two folded boats of the Engleheart type, with collapsible canvas sides, one on the deck by the davits of No. 2 emergency and one on top of the officers' quarters, both firmly lashed down. The rope falls of No. 2 were hurriedly rounded up and one collapsible boat hooked on and swung out ready for lowering.

I stood partly in the boat, owing to the difficulty of getting the womenfolk over a high bulwark rail just here. As we were ready for lowering the Chief came over to my side of the deck and, seeing me in the boat and no seaman available said, "You go with her, Lightoller."

Praises be, I had just sufficient sense to say, "Not damn likely," and jump back on board; not with any idea of self-imposed martyrdom—far from it—it was just pure impulse of the moment, and an impulse for which I was to thank my lucky stars a thousand times over, in the days to come. I had taken my chance and gone down with the rest, consequently I didn't have to take any old back-chat from anyone.

As this boat was being lowered, two men passengers jumped into her from the deck below. This, as far as I know, was the only instance of men getting away in boats from the port side. I don't blame them, the boat wasn't full, for the simple reason we couldn't find sufficient women, and there was no time to wait—the water was then actually lapping round their feet on "A" deck, so they jumped for it and got away. Good luck to them.

With one other seaman I started to cast adrift the one remaining Engleheart on top of the officer's quarters. We cut and threw off the lashings, jumped round to the inboard side ready to pick up the gunwale together and throw her bodily down on to the boat deck. The seaman working with me called:

"All ready, sir," and I recognised Hemmings' voice—the chap I had ordered away long before, and who returned on board to tend the falls, and in whose place I sent Major Peuchen.

"Hello, is that you, Hemming?"

"Yes, sir."

"Why haven't you gone?" I asked.

"Oh, plenty of time yet, sir," he replied cheerily. Apparently the chap had loyally stuck by me all through, though it had been too dark to recognise him. Stout fellow. Later, he slid down one of the falls, swam for it and was saved.

We had just time to tip the boat over, and let her drop into the water that was now above the boat deck, in the hope that some few would be able to scramble on to her as she floated off. Hemming and I then, as every single boat was now away from the port side, went over to the starboard side, to see if there was anything further to be done there. But all the boats on this side had also been got away, though there were still crowds of people on the deck.

Just then the ship took a slight but definite plunge —probably a bulkhead went—and the sea came rolling up in a wave, over the steel-fronted bridge, along the deck below us, washing the people back in a dreadful huddled mass. Those that didn't disappear under the water right away, instinctively started to clamber up that part of the deck still out of water, and work their way towards the stern, which was rising steadily out of the water as the bow went down. A few of the more agile leapt up on top of the officers' quarters where Hemming and I were at the moment. It was a sight that doesn't bear dwelling on—to stand there, above the wheelhouse, and on our quarters, watching the frantic struggles to climb up the sloping deck, utterly unable to even hold out a helping hand.

I knew, only too well, the utter futility of following that driving instinct of self-preservation and struggling up towards the stern. It would only be postponing the plunge, and prolonging the agony—even lessening one's already slim chances, by becoming one of a crowd. It came home to me very clearly how fatal it would be to get amongst those hundreds and hundreds of people who would shortly be struggling for their lives in that deadly cold water. There was only one thing to do, and I might just as well do it and get it over, so, turning to the fore part of the bridge, I took a header. Striking the water, was like a thousand knives being driven into one's body, and, for a few moments, I completely lost grip of myself—and no wonder for I was perspiring freely, whilst the temperature of the water was 28° or 4° below freezing.

Ahead of me the look-out cage on the foremast was visible just above the water—in normal times it would be a hundred feet above. I struck out blindly for this, but only for a short while, till I got hold of myself again and realised the futility of seeking safety on anything connected with the ship. I then turned to starboard, away from the ship altogether.

For a time I wondered what was making it so difficult for me to keep my head above the water. Time and again I went under, until it dawned on me that it was the great Webley revolver, still in my pocket, that was dragging me down. I soon sent that on its downward journey.

The water was now pouring down the stokeholds, by way of the fiddley gratings abaft the bridge, and round the forward funnel.

On the boat deck, above our quarters, on the fore part of the forward funnel, was a huge rectangular air shaft and ventilator, with an opening about twenty by fifteen feet. On this opening was a light wire grating to prevent rubbish being drawn down or anything else being thrown down. This shaft led direct to No. 3 stokehold, and was therefore a sheer drop of close on hundred feet, right to the bottom of the ship.

I suddenly found myself drawn, by the sudden rush of the surface water now pouring down this shaft, and held flat and firmly up against this wire netting with the additional full and clear knowledge of what would happen if this light wire carried away. The pressure of the water just glued me there whilst the ship sank slowly below the surface.

Although I struggled and kicked for all I was worth, it was impossible to get away, for as fast as I pushed myself off I was irresistibly dragged back, every instant expecting the wire to go, and to find myself shot down into the bowels of the ship.

Apart from that, I was drowning, and a matter of another couple of minutes would have seen me through. I was still struggling and fighting when suddenly a terrific blast of hot air came up the shaft, and blew me right away from the air shaft and up to the surface.

The water was now swirling round, and the ship sinking rapidly, when once again I was caught and sucked down by an inrush of water, this time adhering to one of the fiddley gratings. Just how I got clear of that, I don't know, as I was rather losing interest in things, but I eventually came to the surface once again, this time alongside that last Engleheart boat which Hemming and I had launched from on top of the officers' quarters on the opposite side—for I was now on the starboard side, near the forward funnel.

There were many around in the water by this time, some swimming, others (mostly men, thank God), definitely drowning—an utter nightmare of both sight and sound. In the circumstances I made no effort to get on top of the upturned boat, but, for some reason, was content to remain floating alongside, just hanging on to a small piece of rope.

The bow of the ship was now rapidly going down and the stern rising higher and higher out of the water, piling the people into helpless heaps around the steep decks, and by the score into the icy water. Had the boats been around many might have been saved, but of them, at this time there was no sign. Organised help, or even individual help, was quite impossible. All one could do was just wait on events, and try and forget the icy cold grip of the water.

The terrific strain of bringing the after end of that huge hull clear out of the water, caused the expansion joint abaft No. 1 funnel to open up. (These expansion joints were found necessary in big ships to allow the ship to "work" in a seaway.) The fact that the two wire stays to this funnel, on the after part, led over and abaft the expansion joint, threw on them an extraordinary strain, eventually carrying away the port wire guy, to be followed almost immediately by the starboard one. Instantly the port one parted, the funnel started to fall, but the fact that the starboard one held a moment or two longer, gave this huge structure a pull over to that side of the ship, causing it to fall, with its scores of tons, right amongst the struggling mass of humanity already in the water. It struck the water between the Engleheart and the ship, actually missing me by inches.

Amongst the many historic and, what in less tragic circumstances would have been humorous—questions, asked by Senator Smith at the Washington Enquiry was "Did it hurt anyone?"

One effect of the funnel crashing down on the sea, was to pick up the Engleheart, in the wash so created, and fling it well clear of the sinking ship.

When I again recognised my surroundings, we were full fifty yards clear of the ship. The piece of rope was still in my hand, with old friend Engleheart upturned and attached to the other end, with several men by now standing on it. I also scrambled up, after spending longer than I like to remember in that icy water. Lights on board the *Titanic* were still burning, and a wonderful spectacle she made, standing out black and massive against the starlit sky; myriads of lights still gleaming through the portholes, from that part of the decks still above water.

The fore part, and up to the second funnel was by this time completely submerged, and as we watched this terribly awe-inspiring sight, suddenly all lights went out and the huge bulk was left in black darkness, but clearly silhouetted against the bright sky. Then, the next moment, the massive boilers left their beds and went thundering down with a hollow rumbling roar, through the bulk-heads, carrying everything with them that stood in their way. This unparalleled tragedy that was being enacted before our very eyes, now rapidly approached its finale, as the huge ship slowly but surely reared herself on end and brought rudder and propellers clear of the water, till, at last, she assumed *an absolute perpendicular position*. In this amazing attitude she remained for the space of half a minute. Then with impressive majesty and ever increasing momentum, she silently took her last tragic dive to seek a final resting place in the unfathomable depths of the cold grey Atlantic.

Almost like a benediction everyone round me on the upturned boat breathed the two words "She's gone."

Fortunately, the scene that followed was shrouded in darkness. Less fortunately, the calm still silence carried every sound with startling distinctness. To enter into a description of those heart-rending, never-to-be-forgotten sounds would serve no useful purpose. I never allowed my thoughts to dwell on them, and there are some that would be alive and well to-day had they just determined to erase from their minds all memory of those ghastly moments, or at least until time had somewhat dimmed the memory of that awful tragedy.

CHAPTER THIRTY-FIVE *THE RESCUE*

HOWEVER anyone that had sought refuge on that upturned Engleheart survived the night is nothing short of miraculous. If ever human endurance was taxed to the limit, surely it was during those long hours of exposure in a temperature below freezing, standing motionless in our wet clothes. That the majority were still standing when the first faint streaks of dawn appeared, is proof that whilst there is life there is still some hope.

Hour by hour the compartments in this collapsible boat were surely filling with water, due, no doubt to the rough and ready treatment she had received when dumped incontinently from the top of our quarters, with a crash on to the boat deck, there to float off of her own sweet will.

The fact remains we were painfully conscious of that icy cold water, slowly but surely creeping up our legs.

Some quietly lost consciousness, subsided into the water, and slipped overboard, there being nothing on the smooth flat bottom of the boat to hold them. No one was in a condition to help, and the fact that a slight but distinct swell had started to roll up, rendered help from the still living an impossibility.

It was only by the grace of being huddled together that most of us didn't add to the many that lost their lives that night.

Another thing, with the rising sea I realised that without concerted action, we were *all* going to be pitched headlong into the sea, and that would spell finish for everyone. So I made everyone face one way, and then, as I felt the boat under our feet lurch to the sea, one way or the other, I corrected it by the order "Lean to the right," "Stand upright," or "Lean to the left," as the case might be.

In this way we managed to maintain our foothold on the slippery planks by now well under water.

We knew that ships were racing to our rescue, though the chances of our keeping up our efforts of balancing until one came along seemed very, very remote. Phillips, the senior wireless operator, standing near me, told me the different ships that had answered our call. Of these, according to their positions, undoubtedly the *Carpathia* was nearest and should be up with the position where the *Titanic* sank, by daylight.

For encouragement, I passed on to those around, my rough calculation and it certainly helped the struggle to keep up. As it turned out, the information from Phillips, and the calculation, were about right, though poor old Phillips did not live to benefit by it. He hung on till daylight came in and we sighted one of the lifeboats in the distance. We were beyond making her hear with our shouting, but I happened to have in my pocket the ordinary whistle which every officer of the Watch carries. This piercing sound carried, and likewise carried the information (for what it was worth) that it was an officer making the call.

Slowly—oh how slow it seemed—she worked her way towards us. Meantime the boat under us showed unmistakable signs of leaving us altogether. I think it must have been the final and terrible anxiety that tipped the beam with Phillips, for he suddenly slipped down, sitting in the water, and though we held his head up, he never recovered. I insisted on taking him into the lifeboat with us, hoping there still might be life, but it was too late. Altogether there were thirty of us boarded the lifeboat, and later on I counted seventy-five living, apart from those lying on the bottom boards. If a sea got up it was going to take all my knowledge of boat-craft to keep *her* afloat.

As daylight increased we had the thrice welcome sight of the Cunard Liner *Carpathia* cautiously picking her way through the ice towards us. We saw boat by boat go alongside, but the question was, would she come our way in time? Sea and wind were rising. Every wave threatened to come over the bows of our overloaded lifeboat and swamp us. All were women and children in the boat apart from those of us men from the Engleheart. Fortunately, none of them realised how near we were to being swamped.

I trimmed the boat down a little more by the stern, and raised the bow, keeping her carefully bow on to the sea, and hoping against hope she would continue to rise. Sluggishly, she lifted her bows, but there was no life in her with all that number on board.

Then, at long last, the *Carpathia* definitely turned her head towards us, rounding to about 100 yards to windward. Now to get her safely alongside! We couldn't last many minutes longer, and round the *Carpathia's* bows was a scurry of wind and waves that looked like defeating all my efforts after all. One sea lopped over the bow and the next one far worse. The following one she rode, and then, to my unbounded relief, she came through the scurry into calm water under the *Carpathia's* lee.

Quickly the bosun's chairs were lowered for those unable to climb the sheer side by a swinging rope ladder, and little enough ceremony was shown in bundling old and young, fat and thin, onto that bit of wood constituting the "Boatswain's Chair."

Once the word was given to "hoist away" and up into the air they went. There were a few screams, but on the whole, they took it well, in fact many were by now in a condition that rendered them barely able to hang on, much less scream.

When all were on board we counted the cost. There were a round total of 711 saved out of 2,201 on board. Fifteen hundred of all ranks and classes had gone to their last account. Apart from four junior officers ordered away in charge of boats, I found I was the solitary survivor of over fifty officers and engineers who went down with her. Hardly one amongst the hundreds of surviving passengers, but had lost someone near and dear.

Then came the torment of being unable to hold out a vestige of hope.

"Could not another ship have picked them up?"

"Could they not possibly be in some boat overlooked by the *Carpathia*?"

"Was it not possible that he might have climbed on to an iceberg?"

After serious consideration it seemed the kindest way to be perfectly frank and give the one reply possible. What kindness was there in holding out a hope, knowing full well there was not even the *shadow* of hope. Cold comfort, and possibly cruel, but I could see no help for it.

Countess Rothes was one of the foremost amongst those trying to carry comfort to others, and through that sad trip to New York, there were very many quiet acts of self-denial.

Everybody's hope, so far as the crew were concerned, was that we might arrive in New York in time to catch the *Celtic* back to Liverpool and so escape the inquisition that would otherwise be awaiting us. Our luck was distinctly out. We were served with Warrants, immediately on arrival. It was a colossal piece of impertinence that served no useful purpose and elicited only a garbled and disjointed account of the disaster; due in the main to a total lack of co-ordination in the questioning in conjunction with an abysmal ignorance of the sea.

In Washington our men were herded into a second-rate boarding house, which might have suited some, but certainly not such men as formed the crew of the *Titanic*. In the end they point blank refused to have anything more to do with either the enquiry or the people, whose only achievement was to make our Seamen, Quartermasters and Petty Officers look utterly ridiculous. It was only with the greatest difficulty I was able to bring peace into the camp—mainly due to the tact exhibited by the British Ambassador, Lord Percy, and Mr. P. A. Franklyn, President of the International Mercantile Marine Co.

With all the goodwill in the world, the "Enquiry" could be called nothing but a complete farce, wherein all the traditions and customs of the sea were continuously and persistently flouted.

Such a contrast to the dignity and decorum of the Court held by Lord Mersey in London, where the guiding spirit was a sailor in essence, and who insisted, when necessary, that any cross-questioner should at any rate be familiar with at least the rudiments of the sea. Sir Rufus Isaacs—as he was then—had started his career as a sailor. One didn't need to explain that "going down by the bow" and "going down by the head" was one and the same thing. Nor, that water-tight compartments, dividing the ship, were not necessarily places of refuge in which passengers could safely ensconce themselves, whilst the ship went to the bottom of the Atlantic, to be rescued later, as convenient. Neither was it necessary to waste precious time on lengthy explanations as to how and why a sailor was not an officer, though an officer was a sailor.

In Washington it was of little consequence, but in London it was very necessary to keep one's hand on the whitewash brush. Sharp questions that needed careful answers if one was to avoid a pitfall, carefully and subtly dug, leading to a pinning down of blame on to someone's luckless shoulders. How hard Mr. Scanlan and the legal luminary, representing the interests of the Seamen and Firemen, tried to prove there were not enough seamen to launch and man the boats. The same applied to the passengers, and quite truly. But it was inadvisable to admit it then and there, hence the hard fought verbal duels between us. Mr. Scanlan's conquest of the higher legal spheres of recent years proves he was no mean antagonist to face. His aim was to force the admission that I had not sufficient seamen to give adequate help with the boats, and consequently that the ship was undermanned. How many men did I consider necessary to launch a lifeboat?

"What size lifeboat?"

"Take one of the *Titanic's* lifeboats."

"Well," I pointed out, "it would depend greatly on weather conditions."

"Make your own conditions," replied my legal opponent impatiently.

I suggested, as an example, we should take the wind as force six Beaufort's scale.

"Yes," he agreed.

"Then," I added, "there would be an accompanying sea, of course."

"Yes, yes," he again agreed, and fell into the trap which Lord Mersey proceeded to spring, by informing Mr. Scanlan that in the circumstances described it would be impossible to launch any boat.

So the legal battle went on.

Still, I think we parted very good friends.

A washing of dirty linen would help no one. The B.O.T. had passed that ship as in all respects fit for sea, in every sense of the word, with sufficient margin of safety for everyone on board. Nowt he B.O.T. was holding an enquiry into the loss of that ship—hence the whitewash brush. Personally, I had no desire that blame should be attributed either to the B.O.T. or the White Star Line, though in all conscience it was a difficult task, when handled by some of the cleverest legal minds in England, striving tooth and nail to prove the inadequacy here, the lack there, when one had known, full well, and for many years, the ever-present possibility of just such a disaster. I think in the end the B.O.T. and the White Star Line won.

The very point, namely the utter inadequacy of the life-saving equipment then prevailing, which Mr. Scanlan and his confrères had been fighting tooth and nail to prove, has since been wholly, frankly, and fully admitted by the stringent rules now governing British ships, "Going Foreign."

No longer is the Boat-Deck almost wholly set aside as a recreation ground for passengers, with the smallest number of boats relegated to the least possible space.

In fact, the pendulum has swung to the other extreme and the margin of safety reached the ridiculous.

Be that as it may, I am never likely to forget that long drawn out battle of wits, where it seemed that I must hold that unenviable position of whipping boy to the whole lot of them. Pull devil, pull baker, till it looked as if they would pretty well succeed in pulling my hide off completely, each seemed to want his bit. I know when it was all over I felt more like a legal doormat than a Mail Boat Officer.

Perhaps the heads of the White Star Line didn't quite realise just what an endless strain it had all been, falling on one man's luckless shoulders, as it needs must, being the sole survivor out of so many departments—fortunately they were broad.

Still, just that word of thanks which was lacking, which when the *Titanic* Enquiry was all over would have been very much appreciated. It must have been a curious psychology that governed the managers of that magnificent Line. Promotion and service in their Western Ocean Mail Boats was the mark of their highest approval. Both these tokens came my way, and fifteen of my twenty years under the red Burgee with its silver star, were spent in the Atlantic Mail. Yet, when after completing my twentieth year of service I came to bury my anchor, and awaited their pleasure at headquarters, for the last time, there was a brief,

"Oh, you are leaving us, are you. Well, Good-bye."

A curious people!

However, that was not to be for some years, and I was yet to see another of the Line, my old favourite, the *Oceanic*, swallowed up by the insatiable sea.

Having at last finished with the "*Titanic* Enquiry," I again set about picking up the threads and found myself once more signing Articles on the *Oceanic* with many that had survived the *Titanic*. One well-known figure was missing from the Shipping Office about this time and that was "Old Ned," known to all and sundry as just "Ned." Actually, he was responsible for the stokehold crowd, and a tougher bunch than the firemen on a Western Ocean Mail boat it would be impossible to find. Bootle seemed to specialise in the Liverpool Irishman, who was accounted to be the toughest of the tough, and prominent amongst the few that could stand up to the life, where life below consisted of one endless drive. Even the engineers seemed to get tainted with that unqualified "toughness," for they must be able to hold their own with the worst. This type reached its peak in the days of the old *Majestic* and *Teutonic*. The conditions under which firemen laboured in these boats, were inhuman. Little blame if the men did become brutes. The heat of the stokehold alone, when driving under the last ounce of steam, was terrible. Added to this, when in the Gulf Stream, was the intense humidity.

It was no uncommon sight to see a man, sometimes two, three or even four in a watch, hoisted up the ashshoot with the bucket chain hooked roughly round under their arm-pits, to be dumped on deck unconscious. A few buckets of water over them and then they were left to recover. Neither must they be long about it, or up comes the Leading Fireman, who, with strict impartiality, will apply both boot and fist to drive his dogs of war below again.

The instructions were to keep up that "arrow," indicating the steam pressure, at all costs, regardless of body or bones. Small wonder at the tales that used to creep about, of men gone missing after a free fight, when sharp shovels are used as flails.

"So and so missing. He must have gone overboard during the night. Caught with the heat, poor beggar."

Yes, caught all right, but perhaps with the sharp edge of a shovel.

An engineer at one time was seen to go into the stokehold, and never seen to come out, nor yet seen on deck. He was a particularly powerful type of man and brutal withal, who hazed his watch to the limit in the demand for steam, till the stokehold was Bedlam let loose. From that day till this—though never mentioned ashore—his disappearance was frankly attributed to the swift cut of a shovel from behind, and his body shot into a furnace. The truth will never be known, but from then on, an engineer never went into the stokehold unaccompanied by his leading hand.

These were the type of men "Old Ned" was called upon to supply and handle. Originally a fireman himself, he knew all the tricks, and feared none. Tall, keen, alert. Perfect athletic build. A hawk-like eye, and monstrous aquiline nose, that had been broken more times than even he could remember. Slow of movement and quiet of speech, with a voice that came rumbling from way down in his chest.

A couple of hundred toughs, crowding and jostling together, waiting to sign on. "Ned," towering above the tallest, comes through the doorway and makes his way with a hardly a check, surging through, and throwing aside the Bootle toughs like a ship contemptuously flinging off the little waves that would hold her. A shoulder here, an elbow there. Nor would he hesitate to put the flat of that huge hand of his on the flat of some more than usually objectionable face, with the base of his wrist tucked neatly under the chin. If the man was sensible, he stepped back, quickly and sharply, regardless of the curses of those behind him, or how they might retaliate. Arriving at the table, "Ned" quickly says, "*Stand back*" to those who would crowd in with their Discharge books held out. For be it known there will be a full score and more eager to accept every single vacancy. Even "Brutal Bootle" looks with respect on a man who has gained that giddy height, and been chosen by "Ned" for "The Mail Boat." A vicious and resentful crowd they were, and though master of the situation at the pay table, it was a different matter when turning a dark corner in Dockland, as old "Ned" had known to his cost, many a time and often. On the other hand, there was not a pub within a mile or more radius, that he could not walk into and call for enough beer to drown a man, had he wished. No fireman came ashore from the Mail Boat, with his pay in his pocket but "chalked one up for Ned." Even a Chicago gangster might have envied the cortège that finally followed "Old Ned" after signing his last ship.

With the *Oceanic's* comfortable quarters, and bathrooms, there was no call for the tough element, in fact it did not exist in Southampton, where the mail boats were now running from. Again, she introduced a reserve of power that enabled a steady speed to be kept. In fact, the *Oceanic's* records for steady and consistent running have never been beaten. Two consecutive runs of over three thousand miles and not one minute of difference. Three consecutive voyages and only one minute of difference between the times of leaving Sandy Hook, New York, and passing the Wolf Rock off the Scillies.

We were bound home on that fateful August 4th, 1914, when we got the brief message that hostilities had broken out and were advised to "deviate from the recognised tracks." We did deviate, too, for we saw no fun in being captured in a fine ship like the *Oceanic*, right at the outbreak of war. Judge our anxiety when nearing the Irish Coast, on seeing the masts and funnels of two ships coming above the horizon—ships obviously of the cruiser variety. The only question was, *whose* cruisers? Well, anyway, we had to get in sometime, and the chances were they were not Germans—so we'd better risk it. All the same, it was an undoubted relief when at last the white ensign also came above the rim of the sea.

CHAPTER THIRTY-SIX *THE WAR*

ALL the mail boats were potential cruisers, with built-in gun platforms, so it was no surprise on arriving in Southampton to see a shoal of draughtsmen, naval architects, Government representatives, and so forth, hurl themselves on board and turn our well-ordered routine into chaos, and the ship into a man-o'-battle, or an imitation one anyway, for we didn't see ourselves doing much battling with old and antiquated 4.7's.

In due course—and a mighty long one—we commissioned as one of His Majesty's ships, and hoisted the white ensign. Our crew were duly "fell in" (something new for them right away) and asked if they would wish to volunteer to remain in the ship in view of the service for which she would be required.

It seemed rather a futile question to me, and one I could, with the utmost confidence, have given the answer to in the next breath. The men belonged to the ship, had been in her for years, and they had no intention of leaving her unless they were chucked out, which certainly would not happen so long as they had behaved themselves. If she was going " off the run " there might be additional fun, which would be welcome, but beyond that they were not interested. In response to the order "those now wishing to volunteer to remain in the ship, one pace forward *march*," they all quietly walked forward across the deck, to make it evident that it was one very good pace.

The Navy chap was a bit horrified, but I told him to never mind, they understood in the main, what he meant.

Unfortunately, a good sprinkling were Royal Naval Reserve men, and ex-Service men who were quickly drafted to other and perhaps more useful spheres—we were sorry—and believe me, *so were they*.

Our Carpenter and Bosun were informed that they were now Warrant rank, which didn't seem to impress them greatly, till they found themselves each invested with a sword. As old "Chips"—not notorious for either cleanliness or choice of language—asked me, "What the hell am I supposed to do with this damn thing? Take it round with me when I'm sounding ship?"

What disgusted this quaint couple most was having to move their quite comfortable quarters, as it was considered infra dig. to be quartered so near the crew. When told the exact meaning of the words, the Bosun feelingly replied, "Infra dig., eh? If any of my watch is looking for a nice thick ear, let 'em try the infra dig. on me."

Evidently he had not *quite* got the exact meaning, though he certainly had the sense of it, and did not need a sword and new quarters to put a point to it. A mail boat man in a mail boat, is a round peg, fitting nicely into a round hole; a hole that is rapidly squared with the introduction of Navy ways and manners. But when it came to drafting a lot of Hebredian fishermen on us, they were any-shaped pegs, endeavouring to fit impossible holes, naturally leading to utterly impossible situations.

I was promoted to First Lieutenant and Mary of the Messdecks; also the thankless task of trying to get these fellows from the north firstly to understand English as we spoke it, and secondly, when it took the form of orders, to instil in them just what was expected of them, when these orders were given.

There were Action Stations, Collision Stations, Fire Stations, and many other Stations and evolutions, but none that our fellows from the north had ever heard of. Furthermore, it was sometime before they realised that it was necessary to practise these efforts, so as to be ready if and when the occasion arose. After a lengthy explanation of what each individual was to do, where to go, and how to act, when Fire Stations were sounded, the order was at last given to the bugler, "Sound off fire stations." This he did, immediately followed by the "Still," then the indication, "Fire in the forward magazine," and the bugle call, "Carry on." Everyone dashed off, except three.

"Come on, what the hell are you standing there for? Didn't you hear? Fire is in the forward magazine."

Now I ask you, what would you do when a big fellow, with his eyes nearly popping out of his head, replied in sepulchral Scotch, "Guid God, sir, ye dinna say so!"

It was not that they were by any means born stupid, nor were they scared, but they were a bit slow in the up-take. Excellent material, but a wee bit raw, till they became accustomed to "Navy Ways." When anything needed doing they, as with the Merchant Service man, had a perfectly simple method of just slipping into it, and getting it done, without waiting for pipes and whistles and bugle calls.

Our own Boatswain gave an amusing illustration once when an order was given to clear away and lower the gangway ladder. It was a great big cumbersome teak-wood affair, weighing a couple of tons. *His* method in *our* way was to take a few hands, heave it out and lower away, in very short order, but no particular manner, except that the operation embodied the essence of seamanship. But now we were the Navy, and the hands must first of all be piped. Then fallen in. Then told off with their Petty Officers for that particular job. By the time they arrived down on the main deck, and started to get busy, the Bosun was just about boiling with impatience, but being now a Warrant Officer, must not lay his sacred hand to unseemly toil. I watched him, more than a bit amused, as I'd seen him have that ladder out and down, time and again, in the shortest of shakes. He stood it for a while, then with a real Western Ocean Bosun's flow of language, he leapt on to the ladder, yelled at a couple of his own men to "Come on" and to the rest to "get to hell out of it." Breaking all sacred Navy traditions and disregarding his rank, he had the ladder tipped out and lowered down in not much more time than would have been taken to clear it away.

Forcing the Merchant Service man into Navy ways was almost as hard as making water run uphill. Yet, such is his adaptability, that within a very few months of war he clicked his heels and turned to the right about, with the best. In fact, when the war was over, and we were back again in our own happy and respective spheres it took him some time to quit clicking his heels—and get some work done.

With our heterogeneous mixture we were bundled off on the Northern Patrol. Gun crews formed of men who had never seen a gun before, much less fired one. Small wonder then that when with the Fleet one night at "night firing", the ship towing target for us signalled that it was quite all right, "we were *not* hitting her, but *would* we mind firing at the target, which was some few hundred yards astern of her".

The *Oceanic* was really far too big for that patrol,

and in consequence it was not long before she crashed on to one of the many outlying reefs and was lost.

The fog was as thick as the proverbial hedge when she ripped up on the rocks; and in all fairness one could not lay the blame on the navigator—my old shipmate of many years, Davy Blair—trying as he was to work that great vessel amongst islands and mostly unknown currents.

The fact remains that early one morning she caught this outlying reef, and was pounded to pieces by the huge sea then running. Lying broadside on to the reef, with the tide setting strong on to it, she was held there, lifting and falling each time, with a horrible grinding crash. I know it nearly broke my heart to feel her going to bits under my very feet, after all these years. The sensation, as those knife-edged rocks ground and crunched their way through her bilge plates, was physically sickening.

How she held together long enough for us to get everyone out of her was a miracle in itself, and certainly testified to the good work put in by Harland and Wolff.

What with the heavy sea and swift current—to say nothing of the fog—we had our work cut out to get the stokers and engineers away without loss of life. With the seamen, and eventually the officers, although the weather conditions had become markedly worse, the operation was somewhat easier. Our much discussed Hebredian contingent certainly shone that day. The calm and collected manner in which they went about their work, made it seem as if abandoning ship, under such trying conditions as then existed, was of daily occurrence with them—personally I was tremendously glad of their self-reliant help, and proud of their fearless ability.

We stood by in the boats till next morning when another ship of the Patrol turned up in response to our wireless signals. All the same, I couldn't resist taking my boat back alongside what was left, at daylight, to have a last look at my old love—this, despite frantic signals from our rescuer who, as it turned out, had just had information regarding an enemy submarine in the vicinity.

I jumped on board the old hooker for a quick look round. A last glance at the old cabin where I had spent so many comfortable hours—and damnably uncomfortable ones. Then, just as I was rushing out to return to my boat—whose crew were expecting the ship to roll over on top of them every minute, I spotted the ship's clock on the bulkhead. The clock I had looked at so lovingly, when I came below for eight long hours, but whose inevitable fingers I had cursed so heartily as they drew inexorably nearer the last zero minute, when I must at last leap out of my warm bunk to hurriedly dress, and dash for the bridge.

All these and many other memories seemed to lie behind that smug and friendly face. On the impulse of the moment, I seized it in both hands, and tore it bodily from off its wooden wall, and bore it away in triumph.

I still look at it and call up many happy memories —but now on board my own little craft.

I got a severe strafeing from the impatient skipper, who said I was responsible for more grey hairs in his already grey head; I didn't mind his grousing, I had my clock.

I was never so fond of any ship as the *Oceanic*, either before or since, and her loss was like the snapping of the last link that had held me to the Merchant Service, and the White Star Line. Aboard her it had been like carrying my home to the War, but now I felt I was into the War neck and crop.

Back to barracks at Devonport, a cushy job for those that liked to start playing Bridge in the forenoon and continue consistently throughout the day. I'm not particularly fond of Bridge, immediately after breakfast, even if there were a War.

Davy Blair, my old *Oceanic* pal, and I volunteered for a job that we had got wind of in the Flag Lieutenant's office. The main qualification for the men who were to get it, we were told, was that they should be "Hard Cases." Well, Davy and I had both done the Western Ocean, and knew it in its worst moods these many years. If the Mail Boat Service didn't qualify us as far as weather was concerned, then nothing ever would.

We were accepted and told to get fixed up with fishermen's rig, such as is used by the Brixham trawlers. A visit down sailor town soon completed the outfit, blue jersey, smock, rough serge pants, heavy weather cap, and seaboots, making us the imitation of a perfect fisherman. My first disguise! and if I looked as big a fool as I felt, then I'd need to be sorry for the success of our venture.

Davy was given a section of the coast from Newquay round the Lizard including Falmouth to Dodman Point. Here my section started and carried on past Mevagissey, Looe, round by Plymouth, Start Bay, Dartmouth and on past Tor Bay to Teignmouth. A fairly big patrol with a roving commission, to find out what I could get, and report back in a week's time to the C. in C. Devonport. My craft was a pure and simple Brixham smack, with no attempt to disguise the discomforts.

I arranged with my wife to meet me in Brixham, in a couple of days' time, and for her to do a bit of snooping on her own account along the shore side. Also I asked the Flag Lieutenant to take the necessary precaution of notifying the War Stations and Coastguards along the coast and any others likely to trip me up.

We sailed away merrily into the teeth of a S.W. gale and I can truly say, it was somewhat different from sea going in an Atlantic liner.

After cruising along that ironbound coast from Bolt Tail to the Start, we at last got a bit of welcome shelter in Start Bay. The weather easing down, we cruised along close in shore making slowly for Berry Head. Just before opening the Dart, I was examining the cliffs of Penlee Point just outside Dartmouth, with a pair of strong glasses, when I noticed two sets of steps cut in the cliff and leading down to deep water. Nothing terribly unusual, yet odd. However, I tucked it away for future reference, pushed on to Brixham and trotted off ashore to make touch with the Coastguard, as arranged with my wife. Of course in Brixham every one knows everyone; therefore it was perfectly apparent that for one thing I didn't belong, and for another that I was no fisherman.

I trudged out to the Head to find that no lady of that nor any other description had been along nor had they been notified in regard to anyone of my name, type, size, or build, and furthermore, not to put too fine a point on it, who was I anyway?

My advice to them was to get in touch with the C. in C. and find out. Meantime I clumped off back, smock, seaboots and all. Half way down the hill I met an antiquated growler coming up, and sitting in it was the wife of my bosom.

At my first hail the cabby just *looked*, but he did not stop. At the second hail he did stop and leaning through the cab window I informed the lady that I had already been to the coastguard and that they didn't know me from a crow, but were evidently out to satisfy their own curiosity. Well! we'd try and make for an hotel and get some inward comfort. This we did, and as I opened the door of the cab and took the seat beside my wife, an audible whisper went round from the crowd that by this time had collected, "E's got in with 'er."

My wife, by this time, was thoroughly enjoying the War. But I'd an idea that another war was coming, and I wasn't very far wrong. When we got to the hotel my wife went inside to do the chaffering whilst the crowd paraded past the cab window. I took off my smock. Still the interest remained. I sat back in a corner. Not a bit ashamed they just peeped round through the window. At last, completely fed up, I got out of the cab, and stood on the steps of the hotel to give them a really good view. Apparently they decided then and there that I *was* a German spy, and that, without a shadow of a doubt.

My wife came out with the information that they would take us in. But I decided if I was going to be stared at, or run in, it was not going to be in those ridiculous clothes. So back on board I went, and changed into mufti. Of course, that completely tore it. There was not a shadow of doubt left that I had at least a couple of German Cruisers, if not in my pocket, then they were on board the smack, which as I have said, hailed from Brixham.

I wasn't a bit surprised when the Chief officer of Coastguards called, with his retinue, no doubt supported by the local constabulary secreted behind the door. In the meantime I had tucked away a much-needed meal, and in consequence, my somewhat vivid welcome to Brixham had to some extent paled, with the result that explanations followed and we were soon good friends and we remained good friends throughout the time I had that patrol.

The Flag Captain was the culprit, he had completely forgotten to notify anyone.

My wife enlisted the local padre and made one or two useful enquiries regarding Penlee House (where I had discovered the steps) whilst I had a nose round from the seaward side.

The unanimous opinion of our committee of three, was that we did not like the look of the place one bit, and I reported back to the C. in C. to that effect. "All right, that's fine. Take the *Kermac*. Keep your eye on the coast I've given you, and the spot you mention in particular. Push off, but don't get foul of the Military authorities ashore, if you can possibly avoid it."

Being "in all respects ready for sea," I found myself outside Plymouth Breakwater, Captain of the Iceland trawler *Kermac* armed to the teeth with a six-pounder and ready to do battle with the best. Also I had been presented with a nice selection of foreign flags, any one of which I was at liberty to dangle in front of a prowling periscope, as an inducement for him to come up and be sunk. "But you must be careful to break out the White Ensign and haul down your foreign colours before you actually open fire."

Well, that was all right. The orders were quite sound, and I daresay the precaution necessary. All the same I should have been sorry for the sub. that relied upon our choice of the correct flag being hoisted at the precise and exact moment.

As a first effort we went steaming gaily past a War signal station under the *Dutch* colours, and never saw his frantic signals challenging our identity. Of course this extremely suspicious occurrence was instantly flashed far and wide. "Look out for suspicious vessel passing up the coast flying Dutch colours." "Stop and examine her." As it happened we did not pass up the coast; I suddenly took a notion, when off the Start, to push off into mid-channel for the night on the off-chance of falling in with some sort of adventure.

When it was discovered we had disappeared into the blue, then everyone got on their toes and at least one division of Destroyers was despatched to take up the chase. We fell foul of this little lot at daylight next morning, just as we were about to enter Dartmouth, after our night's outing. No doubt the Destroyer Skippers were also on edge after being kept out on a wild goose chase all night. Still, that was no sort of excuse for opening fire before they even got in range. Probably they were a bit befogged after being at sea so many hours, and it didn't dawn on them that once inside Dartmouth I should be reasonably safe, as I could not very well disappear overland or even up the Dart, drawing over sixteen feet. However, having successfully carried out the intricate manœuvre of surrounding me, with guns and torpedo tubes, trained to a nicety in case I did take an ill-advised notion to suddenly submerge or even rise out of the water and vanish in the clouds—the representative of the Senior Officer of the Division came on board, and with due solemnity I escorted him to my cabin and stood him a drink.

Penlee Point is a cliff rising sheer out of the sea, and Penlee House sits thereon facing seaward. Day by day, and week by week our suspicions increased until at last one night I happened to see the occupants flagrantly signalling out to sea with coloured lights. I was now absolutely certain that the house was being used for imparting information to submarines off shore, but I kept the information to myself for the time being in the hopes of being able to bag the submarine. It was more than likely there was only one submarine working here at a time. It is a rocky and risky bit of coast, and for some time I was puzzled to account for the accuracy of navigation that would let a submarine approach with the certainty of getting into the exact line of light for receiving signals. The method of signalling was such that unless you were in the precise line of light the signals were absolutely invisible. I happened on the solution to that problem purely by chance.

We had been over towards the French Coast one night, and were returning in the early morning as usual, to Dartmouth—which I used as a sub.-base. Just as daylight was breaking we picked up the English coastline, which I examined very closely, trying to locate Berry Head, or the Start, in order to get the rough bearing of the entrance to the Dart. By and by the sun rose, and it shone directly on the land ahead, which showed up in a black irregular line. But on this black hillside, I could make out through my glasses a distinct, short, vertical white line, looking all the whiter by contrast with the surrounding blackness. As we approached, this white line became still more and more distinct. From the bearing of Berry Head and the Start (by now well in sight) I knew we must be heading just about direct for the mouth of the Dart, and therefore, this white line must be on the hillside just outside Dartmouth, and above Penlee Point.

Now, back of Penlee House the main road runs, and on the other side of the road is steep rising ground, and on the hillside there are three houses which had always seemed to have an odd look about them, but up to that time I had not been able to put my finger on where the oddness lay. I now discovered that their odd look was due to the fact that they were painted all white. White fronts, white roofs, and even white chimneys.

Coming in from the sea these three houses formed a distinct white line, which if kept in line led you direct to the steps at the base of the cliff. At night, a light in the centre window of each house, kept in line, would not only lead in, but would give the precise distance off the land, when the ridge of the roof of the house in front cut off the light of the house behind. Perfectly simple. Absolutely effective.

A very sore point with the Brixham fishermen was that Start Bay had been closed for years to trawlers, although this bay is noted for its very fine soles. Across this sheltered bay runs a sandy shoal, protecting it from a swell from seaward. Here was the submarine's base, from which she operated in perfect immunity, whilst from 'the house she got her information as to what ships were expected up and down channel.

It was from here she obtained her information that H.M.S. *Formidable* was bound down channel. She waited for her off the Start, and sunk her with pretty heavy loss of life. When that took place, then things did begin to move a bit, but up until then I had steadily bucked my head against the brick wall of Navy Customs and traditions. I was loath to tell all I knew for fear that I should scare my bird away before I could catch her. That nearly happened after telling the C. in C. about some of the signalling I had seen at times. As it had taken place from the shore I suppose etiquette compelled him to inform the O.C. troops of the district. Be that as it may, the very next morning, two British heroes mounted on their chargers, in full uniform, Sam Browns and swords complete, rode up to Penlee House, knocked, and demanded to be told "Why had they been signalling out to sea, and to whom?" The inhabitants of the house were unreasonably reticent, for I don't believe they told a word about the submarine!

It is hard to believe, and the only extenuation one can offer is that it was early in the war. We had not yet taken off our gloves, and that likewise was the reason I suppose why the authorities in Devonport would not consent to supplying me with a depth charge to deal with my lively little quarry. Beyond sending more and more ships for the patrol, till I had a fleet of twenty, nothing would move them. The powers were convinced that the submarine was merely using this place to take in oil. The tune changed when the *Formidable* went down, and they then took off their gloves, and went for her baldheaded, eventually blowing her up off Slapton Sands where she had been hiding all along. Unfortunately, and to my bitter disappointment, I was not in at the death. I was in hospital. Not with honourable wounds, but of all wretched things, with measles!

CHAPTER THIRTY-SEVEN

SEAPLANES AND GRASS LINES

WHEN I was at last released from the Naval hospital it was to find that the fiat had gone forth "all permanent Naval Reserve Officers to the Grand Fleet."

Well, one must take the rough with the smooth, but I made up my mind that I would not spend a day longer on that tack than I could help. I knew only too well the ghastly monotony of battleship life. However, I was in luck, I was not sent to a battleship, but to the old Cunarder *Campania*, now also H.M.S. but even so, there was every prospect of something livelier than sitting in a wardroom drinking Gin-and-It.

She was a comic all right, and we were a comic crowd. Officers and men, R.N., R.N.R., R.N.V.R., R.N.A.S. The only tribe we lacked was Chinamen. I was appointed Watchkeeper, for when there was anything to watch, and Observer for when there was anything to observe. This was not going to be too bad, seaplanes being what they were, or as it turned out, what they were not.

We had many types of seaplane. The majority rejoiced in the designation of "White's Coffins" perhaps because they were painted white, and made quite suitable marine tombstones. Frequently they got off the water, but more frequently they didn't. When they did, I observed. When they didn't I usually got wet swimming to a boat.

When we were practising in Scapa Flow there was always a convenient boat in attendance, or at any rate within hail. When doing P.Z's with the Fleet at sea, there wasn't, which always gave added zest to the game, for if you came down, you stayed down.

On one of these occasions off Iceland, when the Blue Fleet, representing the Germans, had gone off into the blue; and we, the Red Fleet, were going to find them, the *Campania* was ordered to "Up Seaplanes and at 'em." They were got out, but not up! At least, out of a round dozen that were put in the water, one alone took off safely, and that, luckily, or unluckily, according to whether you were in her or not, was mine, and off we flipped to locate the "Enemy."

In front of me I had my Code book, Morse keys and such navigating instruments as were then in vogue, that day of Our Lord; and they were primitive like everything else connected with the air.

Having run out our aerial, I commenced to "keep the Flag informed," or was pleased to think I did.

There happened to be a nice low layer of clouds above which we could hide ourselves, coming down from time to time to have a squint round. Of course, we knew in what direction the enemy lay. That's part of the game. If you don't know that you can't find and fight each other, so what's the use! We eventually made contact and found. There they were, laid out below us for all the world like a fleet of toyships on a bit of blue glass, each surrounded by a bit of cotton wool. So many battleships. So many cruisers. So many destroyers. Heading so and so, at such and such a speed. All this I carefully coded, and as carefully tapped out.

Another call to the Flagship, and a "repeat" of the information—just to make sure; then wind up the aerial and "Home, John," after a good day's work, being quite sure that our side would now win, and we would be the shy recipients of loads of kudos—if not personal congrats. from Jellicoe himself.

But it's one thing to say "Home, John," and another to get there. The "Home" in this case being a fast moving and mighty small unit, somewhere in the sea between Iceland, Shetland and Norway. It wasn't long before we should have been glad to surrender ourselves to the "Enemy," only we'd lost him too! Then, just before we ran completely out of petrol, we found someone and down we came. To our unmitigated relief it was our own fleet, and we were soon swinging at the end of the derrick, being hoisted back on board. The fight, apparently, was over, but to our utter disappointment, such is the fortune of war and bad wireless, they had not heard a word from us since we had left!

Next thing I was put on to teach the young idea how to "Observe." It is a great game teaching others what you don't know yourself. It does need tact, but then this was war. So I went to work and formed my classes, bluffed out a syllabus, and turned out "qualified" Observers.

As time went on we got more and more bottled in by subs. snooping around outside the net defences, with occasional mild excitements, such as a cruiser charging blindly through the nets, fondly thinking the boom was open, only to find himself hung up by the tail with a mixture of nets, and propellers to disentangle when the weather moderated. But for a couple of days there she hung with a S.W. gale doing its very best to make things thoroughly enjoyable for all on board. Some of the chaps told us, when they did get clear, that they were sure she rolled completely over, a couple of times, and came up the other side; but I think that was an exaggeration. A self-respecting ship doesn't do such things!

Then, of course, there was the "Battle of Scapa Flow" when Destroyers and Light Cruisers, playing "follow my leader" slipped their moorings and joined issue with the splashes from each other's falling shell. I think in the final analyses it was quite agreed that it must have been a porpoise and not a periscope in the first instance, that broke surface on that memorable day.

Perhaps the officer of the day who started the commotion had not had enough water in it and seeing the porpoise, let rip. Others, quite excusably, joined the fun, firing at the splashes of the original joker's shells, which were quite easily to be mistaken for an enemy submarine breaking surface.

Whoever the humorist was that started it, he modestly and wisely hid his light under the proverbial bushel, despite a silent, though hearty vote of thanks, for creating the little diversion.

Being H.M.S. we must, of course, carry out our routine with H.M.S. precision. Each little evolution neatly labelled and named. One such was called "Away salvage party," used mainly for the purpose of retrieving strayed or erring seaplanes—and the "Away salvage party" got plenty of practice. Particularly as the skipper refused to have them retrieved in any other manner. One chap conked his engine when *just* out of reach of the ship's boom, and as a goodly breeze was blowing, he rapidly sailed away to leeward, and, incidentally, towards a line of particularly repulsive and jagged rocks. It would have been a simple matter to have chucked him a line, as he drifted past the after deck. But no, that would be too simple. It was a fine day, and the sun shone. We would show the Fleet and the 2nd Battle Squadron in particular (of which we were a unit) just how things *should* be done. With that was piped "Away salvage party."

Up came the crew of the motor boat with fire appliances, life jackets, and what not. Fell in. Told off, and then tumbled into their boat. Now comes the boat to the stern, to take the end of a grass line to the adventuring seaplane, by this time well away to leeward. Off dashes the boat at little short of twenty knots, but the line soon proves to be too short, and, with a quick turn, taken round the mooring bitts on board she is brought up with a sudden and mighty jerk, throwing all the crew on their faces. Fortunately they were too far for us to hear what *they* had to say. Another line is procured and bent-on, then away they go again.

A peculiarity of the grass rope species is (and for which reason it is used) that it floats on the surface of the water, which in this case formed the contributory cause to our popularity.

First came the Dreadnought's picket boat, with a four striper on board. The coxswain watching our evolution, sees not the grass line, which he neatly picks up with his prop, and stays put. "Mark one." Next turn was the pinnace of the Flagship of our Squadron with the Vice-Admiral on board. No favouritism is to be shown even if he is a V.A. Neither does the coxswain take warning by the other picket boat, nor see the line, and the next moment we have him securely hooked. Altogether three boats, including our own (by now quite helpless) were attached to our line, which reached by this time half way across a goodly section of Scapa Flow. (Where was Heath Robinson now?) Meanwhile, the erring seaplane having reached the rocks, is now in an advanced state of disintegration, the crew electing to salvage themselves, land on the rocks, light their pipes, and watch the process of disentanglement. The next day we were the recipients of quite a choice selection of signals. But such was life with the Grand Fleet.

CHAPTER THIRTY-EIGHT
DOVER PATROL

HAVING spent one winter and one summer in this manner, I was not looking forward with pleasurable anticipation to another winter in those latitudes. Darkness at 2 p.m. daylight at 10 a.m., is not funny when there is little or nothing to do. So there were shouts of joy when we heard the good news, with the inevitable introductory preamble "Being in all respects ready for sea," we "were to proceed with all despatch" to Liverpool for refit.

With a bit of luck I was going to see the last of that old hybrid, and she was going to see the last of me. A talk with the Skipper. A little judicious strain placed on a few correct strings and then "Would I like an independent command?" *Would I not.* In due course my appointment to H.M.T.B. 117 came through, just before Christmas day! No matter. I'd willingly sacrifice Christmas Day and a good deal more to get away from that deadly monotony of "Somewhere in the North Sea."

Life was now worth while. Hectic and hard, but more what I was used to. It wasn't long before I distinguished myself in the Nore Defence Flotilla by discovering a bank that wasn't there, and bending my main shaft in consequence. The N.D.F., as we were called, had been given a retreat up Stangate Creek off the Medway, with the parent ship lying at the mouth. One bright and cheery morning, I had difficulty in getting away from my moorings and, as a result, had dropped well "astern of station". To make up, we were doing about 18 knots (instead of the sternly regulated eight for the creek) when my prop took ground. I quickly took a bearing by the buoys, and noted the position.

So much inshore from those buoys there *should* have been deep water, according to the chart. Well, there wasn't, and that was that. Now, should I make the usual statement. "Regret to report having struck wreckage in the Black Deep during the night of so and so," or should I stick to my guns and say there was no water there, and chance my arm. Well, wisely or unwisely, I took the latter course, and got my leg pulled unmercifully in consequence. "A new discovery. Lightoller's bank!" "Ho! Ho! Ho! Had anyone seen Lightoller's bank?" This in addition to shirty signals from the Flag to "go and find it."

The Survey Boat had been cruising around for days and the chap in charge happened to have been a shipmate of mine in the old White Star days. Harbord by name. "Well, Lightoller," said he, "I'm awfully sorry but *I* can't find it." We sounded, and better sounded. Yes, tons of water, where I had said there wasn't! and I began to scent a Court of Enquiry.

Finally, and for no reason, Harbord says, "Let's go off to No. 1 buoy and take a shot." We did, but frankly I don't know to this day what spirit moved him. When the coxswain gave his reading from his sextant, "No," says Harbord, "you must be wrong. Here, take this sextant, and see what you get." He did. "Why hang it," said Harbord, "the *buoys* are all wrong." And sure enough they were. The dockyard had laid every line of buoys, in a wrong position as compared with the chart. Not only was it my turn to do the chuckling, but the Admiral, to signify his annoyance with the dockyard, sent for the *Harvey*, the big survey ship, and made them make a survey of the whole creek and shift every buoy; whilst I felt my halo increase by a good couple of inches!

About this time London was getting it badly from Zepps. We knew quite well when they were coming over, but so far had been totally unable to prevent them discharging their load of bombs, as, when, and where they wished. Periodically, we of the N.D.F. would get the "Executive Signal" and dash off to take up our respective positions in the estuary of the Thames, in the hope of sighting them.

My pitch was just round the Tongue Lightship, and one such night, after getting "Raid Stations" I blinded out to my position and told the Lightship to put up a small riding light. (Her regulation light being a thing of the long past.) But a little glimmer would just enable us to keep station and concentrate on listening, instead of dodging sandbanks.

Amongst my signalmen I had a chap who had the most extraordinarily acute hearing. I've known him hear and describe sounds quite outside the ken of anyone on board. I told Number One—in other words the First Lieutenant—to put him on the bridge with nothing else to do but to keep his ears open. Let him sit down, stand up or go where he pleased; for if we were going to have any chance at one of these blighters, we should have to hear him first. All things set; a Tracer in the breech of our one and only anti-aircraft gun, ship just stemming the tide, and I slipped down into my cabin. Not ten minutes later and the Gunner was shouting down the hatchway in a hoarse whisper, "Zeppelin right overhead, sir." Up on deck like a shot I went, but coming up out of the light I could see nothing. "There he is, sir," said the Gunner excitedly, pointing straight up, and there sure enough he was; so close as to blot out the sky, and so directly overhead that the anti-aircraft gun would not bear. In those days they only came within a few degrees of the absolute perpendicular. Everyone in the excitement of the moment had adopted a whisper, for fear we should be heard I suppose, though what chance there was of that with the row his engines were making, heaven only knows. Calling for the engineer, I told him to give her what steam he could, without touching his fires, in case a spark should scare the Zepp away. Slowly we drew out, whilst No. 1 of the gun, with his eyes glued to the telescope waited for the gun sights to "come on." Everyone was holding their breath, whilst the propeller slowly churned round.

I'd given the order "Action" which the Gunner had supplemented with "Fire, when your sights come on."

At last, "Sights are on, sir," and before the words were out of his mouth, *bang!* and away went the first tracer with its little trail of fire. "Over. Down fifty. Fire!" "Hit!" yelled everyone as the tracer went clean through the Zepp's tail. He was now trying his utmost to get out of range. "Independent," yelled the Gunner, and away with another bang goes the next shell. "Hit again," reports the Gunner.

How on earth we didn't set him on fire, and bring him down, heaven alone knows. Just absolute rotten bad luck.

Then *he* tried to get *us* and at the same time lighten himself by dropping his bombs, for there was no doubt he was badly hit. Another shot gets him and he dips sharply by the tail. "He's coming down," shouts everyone, now thoroughly worked up. But he wasn't. Down came a rain of bombs instead, all exploding as they hit the water, like a Brock's benefit and Crystal

Palace show rolled into one. He'd had enough of it, and was throwing everything overboard, in a frantic effort to escape. By the flash from our gun, he saw where the shots were coming from; so he turned his tail towards us, giving, in the darkness, an impossible target. In the end he managed to get away.

But London was spared that little lot, I was given the D.S.C. whilst our friend Zepp, went back and reported having "Sunk a destroyer in the mouth of the Thames."

I was then promoted to the one and only Dover Patrol. I'm afraid I did not appreciate the honour, and kicked about the shift; just when I was nicely settled in the N.D.F. with my family housed at Minster (on the mud!).

"Did I fully realise what it meant being singled out for a Destroyer of the Dover Patrol?" etc., etc., in the very best naval circumstance and style. Well, no, I certainly did not, but "orders was orders" and I might as well get on with the job.

So, once more, the family packed its grip, and moved along to No. 8 East Cliff, Dover, whilst I reported to the H.Q. and was greeted as follows:—

"Oh, yes, Lightoller. Well, you are of course appointed to the *Falcon*. She's over in Dunkirk working up the Belgian Coast. Carry on, please." With which full, complete information and instructions I was introduced to the intricacies of the Dover Patrol.

The first thing was to find something to convey me across Channel. The Duty Destroyer filled the bill there, landing me in Dunkirk late that evening. I soon spotted a neat little craft lying alongside one of those contraptions of modern warfare—a 13 in. Monitor. The little craft was H.M.S. *Falcon*, of a type commonly known as the "30 knotters." Not a great deal of space unencumbered by guns and torpedo tubes; but palatial, particularly below decks, compared with the Torpedo Boat I had just left. A fair sized wardroom, and best of all, my own cabin to sulk in.

After the usual formalities of taking over from the previous Captain had been got through, the next thing was to try and get to know my own crew. Rightly or wrongly I always like to size up each man individually for myself. Furthermore, I had a strong objection to the splendid isolation usually enjoyed by the Captain of H.M. Ships. Not through any particular desire to rip up hoary naval traditions, but the times being what they were, to my mind a unit was nearer her peak of fighting efficiency when there was confidence and close touch throughout the ship. This applies more, perhaps, to a Destroyer (particularly when on more or less special service, as we were) than a big ship, where everything must be based just on routine—though, frankly, I think a lot of the said routine could be dispensed with without any loss of fighting efficiency.

The fact that I leaned pretty solidly on experience gained through long service in the Mercantile Marine, led to some comical patches at odd times. For one thing, I expected each man to think for himself, and, in an emergency to act for himself. For instance, all the guns were kept loaded with the handle of the breech mechanism lever withdrawn just sufficiently to break contact with the striker. To bring the gun into action, all a man had to do, was to push the lever home, and press the firing trigger. The idea being, that if at any moment a submarine, or, what was more likely, a periscope, broke surface, the man who spotted her— and he was just as likely to be one of the hands round the decks as one of the proper lookouts—would swing the nearest gun, roughly in that direction, push home the B.M. lever, and fire. This, instead of the recognised method of dashing to the Officer of the Watch, and making his report; or to the petty officer of the Watch, who would, in due course, report to the bridge, and by the time the report had made its round the submarine was down again in the vasty deep.

The effect of a man jumping to the nearest gun and firing, was that the whole ship was instantly on the alert; everyone, including the O.O.W. heard the shot, and he dashed to that side of the bridge, knowing at once that a sub. had been sighted, and by the fall of shot he knew the direction in which it had been seen. All this was encompassed in just a couple of seconds of time.

Although this terrible departure from Naval customs distressed many of the R.N. officers and petty officers, they had, in the long run, to admit that it achieved its object, by instantly concentrating everybody's sight and sense on one certain spot of water. The only man who would never admit the slightest element of good in the scheme was the wardroom steward; but he was prejudiced through unwisely standing too near the breech of a six-pounder, when one of the stokers loosed off, at what, later, turned out to be a porpoise. The steward got the breech of the gun in the small of his back, which successfully knocked out all the wind, and what little sense he had.

The Patrol's ordinary job was, of course, to hold the Straits. Our secondary job was to journey up the Belgian coast and annoy the ubiquitous Hun; at the same time protecting the left flank of the British Army, which by now, rested on the sand dunes not far from Dunkirk itself.

To protect our ships, whilst on patrol, from attack by submarine from shoreward, there was a long line of mined nets. The Destroyers, in addition to forming a screen for the big ships, had to keep an eye on these nets, and light special acetylene lamps on Dan Buoys, so that our own submarines could navigate with a reasonable degree of safety at night.

Periodically, the whole Flotilla would indulge in exchanging a bit of hate with the shore batteries. By way of return, the German Destroyers would raid us. But this was usually at night time when the big Monitors were in the harbour. The latter's 13 and 15 in. guns were just a bit too heavy for them, though they did work out a very successful scheme to annoy us, when there was not enough water for the Monitors to get inside the harbour. They evolved what we called an Electric Motor Boat, commonly known as an E.M.B. These were driven by internal combustion, and directed electrically from the shore, by a wire attached to the boat. In the stern was a reel of wire miles long which supplied direction. An aeroplane formed the guiding star and gave directions by wireless back to the station ashore. In the bows, the E.M.B. carried a high explosive charge, and travelled at some thirty knots. In consequence it was almost impossible to hit her. With us Destroyers we could always get out of the way, by either heaving up, if there was time, or slipping our cables if there wasn't. With the unwieldy Monitors it was another matter, for they could neither slip, nor move quickly enough to dodge. The result was, they would see the feather of foam (which was all that could be seen of the E.M.B.), and then they promptly loosed off with every available gun they possessed, with every hope, but little prospect, of registering a hit. Of course, the Monitor had its blister, or bulge, round the water line, so that there was really no fear of her being actually sunk. But, as in one case, the E.M.B. came charging along, everybody blazing away with really more danger to themselves than the precious boat,—and hit the *Terror's* blister a glancing blow, leapt clean up and out the water, exploding on her upper works. No small amount of damage ensued. Forthwith written suggestions were called for from all the Captains of the Dover Patrol, working up the Belgian Coast, as to the best manner of dealing with this "menace."

These boats were absolutely devoted to speed, and, as I knew, carried no skeg, which as a rule protects the propeller from anything in the water, a bit of wood, rope or such like. They travelled at an angle of almost 30° tail down and nose up. That was how this one came to jump the *Terror's* blister and blow in her upper works. Well, gunfire having proved utterly ineffective, I "had the honour to suggest" that as a Destroyer was supplied with one grass line forward and another aft, each said Destroyer should, on sighting an attacking E.M.B., bend the two grass lines together and trail them astern, placing them directly across the course of the oncoming E.M.B. She might, by smart handling, have missed the first, but I'll guarantee she was bound to over run the second, and a few dozen turns of two inch grass line round the prop would quickly put paid to *her* little joy ride.

I was thanked, very courteously, but informed at the same time that "the method to be adopted must be concentrated gunfire." I wasn't altogether surprised, being, by this year of grace—and War—fairly familiar with Navy Traditions and Tape. The grass line was obviously too silly and simple!

However, our side soon retaliated with the C.M.B. —short for Coastal Motor Boat. These were real boats and carried a crew of four. Two engineers, two officers and a twenty-two inch mouldy (torpedo). They had a speed of anything up to thirty-five knots, and later in the war reached forty-five. Originally they were based on Harwich, but not allowed to do anything worth while. Many might wonder why. Well, the story oft told, said that what the Navy couldn't do, no one else was going to get a chance of doing—and collecting kudos! Be that as it may, the High Lights in the C.M.B. world worried the Higher Lights till, in desperation, they sent a Flotilla round to Dover—much to Admiral Bacon's disgust. He promptly pushed them over on to "Commodore Dunkirk," and that's how this collection of splendid fellows, with their wonderful boats, came to be based on Dunkirk, using the Destroyers as chummy ships.

Some of their efforts up the coast were epics. They got the Commodore—a real sport—to send a bombing squadron of aeroplanes up to Zeebrugge. It was well-known that apart from submarines, a division of German Destroyers was also based there, and in the case of a raid on Zeebrugge the latter invariably put quietly out to sea, till the flap was over. Then, as quietly returned. All this was common knowledge, but when the bright young sparks of C.M.B. fame, heard of it, they said, "Why, there's a hell of a fine chance. Turn *us* loose." The Commodore, like a good fellow, sent up four bombers to drive out the Destroyers and then turned the C.M.B.'s loose, who promptly sunk one Destroyer, and put another out of action; all in one perfectly good night's work.

A C.M.B., in effect, was nothing more than a glorified hydroplane, decked-in forward over the engines. Aft she sloped away to the transoms in two complete sections, leaving a lateral gap between. In this gap reposed a twenty-one inch torpedo with its business end facing forward, propellors and rudders aft.

Fitted over the nose in the warhead of the mouldy, was the cup end of a compressed air ram. On pressing the firing key, the ram forced the torpedo along her slides to the rear and into the water. The action of the torpedo striking the water actuated the trigger, which, in turn, opened the compressed air chamber to the propellors, and at the same time elevated the diving rudders. The net result was that sufficient time having elapsed for the C.M.B. to get clear, the torpedo then shot forward on a course identical to that on which the C.M.B. had been travelling when the firing key was pressed.

These boats must therefore steer straight at their objective until they were well within torpedo range; then fire,—and do their best to get away. Even under the cover of night, they needed a modicum of luck to get out of gun range without being hit—once they had been spotted.

It can't be denied that some of these boats did have a spot of luck at times. On one such occasion, just as one chap had loosed off his mouldy and put his helm hard over to pull out of the scrum, his port tiller wire broke. The only thing he could do was to put the helm hard over the other way with the remaining wire, and jam the rudder against the stern to keep it quiet, whilst he—the Skipper—leaned over the stern and repaired the offending wire. Meantime his craft was going all out, some thirty knots, circling round and round. One part of each circle took him clean through the objects of their kind attention—the Division of German Destroyers—who by way of return loosed off impartially, with everything even including revolvers, for she passed some of them within fifty yards, yet not one of the crew was hit, nor the engine, nor any other vital part. The skipper hitched up the wire, got away, and she returned home, none the worse, beyond a few punctures above the water line.

Another time, a chap having let go his mouldy and turned; was making back, when the oil-feed-pump broke down, and the engine instantly seized up. They were still well within sight, even though it was night, so the nearest Destroyer commenced lobbing salvoes of four inch shells at them. First salvo "over," next one "short." Another "over," and so the game went on, whilst the engineers and officers simply sat under the fore deck, alongside the engine, waiting for the cylinders to cool down sufficiently for them to start up again.

Between them and the four inch high explosive shells was exactly half an inch of perfectly good mahogany.

Once the engine cooled, they were all right, as they were supplied with an auxiliary oil feed. But, meantime, they listened to the shells either whining overhead, or crumping short, sometimes heaving sprays right over the boat. Eventually, they also got their engine going, and came away, not a penny the worse.

All the boats were not so lucky, and as time went on, an occasional one, here and there did *not* return. In fact the German Destroyers were not a great while before they discovered a method which effectually put a stop to these little night excursions. We never knew exactly what their practice was, but the evidence was clear, by the increasing number that failed to report. Finally, the Commodore called the circus off.

It isn't to be supposed that the German Destroyer chaps took these attacks sitting down. They retaliated by raiding the Straits again and again, and their method of attack made it very difficult for us to locate them. Usually they worked with a division of four modern ships mounting 4.2 guns. (The Grand Fleet collared all our modern Destroyers, so we had to make out as best we could.) The Germans would come down, when there was no moon and tear up and down the Straits, sinking everything on sight. Trawlers, Drifters, Destroyers, or anything else that came within their ken. Their practice was, on anything being sighted by the leading ship, to instantly pass the word down the line, keeping their own sights " on " till the fourth ship picked up the prospective quarry and fired. The other three pressed their triggers at the same instant. The result was one solid salvo of sixteen or twenty guns and then blank darkness again.

Unless one was near and actually looking that way, it was impossible to get a bearing, for they never fired again at that object—usually there was no need. Over went their helms, and off on another tack. Then another flash, in a totally different direction, and still another of the Dover Patrol had paid the price.

A drifter had been put down in this manner one night, and H.M.S. *Fairey* (Destroyer of our Flotilla) seeing the flash and hearing the report, dashed off in that direction to discover some half a dozen men struggling in the water. He'd got it fixed in his own mind that the explosion had been a mine, and switched on his searchlight to help him to see, and rescue the survivors. The Huns, of course, spotted him at once and swinging round, came up on his blind side and gave him a salvo also. Only one man out of the crews of both ships was saved.

CHAPTER THIRTY-NINE *THOSE DAMNED "R" WORDS*

Up to this time we had been patrolling the Straits singly and independently, but it became a distinctly losing game. So someone had a brainstorm and instituted the "R" words. Every two hours day and night, two words commencing with R were sent out on our wave length. There were also two executive words commencing with R and changed every twenty-four hours, and known only to the Captain. Just imagine how automatically one's reply became to the signalman's, "Rodosto Renoun, sir." "Repulse Retreat, sir," "Revenge Remand, sir," and so on, day in, day out and night after night. As often as not the words would be reported just when one's mind was more than fully occupied with something else.

If and when the executive words did come, all Destroyers rendezvoused at given places in the Straits and formed up into Divisions ready to tackle the wily Hun, with *something* approaching his own weight in metal. The rendezvous of my particular Division was at a position called Y buoy over on the French side, a place I am not likely to forget in a hurry, for I left the best part of two perfectly good propellors there, but of that later.

The night I got into trouble with the "R" words, as luck would have it, Brother Bosche, of the ever fertile mind, had chosen for one of his star turns.

In the first place he was going to carry out one of his well advertised raids on the Straits, and when he had drawn us off after that herring, he proposed landing —or demonstrating a landing—on the sand dunes behind the left flank of our Army. Not only did "Intelligence" know of the raid, but they also knew it was a bluff —but we poor skippers of Destroyers knew not.

The Hun, without a doubt knew his bluff had been called, when our submarine patrol, on the line of mined nets was cancelled for the night, and in the fading twilight there trickled out of Dunkirk Harbour one 15-inch monitor, two 13-inchers, a couple of 9-inchers, sweepers and destroyers. This lot soon formed up, with sweepers out ahead and the accompanying screen of destroyers hovering around, endeavouring to keep station, zigzag and yet not lose sight of the big ship they were attached to. The *Wolfe* was our misfortune, and the skipper of her was a pretty bleak sort of being. Of course, it was my own fault; I should have been on the top line with those infernal words, but it had been no small job to avoid some sort of snotty signal from the *Wolfe* about something done or left undone.

Heaven knows, there were opportunities enough to give cause for those sort of signals, and this blighter never seemed to miss one. I can only suppose that it was during one of those cheering interludes, that the signalman must have come with his Remumbo Rejumbo, or whatever the executive words were that night, and I had or hadn't said, "All right, signalman." Anyhow, the next thing was, we got the shaded "M.K." from our friend of the torpid liver.

"M.K." translated, means "Proceed in execution of previous orders," in other words "Shove off." Well, we shoved off, hard aport, full speed, whilst I tried to collect my scattered senses. It was pitch dark, and no sign of another destroyer who might have given me the tip. "Number one, what do you suppose the M.K.

was made for?" I asked. Number one hadn't the remotest idea, nor had anyone else, for by this time I had taught them all to use their own individual think-boxes.

There was nothing for it but ignominiously return and "Request further instructions," in other words, ask for it. And we got it! "Take station astern," was the signal. Dirty dog! He wouldn't even give me a hint. With our tail tucked neatly between our legs we crawled along astern. Suddenly, with a blast of intelligence, "Signalman," I yelled as loudly as I dared, "What were the last of those two damned 'R' words you gave me," and sure enough they were the Executive words by all that was holy and I had slipped up on them. "Signalman, make the interrogative M.K.," meaning, "*Request* permission to proceed in execution of previous orders." Back came the reply, "Approved," and no rider, for a wonder. "Hard aport," once again, and "every ounce of steam you can give her down below there." Sandbanks on one side, and mine nets on the other. (Eight knots was a safe speed, we were making twenty-five.) No matter, we *must* make Y buoy on time. At all costs we must not let our Division down.

What added a certain amount of zest to our midnight blind was the fact that only a few days before the *Gypsy*, another of the Flotilla had been making a similar dash, *in daytime*, and had made a collection of some of those nets with her prop. She was towed in, later on, and put in Graving dock. Shores had been placed, and the water was just leaving her when it was discovered, by the then scattering crowd of dockies, that she had a nice little bunch of grapes hanging, all entangled, from her props. The grapes, in this instance being mines, still attached to bits of net.

We had no ambition to collect either nets or mines,

and in point of fact didn't, but in due course, "made our numbers" to the Senior Officer of our Division.

Off we went hunting the hoary Hun; a job every man jack preferred to dancing attendance on the snotty old *Wolfe*.

He was out that night all right, but we couldn't make contact with him. Blindman's buff is not an odds on game with the coast of England and France for boundaries. Maybe he sensed we were after his hide, or perhaps he had been told to play a bluff. Anyhow he returned to his lair with an empty bag that good night.

Later on, the usual signal came through, "Resume normal conditions," which again translated means "get on with your various jobs." Ours was to get back to Dunkirk, and coil down, preparatory to the next jaunt up the coast.

Dunkirk itself was no health resort in these times. At night the Germans sent their bombers over, and by daylight, with all the impudence in the world, their tame photographers to take record of the wreckage.

Often and often, after a night of strafing, when bombs had been dropping everywhere, and great gouts of flame going up, accompanied by crash after crash, one would think, "Well, there will be no Dunkirk when the day breaks after *this* little lot." But no such thing. A couple of lamp-posts down, and a few windows broken would be the sum total of damage. The inhabitants, in fact, made a well-earned boast, that during the whole time, the tram service was never once held up on account of raids. Brother Hun tried very hard to get the Commodore's office, in return for his little efforts with the C.M.B.'s, but though time and again he had to have the windows replaced, they never managed to get a direct hit. Certainly they compelled him to give up using glass and resort to wood in the window frames, but that did not stop the good work going on.

Sometimes, to vary the nightly programme, the Air Force would place landing lights on the beach and encourage the wily Hun to bomb them. He did, and then would take bearings from the landing lights and turn his attention on the town—as he thought; but, owing to the misplaced lights, he put his bombs into the inner harbour where *we* lay, which was not so good. He caught the destroyer ahead of us one night with a bomb under his stern, which though it sank him by the stern—by a stroke of luck—did not set off his depth charges. If they had gone off, we should all have gone up. Another target he tried hard for, was the ammunition ship lying in the inner dock. She was loaded with 15, 13 and 12-inch high explosive shells, and was a continual source of annoyance to the inhabitants of Dunkirk, for if they had hit the ship, the whole town would have shifted.

The Captain and crew of the ammunition ship took their risk in a curiously philosophical way. Briefly, their argument was, "What's the difference between sitting on one, or one hundred H.E. shells—be they five or fifteen inch, if either you or the ship is hit? The result is the same anyway." I suppose they were right, when you look at it that way.

Every day, one destroyer was told off for "Cross Channel Duty," with despatches and so forth, for or from Dover. In fine weather, this was always the best job, as it let one out from the everlasting patrolling at comparatively slow speeds in company with the Monitors. Crossing Channel, there was always the chance of having a few shots at mines floating about or a possible strafe with a submarine. The Straits were strewn with the former, and it was good sport trying to hit them in a seaway. If they were British, then it was quite safe to go close up, despite orders to the contrary, and sink them at close range. I only knew one to ever explode. Even then, it only sent the ring of the cap whirling in the air. This so resembled a man throwing his own cap in the air, that the whole Watch, viewing the affair from our decks, just cheered to a man, on the impulse. If, on the other hand, it was a German mine, you opened fire and kept at a respectful distance, it was not advisable to take liberties with those chaps.

After the close shave I had had up the Belgian coast, through messing up things by missing the "R" words, I took Number One and the Yeoman of Signals into my confidence, and shared the secret words. Orders or no orders about utter secrecy, I was taking no more risks, and I slept sounder in consequence. The result was that one night, some weeks later, after the endless repetition of two hourly "R" words, we suddenly got the Executive again.

This time our luck was in and we caught our wily friend, and gave him a good trouncing. His report was that he had suffered no damage, whereas on the other hand, he had sunk two British Destroyers. This was not exactly correct though we did get two badly damaged. Still, not by any means sunk, they both got back into the harbour. One was torpedoed in the stern and with the other the best part of her bows gone. The former was the *Zulu*, and the latter the *Nubian*. With unlooked for economy the Dockyard cut each in two, and as they were sister ships, joined the forward end of one to the after end of the other and with unexpected humour, called the result H.M.S. *Zubian*.

Dover harbour, after Dunkirk, was Peacehaven, even though there were few moonless nights when the place was not raided and bombed. One of the worst occasions started in broad daylight, at Folkestone, where the Canadian troops were in camp. It was the afternoon of a very fine day, and we were out on the Channel Patrol which included Dover and Folkestone. I had taken over the bridge in the afternoon, and sent the Officer of the Watch down for a smoke, when there was a big splash thrown up, right close alongside. I naturally thought I must be fouling some big-gun range, but I had had no notification of anything of the kind and therefore it was their fault if they hit us. Another splash. Then, being quite close in shore, I could see huge columns of earth being thrown up in the air, very close around where the Canadian Camp should be. The next minute our look-out reported, "Enemy aeroplanes overhead," and sure enough they were. A dozen or more Gothas had come overland and tackled the Canadian Camp. Seeing us they thought they would have a go at us as well. Then one of our Blimps came sailing placidly along, having been recalled to her hangar. She couldn't see the Gothas above her and, as her Commander told me later, he couldn't understand what on earth I was trying to do, blazing away, as he thought, at him. Actually I was trying to beat off the Huns who, by now, had turned their attention to the Blimp.

Next they paid a visit to Dover, and then I did spend an anxious half an hour or so for my wife and kiddies were there, almost exactly under where the damned Huns were dropping the last of their bombs, spotting, and dropping at their leisure. Our anti-aircraft defences were not what they might have been.

I found out later that my wife had been sitting on the verandah when the fun started, and there she remained quite unperturbed, with a pencil and a bit of paper, spotting the shots from our batteries. To their everlasting credit be it said, that they did bring down two of the blighters.

Summer time in the Dover Patrol was not bad tack, as the war went. For one thing we could pretty well be sure of supplementing our larder now and then with fish. The Admiral had two trawlers working for the Staff, and we used to keep a bright lookout for them coming in with their catch. We were always sure of twenty or thirty pounds of fish in exchange for a bit of tobacco. Sometimes we would get a few on our own by putting down a small charge, one day with amazing luck. It was just alongside the Varne Shoal we fired a sixteen and a quarter pound charge of guncotton and raised well over two tons of cod. When we saw them coming up stunned it was "Away all boats." Actually we got on board a ton and a quarter, and we must have missed twice that amount through them coming to and swimming off. Naturally, we thought we had happened on the home of all cod, and in consequence I "fell in" the hands and swore them to secrecy. But what was the use. We distributed fish to the whole of the flotillas and, of course, everyone wanted to know where we had got the catch. The secret, naturally, leaked out, as everyone had a special chum on some ship, who in turn imparted the information to his Skipper, the consequence was that everyone was seeing a "submarine off the Varne Shoal," so that between us, we nearly blew the blame shoal away.

There were submarines in plenty so everyone had good excuse. Now and again someone succeeded in nailing one, but it was fairly rare. One night a chap had the audacity to come up and shell Dover. Another time they bagged one of our own submarines, set to watch the Gate in the line of nets stretching across the

Straits; which just shows their knowledge of what was going on. They were not even supposed to know of the Gate in the nets, let alone the submarine set to watch. They did though, and came down, as I have said and torpedoed the poor devil. We tried mining some of the routes they fancied. One of these was around the Gravelines Buoy, a little west of Dunkirk. Our Layers put down a triangular minefield with the Gravelines buoy at the apex and the Haut Frond buoy in the centre. The Germans, with their warped idea of humour, came and laid another exactly alongside it, and thereby trumped our trick. In fact, we actually had to remove ours altogether as in the end it became more harmful to us than the enemy.

CHAPTER FORTY — BLUNDERING THROUGH A MINEFIELD

Before our minefield was actually removed, we in the *Falcon* went through it.

It happened this way. Another Destroyer and ourselves had been doing Escort Duty for Troopships across to Boulogne and had finished for the day at Folkestone. Then we had to make the best of our way back to Dunkirk, ready for next day's duty.

It was pretty obvious that we were going to have fog, and a thick one; in fact, it was already shutting down as the last transport got into Folkestone. The question was, should we shove off and try making Dunkirk with the possibility of a night in, or take the safer course and ask permission to moor up in Dover. There was no doubt whatever of permission being readily granted, in view of the weather conditions. But I knew full well that if during the night it should clear up—and quite likely it would—we should get the pertly authoritative "M.K." and have to shove off forthwith.

We were Senior Ship so I had to make the decision.

Well, I made up my mind *I* was going to try for Dunkirk and the night in, but the *Racehorse* could please herself. I would not hoist the "One Pennant A," which means "Form Line Ahead," or in other words a definite order for him to take station astern. I gave him a compass signal which merely indicated what course I was intending to steer and the speed, viz. twenty knots. He could then make his choice as to whether he would take a chance and follow us, or go into Dover.

Frankly, I did not think he would come, so jumped right off into the fog at twenty knots and I was a bit surprised to see him a little later loom up astern, having picked up our wake and followed it up till he sighted us.

Two fools instead of one!

We must steer straight for Calais, this being the only reasonable course. Make Calais Green buoy, a mile off shore and then turn up along the coast and try, as best we could, to strike the entrance to the Gravelines Channel, between the side of the minefield and the shore. It would have been utterly crazy to have tried to strike the channel at an angle, on a straight line from Folkestone, as we then should, a thousand to one, either misjudge and run into the minefield, or overrun and hit the beach, which at the best of times is low and difficult to see. We calculated most carefully the exact time it would take us at 20 knots from the Folkestone Gate to Calais Green buoy; also the course and then let her go—trusting to a considerable element of luck not to ram anything meanwhile. If we ran our time and distance to the buoy, that should bring us a mile off shore and allow us exactly three minutes to come and go on, before she was due to pile up.

Time up, and still no buoy in sight.

"Let her run for a minute and three-quarters."

That brought us within 500 yards of the beach, and heading for it at 20 knots.

Quite near enough, so immediately the 105 seconds was up and still no sign of the buoy, over went the helm, hard a starboard and up she came on to the course for Gravelines buoy, which we ought shortly to make on the port bow.

Time up again and no Gravelines Pile Buoy. Another half minute and I would slow down and take a sounding.

Suddenly the gunner called out "There she is, sir," and sure enough, there was the big Pile Buoy, but *red* instead of *black*. Number One was the first to spot the colour and growled, "By God, it's not Gravelines, it's Haut Frond," it was indeed, and we were just exactly in the middle of the minefield that had so successfully blown up five of our own ships already. All the officers were on the bridge and pretty well all hands on or around the decks, so everyone saw where we were and knew full well what the chances were. We kept on at the 20 knots (it was the only thing to do) but brought her slowly round so as to disturb the mines as little as possible, till she was on the bearing for the Dyck Lightship; and then, just held our breath.

Would she go up or would she come through?

I stood facing aft to watch if the *Racehorse* went up, which to my mind would have been a worse catastrophe than going up ourselves, for I had led her into it.

The relief when at last we sighted the Dyck and the still greater relief as the *Racehorse* swung round in our wake into the channel, can well be imagined. We were all right now and would get our valued "night in" in our bunks. Having made fast in Dunkirk with the *Racehorse* alongside, Welch, the Skipper of her, came on board to have dinner with me. "Damn good course you made, Lightoller."

"Oh, yes? See all the buoys?"

"All except Calais Green," said he.

"Did you see Gravelines?"

"*Of course*, you went round it."

I then told him. "We went round Haut Frond."

He stared, for a second, as the full meaning sank in and then, with a world of expression, just said, "Oh, Hell."

Evidently we were not meant to add our names to the many who are represented by the memorials, standing to-day, one on each side of the Channel. Silent testimony to the many brave fellows who played and lost. My own hat comes off, more especially, to the crews of the trawlers and drifters in the Dover Patrol. They were continually raided by Huns armed with the very latest guns, 4–2's, fifteen to a salvo, against the drifter's puny little 6-pounder. Why, they hadn't the proverbial cat's chance. Even we Destroyer chaps had little enough chance when we came up against a division of those modern Destroyers. But then we had some sort of armament to hit back with and anyway it was our specific job. Not so with the trawler and drifter men, they were just like sitting hens and the Huns deserved just about the credit a sportsman would get in like circumstances.

However, we managed at last to put a stop to both the above and below water raids by instituting Lightships burning flares of three million candle power, at irregular intervals. These lit up the whole Straits. Added to this, we mined the Straits at varying depths, so that no submarine could venture below the surface at all. If she was on the surface when one of these lights went off, then she *must* dive, or be sunk by gunfire. If she dived, it was merely the worst choice of two evils, for she was almost certain to touch off one of the mines.

It effectually put a stop to their activities in the Straits of Dover and from then on the strain eased up considerably.

The Straits, from a weather point of view, is one of the very worst places in the world for a ship of the Destroyer type. The seas are just big enough for her to make the worst possible weather in the worst possible kind of sea. Actually it is the tremendous current that makes the sea so bad. I have seen the *Falcon* burying herself right up to the bridge, when only making about four knots. On some crossings a hand had to be stationed on the telegraphs all the time and the utmost speed we dared make at any time, was three or four knots. Frequently I have had to stop and even then she would barely ride up to those huge, wall-sided seas. I've had bad weather on the Atlantic and driven hard into it year after year, but I can safely say, even that was sometimes child's play compared with what we had to contend with, during some of the S.W. gales in the Straits.

Those who had had Atlantic experience stood it best. Many of those who had not, simply cracked up. With the Skipper of one Destroyer, his hair went completely white.

Winter was naturally, much the worst and often I have come off the bridge after one of these nights and had to wash off with warm water, the thick crusted salt, that had gathered round my eyes during the night. If you rub any of that sea salt into your eyes, you certainly do know all about it. Having got rid of the thick of the salt one then proceeds to thaw out; for even with thick underclothes, a heavy suit and a suit of Duffle over all, the cold pierces through. You can go on the bridge at dusk all nicely dry and every stitch individually warmed, yet by about three a.m. the cold has got through everything and from then on till daybreak one gets steadily colder, and stiffer.

I had two and a half years with the *Falcon* in the Patrol and though I enjoyed them, I think they were two of the hardest of my life. Even in the harbour of Dover, there was no rest day or night with a S.W. gale.

Whoever the bright boys were who designed that harbour and breakwaters, they certainly had not the remotest relation to sailors. If they had merely consulted anyone of the Cross Channel skippers *and taken his advice*, the harbour would not have been the ghastly failure it has since proved. Open, as it is to a S.W. gale, no small craft can lie there with the slightest degree of comfort. The tide has been allowed to sweep across the entrance, so that big ships cannot enter except at stated times and of course, mail boats (for which it was designed) cannot wait for those times. The net result is that it has been practically abandoned. Even Destroyers with all their immense engine power and ability to manœuvre, often found the utmost difficulty in picking up their moorings and making fast to the buoys. Many a time they would have to give it up and anchor in the Downs.

CHAPTER FORTY-ONE *SCROUNGING LEAVE*

The Destroyer Flotillas in Dover were always kept at "Five minutes' notice," which meant they must be prepared to slip their respective buoys within five minutes of getting the M.K. The custom throughout the Flotillas was to keep everyone on board, except the mailman and wardroom steward, whose duties took them ashore and, of course, all Skippers went ashore.

This lack of freedom did not make for happy ships, particularly with the shore so near and crowds promenading up and down the seafront. If any Skipper did let any of his men ashore, *he* took the risk and chanced a good scrubbing if by chance the M.K. was suddenly made and he had to put to sea and leave any of his crew behind; as, unless the man hid until the ship returned, he was sure to be ticketed by an M. P. and that would, of course, give the whole show away.

However, the *Falcon* never came in without at least one Watch getting a few hours to stretch their legs and we managed thuswise.

As soon as we got to the buoy, the whaler and dinghy were at once called away and the men concerned being already dressed for the beach, were landed. All were on their honour not to leave the seafront, or, if they did, for one or more to remain and keep an eye on the ship and in case the "Recall" was hoisted, to be able to make touch with the others, the whole party to be in the boats within four minutes, leaving one minute to get on board.

(On more than one occasion I had to slip and pick up the last boat as I went past the pier end.) I must say the Powers were very lenient and winked at a good deal, so long as I was not caught out—though it was freely prophesied, both afloat and ashore, that one day we should get our Waterloo!

We were cutting it pretty fine, I knew, but somehow, we managed it. Of course, in the first instance, I had fell in the hands and explained the situation clearly; if they let me down, I should get an almighty scrubbing —perhaps a Court of Enquiry and they would get no more Special Leave, as it was called.

However, it worked like a dream. It kept the men as happy as sandboys, gave them something to look forward to and talk about in the night watches and, what is more, I never had a man up for punishment the whole time I had command of her.

I gave Number One complete discretion as regards granting leave, with the result that there was not a smarter ship in the Division, or even in the Flotilla. Number One need only threaten to stop the Watch's "Special" if someone was not up to scratch, for the remainder of the Watch to turn on the offender and nearly rend him to pieces. I really think they valued that hour or two of Special Leave far more than any legitimate leave. Partly, I suppose, on account of the element of risk, partly because they could swing it on the other ships, but mainly as sheer relief from the deadly monotony of each other's company in such confined quarters.

On one occasion I had to leave one man short. Twice with two men short, but the crew had a funk hole arranged for just such a happening, where the miscreants hid their sorrowing heads till the ship returned and their chums brought up a current Leave Chit.

Personally, I had my own private recall signal, which I could always see from the house—situated as we luckily were, on the seafront.

One night when it was blowing a gale of wind from the S.W. and the usual beast of a sea was rolling into the harbour, I was pacing up and down the dining-room keeping an eye on the ship, when suddenly I saw the "Recall."

Grabbing my greatcoat and slamming my cap on my head, I dashed off for the Naval Pier, where the whaler would be waiting. I arrived at the end of the pier soaking, but there was no whaler. I dashed into the signal hut, to tell them to make a signal to the *Falcon* for her to send the whaler in at once. A signal-man had just commenced taking in a signal at the time and he pointed to his pad. I, to my horror slowly read word by word, as the signal came through from my First Lieutenant. "*Falcon*–to–Capt.–D.–stop–regret–to–report–having–been–rammed–in–the–stern–by–*Nimrod*–and–cut–down–to–water–line–stop." Here was I ashore (where I had no business to be) and she, perhaps sinking! I couldn't break in on the signal and tell them to send the boat; I must stand helpless and impotent, waiting for the remainder of that signal, whatever it might mean.

Dimly, through the swelter and rain, I could see her rolling heavily in the seaway and to my perfervid imagination, she seemed distinctly deeper in the water. Was she sinking? All this and much more flashed through my mind as I stood almost holding my breath, until the signal-man continued and to my utter relief, I read, "Water–well–under–control–stop–in–no–immediate–danger–1030."

Just then, the whaler came alongside the pier and in I jumped.

Dark and raining though it was, there was a very obvious grin on every face. With very good reason too!

We were due out on patrol the next day and would have been out over Christmas Day in that S.W. gale. Even if it eased up the sea would have been beastly. Now we were in harbour and there was every likelihood of staying there. No wonder there were smiling faces. The next week, thanks to our good friend *Nimrod*, saw us on our way round to Portsmouth, for a refit and to repair the damaged stern.

During our two strenuous years of service in the Patrol, we had a marvellous run of luck and escape from accident. Apart from making violent contact between my propellers and Hills Bank, just outside Dunkirk, we hadn't scratched the paintwork. But the *Nimrod* seemed to have broken the spell and her effort turned out to be the opening chorus to a whole chapter of accidents—with Finis written at the end.

The next trouble started through going up Portsmouth Harbour at 16 knots, exactly the same speed I used in Dover, or anywhere else for that matter. What I didn't know, was, that the rigid maximum for Portsmouth was 8 knots. Furthermore, it happened to be a very high tide and we sent the water shooshing right up the streets, which in many places are just on highwater level. Evidently there was some delay or difficulty in locating the actual culprit, but the authorities, though much too late then to impale the criminal, consoled themselves by determining to catch us on the way out, when they thought we should, no doubt, do the same trick. Well, we didn't and for the very good reason, that the whole harbour was shrouded in a regular peasoup fog.

From leaving the wharf we saw not a thing till we got to the forts at the entrance to the Harbour (neither could anyone see us). Then we saw nothing till Beachy Head and only a glimpse of that. The fog still thick as a hedge, we made the best of our way to the entrance to Dover, which although buried in fog, we managed to make our numbers and get permission to enter by sound signal, we made fast to a buoy for a couple of hours and when it cleared went into Granville Dock for a boiler clean. Then came the second patch of bad luck. We rather prided ourselves on being able to slip our buoy and make fast in Granville Dock in the record time of nine minutes, where others sometimes took the best part of an hour. I used the same old speed, namely 16 knots, a speed which gave one perfect control with those powerful engines. It wasn't altogether swank that induced me to use that speed, it was the fact that I knew from experience, a Destroyer, like an Atlantic liner, is easier handled at a high speed.

We had landed the man who usually attended the engine-room telegraphs, as he was also the mailman. The Yeoman of Signals, who ordinarily would have been on the Searchlight Platform, was taking duty at the telegraphs.

To handle the telegraphs he had to stand facing aft and the result was that he did not see the flag of a diving party working at the Dock Entrance. Worse still, he didn't see that they had the red flag mastheaded, signifying the diver was down. The diver, by curious coincidence, was working on the wreck of a Destroyer, that had come to grief in a gale of wind and sunk for the very reason that the skipper was not using enough power on his engines and thereby lost control of his ship. As a result, she fell on the stone knuckle, smashed up and sunk.

When the Yeoman did, at last, see the flag, and reported it to me that divers were down, it was too late to stop her. If I had then come astern on the engines I should only have churned up the water and endangered the diver still more. So I did the best I could in the circumstances and just stopped the engines, letting her run with her own way.

The Commander in charge of the diving party was naturally mad, thinking I had purposely ignored his flag. Still, if he had come to me I would have explained how difficult it was to see his old flag, which was abominably dirty, and was up against a brick wall a few shades dirtier.

Worse was to follow.

Having passed the diver, we at once went to our 16 knots again and shot in through the lock gates. At the best of times with the dock empty it was always touch and go getting through these gates and swinging at an immediate right angle. This time there was, by further rotten luck, a transport lying in the far corner, where we had to moor.

Immediately the stern was clear of the end of the lock, as usual, I put the helm hard a port and went half speed astern on the starboard engine which should swing her round eight points in her own length. Unfortunately, the Yeoman instead of putting the starboard telegraph to half speed astern, put it ahead. Seeing she was gathering way instead of stopping, I gave the order "Full speed astern both." He then put both telegraphs to "Full speed ahead." Of course, she just leapt across the dock and though, in a couple of seconds more I did succeed in getting the "Full Speed Astern" she crumpled up her bow like a piece of paper on the transport in the corner.

The Yeoman was a good fellow and owned up to his mistake like a man, when I taxed him with how it had happened. So I told him not to worry, I would get him out of it somehow or the other and I wended my way round to Headquarters, to report my mishap.

I was saluted with "Hello, what have you been up to?"

Naturally thinking Captain "D." alluded to my little mishap in the dock, I started with,

"Well, you see, sir, the telegraphs were unfortunately put the wrong way and before I could regain control, we crashed into the transport. I'm awfully sorry, sir, I'm afraid it means another dockyard."

He asked me what on earth I was rambling about.

"Aren't you speaking about my smash in Granville Dock, sir?"

"Am I the devil! You've been reported by the C. in C. Portsmouth for leaving that harbour at an excessive speed and now you have just been reported again for passing a Diving Party also at an excessive speed. On top of that you tell me you have crashed in Granville Dock and rammed a Transport. You can't think of anything else while you are on the subject, can you?"

It needed a deep breath before I could start in and tell him, that in the first place, they were infernal liars in Portsmouth, that the Diving Party's flag was too dirty to distinguish up against the brick wall and, finally, that the Yeoman in consequence was so upset, he forgot he was facing aft and put the telegraphs to Full Ahead instead of Full Astern.

I must say I was really a bit surprised myself, when at last he did seem to come round to my point of view.

Of course I explained how in ignorance I had entered Portsmouth and gone up the harbour at an undoubtedly excessive speed, but that the Dockyard authorities had been too slow in the uptake to hang the blame on the *Falcon*. Furthermore, that I knew full well they were out for my blood and had determined to catch me on the way out. Not only was I just as determined that they should not catch me, but in any case they had been completely defeated by the fog. When I suggested that Dover should call for a weather report on the date in question, I think Captain "D." saw the joke and called. They must have settled it between them, for I heard nothing more of that little episode.

To the Commander of the Diving Party I submitted an abject apology—and suggested he should requisition a new flag, more in keeping with his dignity and the importance of the work he had in hand—or send the old one to the laundry. I heard nothing more from *him*, so that was another out of the way.

Next, I was asked what punishment I proposed to mete out to the Yeoman of Signals—since in the Service the punishment must always fit the crime. I submitted that he was a damn good man—that it wasn't his job on the telegraphs anyhow, furthermore, if he had been in his proper place, on the signal platform, he would have seen the Diver's flag and, in short, I didn't propose to do anything.

"But you *must* do something in order that I can report that the necessary disciplinary steps have been taken."

"All right, sir," I said, "I'll reprimand him" (which is the lowest scale of punishment on the list). Even so, it would still have gone on the Charge Sheet and might have affected his promotion, just then due.

After thinking it over, I had him fell-in and just said, "Consider yourself reprimanded." (The only point was, that I had not reprimanded him.) I walked away chuckling to myself at the blank look of the Master-at-Arms, trying to puzzle out what he should enter in his precious book. Finally he appealed to the First Lieutenant, who, in turn, asked me what I wanted entered. I told him I was not a bit interested in what was entered; with the result that nothing was entered and the Yeoman in due course got his promotion without losing a single day.

Just out of sheer cussedness it would seem, the crew, being Portsmouth men, we were sent up to Hull to refit and whilst there, the orders came that the whole of my Division was to be transferred to the 6th Flotilla with its base on Immingham, at the mouth of the Humber. We were finished and had unwittingly said good-bye to Dover and the hectic life of the Dover Patrol. Most of us were frankly sorry, for although it had been a life that called for the best in a man—and took the most—still it was *real* life and the one and only stretch of sea where one was in close and constant touch with Jerry the Hun.

The reason for our transfer was that with the new minefield laid and the installing of Lightships with their three million candle power flares, the Straits had become a shade too unhealthy even for the ubiquitous Bosche. In fact, one could safely say, after many years of experimenting, that the Straits were absolutely and effectively closed.

CHAPTER FORTY-TWO *LOSS OF H.M.S. "FALCON."*

The North Sea was also in the process of being closed in much the same way, with the result that concentrated submarine warfare was being waged on our North Sea Convoys.

I suppose our Division should have felt duly elated at being chosen to join up with the 6th and help deal with this fresh underwater effort. Perhaps it *was* a feather in our heavy weather caps. Anyhow, it didn't matter, for if we had dismally sung our requiem to the Dover Patrol, we certainly were in good time for the opening chorus on the East Coast. They turned their submarines out on us, as the Yanks say, "Good and plenty."

The stretch they devoted most of their attention to, was between the Firth of Forth and the Humber. Further south the Convoys were more or less under the protection of sandbanks. Poor old *Falcon*. She was not destined to see much service up there. The second night out we were cut in half and sunk.

It's a risky job working a Convoy at night time without lights. A slight misjudgment, like the Gunner made as Officer of the Watch and it is all over. A Destroyer's plating is only three-sixteenths of an inch thick, so there is not much to come and go on. We were almost cut through. In fact the forepart broke off during the night and sunk. Before this happened I had ordered "Abandon ship." First, the engineers and stokers were got away on to a trawler. That made her more workable, but it was not long before it was very evident she was not going to last the night. So, later on, the general order, "Abandon ship" was carried out and every one was sent away, except the First Lieutenant and the Gunner, who stayed on board with me, until she went altogether.

There was just the possibility of getting hold of a trawler and towing the after end in, if it would float long enough. If it went down, we went too, but we always had the chance of being picked up. What did trouble me was the fact that one of the depth charges wouldn't set to "Safe" properly. It is the Gunner's job, when there is any likelihood of the ship sinking, to put all depth charges to "safe." When he reported, he imparted the cheerful information that there was a sporting chance that one of them would go off if the ship sank.

If one of them did go off then the whole blame lot would undoubtedly follow suit. In that case it meant that all three of us would get a good start on the way!

It was a bitterly cold night in February, raining and blowing to beat the band and we were wet through and mighty cheerless. The wind being strong from the westward, we were steadily drifting out to sea and across towards the German coast. I really don't know why I stuck to her, as obviously, she was bound to go down before long. I suppose it could only have been one's natural reluctance to leave your ship whilst she still floats.

About midnight the fore part, after wobbling about, independent of the rest of the ship, broke right off and sank. The after end was down at an angle of about 30° at the time and steadily sinking. There were no boats as they had all gone away with the crew. The whaler did stand by until the crew was exhausted with the cold and wet.

I was also frightfully anxious about one of the stokers who had been badly scalded in the stokehold, when some of the steam pipes burst, immediately after the collision. He had been put on board a trawler, as it turned out later on, but even the help they were able to give him was of no avail, he died.

The dreary night dragged out its cheerless prospect. There was nothing we could do and we had nothing to eat—though the Gunner did manage, after much effort, to get a fire going in my cabin and make some tea. That drink of scalding hot tea put new life into us.

By 1 a.m. she was getting very low and at a still more acute angle. It seemed it could only be a matter of minutes before she took her final dip. How the minutes dragged by with nothing to do. It was bad enough in the *Titanic*, but in that case there was plenty to occupy both our hands and our minds.

Two o'clock came and she was still afloat; 2.15 and the end was surely near. Then, without a moment's further warning, a bulkhead suddenly carried away and she sank like a stone, almost to the minute the *Titanic* sank and we were, as then, left swimming around in the icy cold water.

As the ship disappeared under the waves, our one and only thought was, "Are those infernal depth charges going off under us, or are they not?" It was not a bit of use doing anything whatever till that question was settled. So we just paddled and waited. After a minute or two it was evident they were not, so that was one relief. We joined up with some wreckage and swam and whistled and shouted, in the hopes of attracting someone's attention. About half an hour later a trawler hove in sight and, near as a toucher, ran us down. Had I not had the usual officer's whistle in my pocket, I believe she would.

We were taken on board and given blankets and a good hot drink.

It had long since become the rule in the Navy that whether a ship was lost through negligence, accident, enemy action or what not, a Court Martial must be held, whereby the Captain is either blamed or exonerated. It was a good practice. Then, as in the case of the *Falcon*, there was no stigma remaining. Poor Gunner, he thought there was going to be some stigma all right and had made up his mind from the outset, that he, at any rate, was finished, as far as the Navy was concerned. He would be sent back to big ships and never get another chance of a Destroyer (which is everybody's aim and ambition.) "Well," I told him, "you just wait and see."

Eventually we got into harbour and went through the usual formalities attending the loss of one of H.M.'s ships. Gunner still one hundred per cent. pessimistic. Then came the great day of the Court Martial. Deputy Judge Advocate up from Whitehall and quite a big show. Plenty of three and four stripers to collect sections of our hide.

By the time the Court had assembled, the Gunner was just completely down and out. I still told him the same Asquithian story, "Wait and see." I assured him, somewhat blindly, that the tale was not yet all told and anyway I had an idea in the back of my mind that things were not going to break so badly as he thought.

I'm afraid the solemnity of a full blown Naval Court Martial, with all its traditions and red tape did not strike me as as awe-inspiring as it might have done. I know I inadvertently and ignorantly broke a number of those Naval relics. The first tradition or custom to go by the board was for the prisoner (that was me) to appear without a "Friend." It's the custom for a "Prisoner" to choose someone well versed in legal lore, King's Regulations and so forth, to act as his sort of Naval Lawyer. I chose the Navigator out of the Barracks, simply because we were very good friends. But it so happened that on the great morning when escorted by Provost Martial (in ordinary walks of life he'd be called the Bobby) and I called for my "Friend," I found him wading knee deep in charts. Half jokingly he said, "Look here, old man, can't you manage without me? I'm frightfully busy." I said, "Yes, of course. Don't bother. I'll manage fine" and marched off quite happily.

The proceedings commenced by reading over a Narrative of Events which I had had prepared, instead of being cross-questioned. This, in itself was no small departure I found out later, but on the other hand it saved quite a lot of time. I had carefully tabulated and typed several copies of all that had occurred on that eventful night, hour by hour and even minute by minute, adding a rider to the end to the effect that "The highest traditions of the British Navy were maintained throughout." I also gave the Gunner a good boost up by saying: "Especially would I bring to the notice of the Court the behaviour of the Gunner, Mr. Shonk, who remained with me on the wreck, and maintained an attitude of utmost cheerfulness," etc. etc., "who frequently went down the after stokehold reporting conditions to me and at other times, made tea and played the gramophone." The tea and gramophone touch was perfectly true, but I included it partly as a joke, when I was writing the narrative and never for an instant thought it would be read out before the whole Court. I can yet see the Judge Advocate (who, to my horror, said he would read it to the Court), with solemn jowl reading out loud and me wondering if there would be an earthquake when he came to the last item. However, it just seemed to strike the right chord and caused a grin—much to my relief. Next thing, the President spotted that I was without a Friend and he promptly stopped the proceedings. "The prisoner has not got a

Friend," he said in a shocked voice. I, like an ass, said, "No, sir, he said he was too busy and would I manage without him."

I didn't realise just how ridiculous the statement was. About on a par with a chap who is being tried for murder and who tells the judge, that his Lawyer is away playing golf.

The Court plodded steadily through the set questions, and cross questions, asking me, as each witness finished, "If I wished to cross-examine."

Of course, I didn't. I just wanted to get the thing over and the Gunner out of the soup. Not till the Gunner had been called and examined—and hide it as he might, the fact that he was the culprit stuck out a mile. Then again came the formal question, "Do you wish to cross-examine?" and on the impulse of the moment I said, "Yes, I did." Though for the life of me I could not have said why.

I think they all thought I was now going to pin the blame irrevocably where it belonged. Well, they were *wrong*. I was out to soften the going for the Gunner, for he was looking pretty bleak, poor devil, as of course he did not know what *I* was getting at.

I started in: "How long have you been in Destroyers?" "How long have you been under my command?" "You have been Officer of the Watch?" "You have been in sole charge of the Watch?"

Here the President got my idea but suggested quite kindly that I should not ask leading questions. I apologised and set out again.

"Have you had full charge of the bridge at night on patrol?"

"Yes, sir."

"You have had full charge in the Downs, with a Convoy getting under weigh?"

"Yes, sir."

Then, before I realised quite what I was doing, I reverted to leading questions.

"You have never been reprimanded by me for getting too close to anything?"

To all of which he replied, "No," and "Yes," just as the questions required, wondering what on earth I was heading for. As a matter of fact I hardly knew myself.

"You have had to manœuvre in amongst ships in the Downs?"

"Yes, sir."

"You have never had an accident."

"No, sir."

"You have had full confidence in yourself?"

"Yes, sir."

"You still have full confidence in yourself now?"

"Yes, sir."

And with that I sat down.

I think the President saw my game as it developed and wanted to help. The outcome was that after the Court had adjourned to consider the verdict and duly returned, we were again called in. The hilt of my sword towards me (signifying *I* was exonerated). The D.J.A. then read an eulogy that fairly made me blush and the Gunner's eyes stand out like hatpegs. In short, the Court had "found" that far from being to blame, they had really discovered in us potential heroes by sticking to and going down with our ship.

But, what was more to the point, the Gunner went to the biggest Destroyer building, ditto the engineer —who had been scared stiff he was going to be scrubbed for leaving the ship, whilst we other three stuck to her. The same thing happened to Number One who also went to a big Destroyer.

CHAPTER FORTY-THREE *NORTH SEA CONVOYS*

I WAS lucky enough to get appointed to the *Garry*, the biggest Destroyer up there. The Admiralty, as a matter of fact, kicked about giving her to me, but our Admiral stuck out and sent me to her, but it was a month before Whitehall confirmed my command. She was a Commander's command R.N. and I was only a two and a half striper R.N.R. I got her in the end and a fine ship she was too, though a wet one.

No more patrol work. My job now was to work the Convoys altogether. Pick them up on their way across from Norway and escort them down to the Humber. After that they were more or less in safety. At that time we were losing as many as six ships out of a single Convoy by submarine attack.

The concentration of submarines in the North Sea was now one of the greatest menaces of the War and it was a mighty big problem how to meet it. The Grand Fleet would not part up with a single Destroyer, on the grounds that they couldn't be spared and here we were with boats that should almost have been on the scrap heap, to deal with the vital problem of sea-borne supplies.

Apart from the losses to the country, as a Merchant Service man it made one furious to see these ships sunk on sight, without a chance of them defending themselves, much less retaliating. What a hope, with about forty ships travelling at eight knots, in four lines ahead. The loss of shipping in the North Sea had got so bad that at last someone got a very severe rap over the knuckles and an Admiral was shoved on the shelf.

After seeing the method of convoying I was not altogether surprised at the numbers sunk.

The approved plan of protection was for one Destroyer to go ahead of the Convoy, about a mile or a mile and a half. One other Destroyer on each side, abeam and a fourth astern. To my mind an utterly inadequate disposal, particularly when one takes into consideration the method of attack.

A submarine sights a Convoy, knowing beforehand exactly when it is expected. She arranges her speed so that she can get a preliminary "sight" before the head of the Convoy passes. She then submerges and rises again for a second sight and to fire, when the main body of the Convoy comes into her line of vision. Hardly ever did they loose off, what is called a "Browning" shot, that is a blind shot into the Convoy as a pack. They deliberately picked their ship and with only one Destroyer to contend with this was easy. The Destroyer ahead had passed them and the Destroyer astern of the Convoy was miles away. So, providing she could keep an eye on the one abeam they were comparatively safe. Events and the position of the majority of ships lost, all went to prove this.

I had some heated arguments with the authorities on the subject, as when in charge of a Convoy I insisted on my own disposition, placing one Destroyer on each side abreast of the leading ships. The other two abreast of the last ships (the most we were ever allowed was one division of four Destroyers to a Convoy).

My contention was that the submarine took a sight just before the head of the Convoy came abreast of her. Her second sight was taken and the shot fired when half the Convoy had passed. By my method she could be spotted taking her first sight by the Destroyer abreast of the leading ships and if not then, would stand every chance of being seen and downed when she fired, by the Destroyer abreast of the rearmost ship.

I was allowed to continue with my "Theory" after I brought down six Convoys, averaging forty ships and lost only one and over that I claimed to have sunk the swine that bagged the ship, but I had no conclusive proof. I saw her periscope as she fired and put down fourteen depth charges all round her. If she wasn't smashed up and put down, I'm a Dutchman. We had the meagre satisfaction of a general signal being made to the effect that "the *Garry's* attack was brilliantly conceived and well carried out." Still that was something.

There had been so many reports of submarines sunk, that perhaps a little scepticism in high quarters was not altogether unwarranted. But it was small satisfaction, when one knew for a *certainty*, that one had been downed. The trouble was getting the exact position and later on locating him in that depth of water. Of course, if you blew him open and conclusive evidence came to the surface, that was sufficient. The only other alternative was to ram the submarine, as I was fortunate enough to do later on and then there could be no quibble.

It was a sickening experience to hear that deadly clanging crash, see a column of water leap up alongside a merchant ship and the ship herself tip up and go down, often in a minute, perhaps in only a few seconds, and at the same time, knowing full well that at least half her crew had gone with her. This concentrated submarine attack on the Convoys up and down the coast took a toll that tightened many a belt.

The *Garry* managed to collect quite a bit of credit one way and another. Some merited and some not altogether merited.

On one occasion, bringing down a single ship of considerable speed and something especially valuable, we were passing the Wash (rather a notorious spot for losing ships to a submarine that was reputed to lie there). We met the Destroyer on patrol and knowing also from experience that it was a good spot for fish, I made a signal, "Going to drop a depth charge. Will you pick up the fish and bring some in with you?" He followed at a respectable distance astern, ready to drop his boats in the water and pick up the fish. Just as we opened up the Wash, I dropped two depth charges, one on each side of the Transport, having previously warned him, so as to avoid giving those on board an unnecessary jar.

To be in the vicinity of a depth charge when it explodes is to get both a mental and physical shock of the first water. Unbeknown to me there must have been some Big Bug on the Transport, for, to my surprise, the Admiral got a most effusive letter commending the "Defensive Action of the *Garry*, etc., etc." Little did he realise I merely wanted some fish.

A little later I nearly got caught out at the same game.

With another Destroyer we were bound up for the Firth of Forth to pick up a Convoy coming across from Norway and as we were due to be in a locality where I knew there was good cod, I made the other chap a signal that I was going to drop a depth charge at 7 a.m. and would give him some fish for breakfast. When 7 a.m. came, as bad luck would have it, we met a ship coming down, escorted by a Destroyer (miles ahead of her) and a Blimp. The Destroyer, being out of range and hearing, I determined not to be done out of our fish, so let go. The Transport thought he had caught a packet at first, but, to their relief they found it was only us at our games, whilst we lowered our boats and picked up a nice catch for both ships' crews. Whilst our boats were in the water, the Blimp came nosing around, no doubt just out of sheer curiosity, wondering what we were doing. It would have been all right if he had left it at that, but he didn't and a few days later I got a signal from the Admiral of the East Coast, to "Report what your boats were doing in the water on such and such a date in latitude and longitude so and so." Well, I couldn't say we were looking for a submarine with the ships' boats and I was not going to say we were picking up fish for breakfast, so, knowing the Navy mind, I signalled in reply, "Re your 0014. Submit boats were examining objects on surface of water." It was quite true and as I heard nothing further, my reply was evidently satisfactory.

As far as possible we used to work in two divisions. One with R.N. men in command and the other with R.N.R. chaps in command. This set up a useful bit of rivalry and it was due to this disposition that I was able to prove out my "Theory" of effective defence on Convoy escort.

If I was Senior Officer of Convoy, the instructions were, "Act first and report afterwards." They were encouraged to think for themselves and take the risk. The result was, that each Destroyer was as good as a Division, in that she was an independent unit free to do what she pleased, within reasonable limits. If a submarine tried its games, each ship went for him as and how she could. Everyone concentrated on the spot without waiting for signals and from every angle. As she came within possible range of where the submarine might then be, she commenced to let go depth charges. Other Destroyers coming into the fray from different angles, also let go. Whilst the M.L.'s also tore about letting go indiscriminately. Each one had to keep a mighty close eye on the business end of a ship crossing his bows, or he might find himself gaily sailing over a spot where a depth charge had just been sown, with every chance of it coming up through his bottom. In point of fact it's not safe to be within a couple of hundred yards when one does detonate. A Destroyer, for instance, should be making her twenty knots when she lets go, if she's not going to risk blowing her own bottom in. To obviate this risk, with the trawlers, which had not the speed to get out of range of their own depth charges, they were fitted with depth charge throwers, which flung the charge out abreast of them to a safe distance. Those ships dropping them from their sterns, you could keep your eye on, but even then it was hard enough to keep clear, but when three or four trawlers joined in the crossword puzzle and lumped off their depth charges in all odd and sundry directions, the confusion certainly became worse confounded and the water for a mile or more around, a churned up mass, with each ship steering in every direction. It was a miracle that we never had a collision.

Occasionally we scored with a direct hit and then there was definite proof. Other times just a spread of oil, big or little according to the damage done. More frequently just nothing at all, though that didn't say we hadn't sent the sub. to her last account.

Neither "verbal proof" nor "traces of oil" were accepted as evidence of a bag. Bring in a body, or any part of the internals of a submarine and you were duly credited. But that was mighty difficult when it is considered what a small amount of buoyant substance goes into the structure of one of these underwater craft. Even then, nothing less than an absolutely direct hit would bring it out. Many a time and often, I was convinced in my own mind and to my complete satisfaction, that we had put one down, but lacking any sort of acceptable proof, I merely submitted the time honoured report, without any claim—just resting on the satisfaction of another Convoy delivered intact.

We got our second "unofficial" sub. off the Firth of Forth one night. I call it unofficial, since we again couldn't claim, though in this case also there was not a shadow of doubt. We had brought along one of the big Convoys across the North Sea and, passing the Firth, those that were bound there had broken off.

It was a ticklish job, this breaking off. Pitch dark and no one showing the glimpse of a light. A dozen or more ships to break away and worm themselves clear of the Convoy, steering a course at an angle to the other ships, crossing one ship's stern, another's bow. Only a suspicion of broken water to be seen in the dark and then merely a guess as to whether it is from a ship's bow or her propeller. The man on the bridge must judge right and quickly, for a mistake means not only the probable loss of his own ship, but may involve half a dozen others coming up astern. Added to this, there were always two or three Destroyers breaking off at the same time. Still, I never saw an accident; all credit to the men in the Merchant Ships.

The night to which I was alluding, those ships bound in for the Firth had broken off and the rest of the Convoy had formed up again. I had just taken the *Garry* round the rear end of the Convoy to see there were no stragglers and was making up again to the position we always kept, on the seaward side of the rear ships of the Convoy, when a submarine, thinking the whole of the Convoy had passed, came up and broke surface with his conning tower.

As I have already explained, we kept all guns loaded with the breech mechanism lever just withdrawn. All that *any* man had to do was to push the B.M. lever home and fire. The look-out at the after end of the ship, whose station was alongside the after twelve pounder, saw the submarine break surface—and here was where our system came in. Instead of rushing to the bridge to report and so losing sight of his object, or even yelling along the decks in the hope of someone passing the word, he at once trained his gun on the submarine as she rose and let fly.

Standing on the port side of the bridge, I happened to be looking seaward on the port quarter, when the After look-out fired and though, in the pitch blackness I couldn't see the submarine herself, I could distinctly see the impact of the shell as it struck the hull and exploded inside. It was all over in a split second, the flash of the gun, the crash and explosion, the impact of the shell on iron and the following much smaller flash. The whole procedure was just a mental photograph, clear and distinct and I'll take oath on a stack of Bibles a mile high, that that submarine still lies in the deep water away north of St. Abbs Head.

But would that have convinced the Authorities? Not a bit of it. So I saved myself the trouble of claiming and gave just the usual, "I have the honour to report that on such and such a night at such and such a time, in lat. and long. so and so I sank a submarine by gunfire, etc.," all of which I've no doubt, raised a sympathetic smile—and, small wonder, they'd heard the tale before. They wanted PROOF.

CHAPTER FORTY-FOUR
DESTROYER v. SUBMARINE

A few days later another Destroyer gave proof enough, and here is an example of the luck of the game. One chap may be on his toes all the time and never get his chance, whilst another comes along and simply falls over a submarine. (The War, as far as we were concerned had long since resolved itself into the state of Submarine versus Destroyer.)

The Captain of this lucky ship and I were very good friends and former shipmates and we used to knock around together a lot. The *Garry* happened to be lying alongside, when my pal Grant came ashore on his way to hand in his written report of how, where and when, he came to sink this submarine and to capture her entire crew. Seeing the *Garry* alongside, he just dropped on board for a minute's yarn. Of course, I heartily congratulated him as soon as he showed his nose in my cabin and asked him just how he had managed to ram and sink this submarine, which was quite a modern one and carried two four inch guns, against Grant's measly 12- and 6-pounders. He shoved his report into my hand and told me to read it, when I would then know all about it.

I read all the usual preamble and trimmings, till I came to where he "sighted this submarine whilst in his position astern of the Convoy." "Astern of the Convoy?" I said. "Why you are the one, above all others, who condemns that method of following up astern. How the devil did you come to be there?"

He laughed and after swearing me to secrecy told me his tale.

It appeared some slight trouble had developed in his engine-room. The engineer came on the bridge and asked permission to stop the engines for half an hour or so. Instead of following the correct routine and making a wireless signal to the S.O. of the division and having, perhaps, to state whys and wherefores, he said to the engineer, "Well, if it's only going to take half an hour, I'll slip round astern of the Convoy and stop her. Get through as soon as you can and we will put her to it and pick 'em up again and no one will be any the wiser." The repairs took a bit longer than the time stipulated and Grant got a bit anxious. It was pitch dark and there was just the horrible chance that he might lose the Convoy altogether and then he *would* get a sound scrubbing, if he was found wandering around looking for a Convoy, when daylight broke. The result was that when the word did at last come from the engine-room that they were "ready to proceed," Grant at once put her to twenty knots, intending to slow her down when he had run his distance to within a couple of miles of where the Convoy should be and then pick them up at an easy speed, for it was far too dark to see more than a hundred yards ahead. As it turned out, Grant's underwater friend had heard the convoy lumbering along and as it was far too dark for him to even take a "Browning" shot, he had submerged till the ships had all passed overhead. When they were past and even the Destroyer that, as he knew, in some cases trailed out astern, would, he judged, be well out of the way, he rose to the surface intending to lie there and get a breath of fresh air till daylight.

The first thing they knew was Grant came blinding along at an absolutely unheard of speed, for a Destroyer following up a Convoy, hitting them half way between the conning tower and tail. As Grant said, he "never saw a blame thing till he was right on top of him and couldn't have missed him if he had tried." Grant actually went right over, doing little or no damage to the submarine. The skipper of the submarine got a horrible shock, on seeing a Destoryer shoot out of the darkness and, literally, leap over him. He fully thought that Grant's ramming had been intentional, also that his sub, would be damaged and being unable to submerge, would be sunk by gunfire. To avoid this he ordered the Kingston flooding valves to be opened and took to the one and only boat and sang "Deutchland über Alles" whilst his ship went down. Meantime, Grant, who had ripped the bottom out of his ship, had just time to signal the S.O. of his Division, take to the boats and *his* ship went down. All he could do now was to await the coming of a Destroyer to pick them up—unaware, of course, that the submarine had opened her Kingston valves and abandoned ship. It was a perfectly calm night and as they could hear the Germans in the distance singing their song of success, Grant's crowd retaliated by joining the marine musical comedy with "Rule, Britannia." When the S.O. arrived on the scene and heard the row, as he said, he thought everyone must have gone completely crazy. But the utter disgust of the sub. skipper can best be imagined, when a bit later on he learnt the facts of the case.

In the first place he had surrendered to a ship, which he could have blown out of the water and in the second place he had sunk his own ship when there was no need, as Grant having ripped the bottom out of his ship had already gone down.

The very next day "Capt. D" came along to me bubbling over with satisfaction, "There you are, my lad, Destroyer astern of the Convoy rams and sinks a submarine. Where is your 'Theory' now?" This went on for a good half an hour and I could see the re-adoption of the rotten old method and with it the losses in ships going up and up, instead of coming down and down. There is nothing for it, I thought, so here goes.

"Now look here, sir, if I tell you something will you promise faithfully to keep it under your own cap and not let it influence your appreciation of Grant's little effort?"

He promised and I'll say his face was a study when I told him the inside history.

All Capt. D. said was a very heartfelt, "Well I'm damned."

But we heard nothing more of reverting to the old method. Grant's stock went up with a bound and he was put alongside the wharf to act as flagship whilst in port.

The grades of favour were very marked and quite distinct. That ship, highest in favour, got the wharf job and one could go ashore any time. The rest of the flotilla laid at the buoys. The next in favour nearest to the wharf and so on up the line of buoys and down the scale of grace. Those farthest away, being the bad boys of the family, were not likely to forget their misdeeds or misfortunes either, as the last two or three buoys came right abreast of a Fish Manure Factory.

In summer time with an off shore wind, which it usually seemed to be, you could cut the air with a knife. Not a port or a skylight could be opened. The *Garry* knew every grade and stage in the manufacture of the fish manure. Not content with the perishing stink, those farthest up the line also got most of the odd jobs chasing submarines. Sometimes real, but more often fictitious.

Someone outside sees a porpoise and, on the off chance that it is a Tin Fish, makes a signal that they have sighted a submarine. Next thing the ship alongside the Wharf hoists " *Garry* and *Stour*. Raise steam for full speed with all despatch. Proceed to position so and so and search for submarine reported in that vicinity." Off you go and so spend the best part of the day that you might with luck and good conduct, have spent ashore. After being roped in for this little joy ride a couple of times, instead of spending the best part of the day searching for a submarine (if not actually fictitious, at least certain to be miles away by the time we had got down the Humber and out to sea) I evolved the plan of "sighting" the sub., dropping a packet of Depth Charges, making the necessary report and returning to our smelly buoy, with everyone perfectly satisfied.

If there happened to be any sort of a breeze from the N.E. then every member of the crew was more than satisfied to get back to the quiet of the buoy, fish manure notwithstanding.

What a coast it is in a N.E. Gale. To zigzag along with a Convoy, day after day, doing a bare 8 knots, is enough to try the stomach of a lion and the heart of a Saint, and what a sight to see those forty odd ships constituting the Convoy picking up their anchors and, one by one, steaming out round the Spurn, as daylight broke and into the driving gale. One minute in a mill pond, the next diving and thrashing about with clouds of spray flying across the decks.

As S.O. we had to wait (and how willingly we waited) under the lee of the Spurn, till the last ship had picked up and got out. Convoy orders from the Convoy Officer delivered on board and then we were for it. A cold winter's morning and a sea like nothing on earth. Out we would have to go, with nothing for the next couple of days and nights but roll, roll, roll. The one saving grace of the bad weather was that it made it impossible for the submarines to attack with any degree of accuracy. Furthermore, if an attack were made anywhere near the surface, there was a ten to one chance that her conning tower would show between the seas and that would soon put paid to her little efforts.

It was bad enough on the surface, but it must have been hell for those chaps under water. No wonder one heard of all sorts of wheezes to get rid of their Mouldies and return to the Fatherland. Still, by far the majority of their ships were manned by men of pluck and resource, the only pity being, that it was expended on such an unworthy cause.

The man that could sink a merchantman, from below the surface, without giving him the ghost of a chance, must have had a mentality lower than the worst aborigine and heaven knows, they glory in some pretty filthy practices.

Anyhow, that was my feeling about them and their work, so I suppose there was little wonder that when one did surrender to us I refused to accept the hands-up business. In fact, it was simply amazing that they should have had the infernal audacity to offer to surrender, in view of their ferocious and pitiless attacks on our merchant ships.

Destroyer versus Destroyer, as in the Dover Patrol, was fair game and no favour. One could meet them and take them on as a decent antagonist. But towards the submarine men one felt an utter disgust and loathing; they were nothing but an abomination, polluting the clean sea.

We had made the usual rendezvous "somewhere in the North Sea." Picked up our Convoy and had got nearly down to the Tyne. Forty odd ships, four Destroyers, six M.L.'s, six armed trawlers, one Convoy Leader and two Seaplanes. (The latter needed nearly as much looking after as the ships, for they were for ever coming to grief.) Up till then we had not lost one ship, though there had been two pretty sharp attacks. We were cruising steadily along when suddenly up shot a periscope between the *Garry* and the Destroyer, zigzagging off the leading ships, just where he *would* come up to take his shot. Instantly the order was given "Full speed, Action." The *Garry* leapt ahead for the vital spot, just ahead of where we had sighted him and down went the first Depth Charge, almost immediately followed with a second, a third and a fourth.

Had he fired? Would we see that terrific column of water leap up alongside one of our ships, to be followed by that metallic clanging crash, signalling the doom of yet another victim to these unsporting beasts. Suddenly the lookout on the searchlight platform bellowed at the top of his voice: "Submarine breaking surface on the port quarter, sir." Sure enough, our last Depth Charge had brought him up. "Hard aport. Submarine red one—two-o. Five hundred yards. Independent, Open Fire." Having set that ball rolling I then turned my attention to the good old *Garry*. By now she was dancing up to her 20 knots and swinging her head round in the direction of the enemy. Would he come to the surface and retaliate with his heavier metal, or would he submerge before we could get at him. The forward 12-pdr. settled the question as to whether he would, or could submerge, by a direct hit at the base of his conning tower. Now the other guns were getting the range, but so far, what with the ship swinging so rapidly and increasing speed, accurate shooting was impossible. Now the submarine was coming still more to the surface.

"We shall get him. Steady the helm. Steer straight at him Coxswain."

"Aye, aye, sir," comes the quiet reply and the *Garry* tears through the water with ever-increasing speed.

Four, three, two hundred yards. At one hundred the order was,

"Prepare to ram."

And, with a crash, we are on him. Now there is no question about losing him. All the same it was a glancing blow, though it has ripped our own bows wide open. Has it ripped him up sufficiently to put him out of action?

"Hard-aport, Coxswain," and round we go again.

Shall I risk another run at him, as he is still showing up on the surface? I knew the *Garry's* bows must have been seriously damaged and mainly under water. Still, at all costs, he must not escape, so, once again we race through the water and settle the matter by hitting again and this time ripping her up completely and ourselves as well. Down went "U 110" where she belonged, (last—according to Von Lucknow—to be sunk in the war) and down we went by the bows.

I left the rescue work to the others, who picked up fifteen out of the water and then took stock of the damage we had sustained. No doubt it was serious and the vital question now was, should we beach her, make for the nearest port, or should we chance it and *try* and get back to our base in the Humber?

After holding a council of war we decided that we might just about be able to float long enough if we proceeded slowly stern first throughout the night, for the hundred odd miles that lay between us and the Spurn. Having made the decision we started off, but that night stands out as one of the most anxious nights I have ever put in and I have had a few.

If I got her back and rounded off the job, so much to the good and all the more credit. If she couldn't float and I had to beach her, she would probably be pounded to pieces and I should be blamed for not making for the nearest port. If she sank out of hand I should get soundly scrubbed for the same reason—and heaven alone help me if I lost any lives in the process.

Well, we tommed down the forward mess decks, above where the bottom had been ripped out, shored up bulkheads and hoped for the best. We could make just 8 knots and signalled our base to that effect, "Returning under own power stern first eight knots." The signal that we had rammed twice and sunk a submarine had already gone through and, as I was told afterwards, the Engineer-Admiral brought all his influence to bear, for us to be ordered into the Tyne. His contention being that having rammed the submarine twice, we couldn't possibly float all through the night, let alone navigate her back to the Humber. Naturally, the Admiral and Captain "D." wanted her back and, as they told me later, "they knew I would get her back if I could and anyway I had been long enough at sea to decide for myself, just what was best to do."

It was a very doubtful best, but we did it and daylight in the morning, saw us rounding the Spurn, where two tugs were waiting to help us limp back to dock.

But it was touch and go.

By the time we got her into dock her bow was deep down in the water and her stern cocked up in the air. Water was well over the mess decks and the last bulkhead was bulging ominously. If that went, we went. However, it held and we got her safely in. A carriage and pair might have driven through the gap in her bows, where the armour plated conning tower of the submarine had caught her.

Of course, everybody was very nice. Congratulations and decorations all round. Mine was promotion and a bar to the D.S.C. All hands were given a welcome bit of leave, whilst the *Garry* was placed in dry dock, where the dockyard maties simply ran round the crumpled bow with oxo-acetylene flames and cut it right off.

Within a very few weeks the new bow was on, the last coat of paint was dry, stores on board and once again she was ready for sea—not a trace of the war scar left.

I didn't go to sea with her, but transferred command to a bigger ship in Portsmouth then fitting out for Special Service.

As it turned out, I didn't take this ship to sea either, for the War ended abruptly. Guns were secured and warheads came off torpedoes.

The excitement of the fight was over and ships proceeded "On their lawful occasions" unmolested.

No more convoying needed. No more attacks to stave off. Salt had gone out of the Service, the crazy War was ended and conditions changed in a night. Then why hang it out? Common sense said, go whilst the going's good. Leave whilst the flavour of excitement still remains—don't wait till the taste grows stale.

Despite surprised remarks of, "Why this unseemly haste?" Within a week I had "Paid off" my ship, demobbed and reported "Back for Duty" with the Greyhounds of the Atlantic, back to the White Star Line.

CHAPTER SIXTY-FIVE   *I "BURY THE ANCHOR"*

I FOUND things a bit raw in the Merchant Service and discipline more than a bit ragged, mainly due to the exigencies of War.

Merchant Service Men were thoroughly fed up with being made stool pigeons, for everyone and anyone to shoot at. They had suffered terribly and far more than was either necessary or right. The losses had been frightful and the sufferings more awful than can well be conceived. There was some element of truth in the saying that "Men went in the Navy for Safety."

I was appointed to the *Celtic* and my hands were full for a few voyages, licking her into shape. The men were completely out of hand—though that did not trouble me much. I'd handled them all my life and my sympathies were wholly theirs, so we soon found common ground.

Very quickly, in fact all too quickly for my liking, she settled down into a steady routine, with a splendid, hard-working crew.

Perhaps it was because I brought back no Navy ideas to the old Merchant Service, that enabled us to see eye to eye. The fact remains, she went through her transmogrification as quickly as any ship of the Line and with the least trouble.

Once steadied down in the regular run, life dropped into its same old grooves.

On the English side the memories of war were an open sore. On the American side they were still busy winning it. It was quite amusing, in a way, to hear how pat everyone had the figures of the huge amounts the U.S.A. had sent to "Yurrup." So many millions of shell, so many millions of bully-beef—both classed in much the same category.

They were still three thousand miles distant from the War.

After a time one got used to the child-like simplicity with which they made statements that showed, only too well, that they had never even been on the fringe of the Fight.

For my part, the peace time routine palled and it was only a few short months before I decided to have done with it and seek some excitement ashore—I got it all right, but that has nothing to do with *this* story.

There used to be a fine picture in the front of old Todd and Whall's Seamanship (a book familiar to all apprentices) when first I went to sea. It was a picture of the s.s. *Celtic*, the old *Celtic* of the White Star Line, driving her way to westward. A big fourmaster with twin funnels and somehow I got to look on her as the height and summit of my ambition.

Years passed. Ships came and ships went. Now one Company and now another. Off on the trail and back to sea. The war blazed up and burned out. Yet it was a curious coincidence that for my last ship I should find myself in the modern edition of my boyhood's ambition; the R.M.S. *Celtic*. And it was in my cabin on board this ship that I finally wrote my resignation and said good-bye to the Sea.